Wiliam O'Connor Morris

The French Revolution and First Empire

An Historical Sketch

Wiliam O'Connor Morris

The French Revolution and First Empire
An Historical Sketch

ISBN/EAN: 9783337270872

Printed in Europe, USA, Canada, Australia, Japan

Cover: Foto ©ninafisch / pixelio.de

More available books at **www.hansebooks.com**

THE

FRENCH REVOLUTION

AND FIRST EMPIRE:

AN HISTORICAL SKETCH.

BY

WILLIAM O'CONNOR MORRIS,

SOMETIME SCHOLAR OF ORIEL COLLEGE, OXFORD.

WITH AN APPENDIX UPON THE BIBLIOGRAPHY OF THE SUBJECT AND A COURSE OF STUDY BY

HON. ANDREW D. WHITE, LL. D.

PRESIDENT OF CORNELL UNIVERSITY, ITHACA, N. Y.

NEW YORK
SCRIBNER, ARMSTRONG & CO.

GRANT, FAIRES & RODGERS,
ELECTROTYPERS AND PRINTERS,
52 & 54 N. SIXTH ST., PHILADELPHIA.

Dedicated to

HENRY REEVE, ESQ., D.C.L.

AS A MARK OF THE REGARD AND ESTEEM OF

THE AUTHOR.

PREFACE.

It is unnecessary to say that, in an epitome of this kind, innumerable details must be altogether left out, and that a small space only can be allotted to even important occurrences which would be set forth at length in a complete narrative. Nor has it been possible for me—my object being to describe the principal facts of the French Revolution and First Empire—to comment largely on the institutions of old France, or to show fully how they contributed to the events that followed 1789. An abridgement cannot be a real History; and, apart from defects peculiar to it, I am conscious that this volume must at best be an imperfect miniature of the grand drama of human action and life which it endeavors to delineate. Still I am not without hope that I have represented, in something like exact outline, the great features of that period of trouble and war through which France passed from 1789 to

1815; and I trust I have placed events in their true proportions, and that the opinions I have expressed are correct and moderate. The present time, it must be allowed, is favorable for a publication of this kind, even though it purports to be only a sketch. French and English literature has of late years teemed with documents of the greatest value on the Revolution and Napoleon I., and I have carefully studied most of these sources of information. The events, too, of the war of 1870 bring again before our eyes what the Emperor achieved in the field, though victory has shifted from the standards of one race to those of another; the national defence of France in 1871 reflects light on that of 1793; and in the crimes and madness of the lately suppressed Commune of Paris, we see an image of the Reign of Terror.

DUBLIN: *February* 3, 1874.

CONTENTS.

CHAPTER I.

STATE OF FRANCE BEFORE THE REVOLUTION.

	PAGE
General character and results of the French Revolution	1
It exhibited vividly the peculiar features of the French national character	2
The Monarchy of France before the Revolution; abuses in the system of government	4
The Church and the Nobility. Why these Orders had become generally disliked	6
The power of the ruling orders was divided and decayed, and consequently weak	8
Dissensions between the Crown, the Church, and the Nobles, and discredit of all authority	9
State of the Commons of France. The middle classes; how they were cut off from the People, and the results	11
Condition of the Peasantry	13
Of the population of the towns	14
Destructive and sceptical tone of contemporary French Literature	14
The progress of evil continued down to the Revolution	15
Brilliant anticipations of the future in France	17

CHAPTER II.

THE STATES-GENERAL AND NATIONAL ASSEMBLY.

1789	Meeting of the States-General	19
	The Commons declare themselves the National Assembly	20
	The oath of the Tennis Court, June 20	22

	PAGE
1789 Dismission of Necker, and formation of a reactionary Ministry	24
Rising in Paris	24
Mutiny of the French Guards and insubordination in the Army	25
The Commune, the National Guard	26
Siege and storming of the Bastille, July 14, 1789	28
Beginning of the emigration of the Nobles	29
Recall of Necker	29
The King sanctions what had been done in Paris	29
The Tricolor Flag	30
Risings in the Provinces	30
Legislative measures of the Assembly	31
Sudden abolition of the feudal burdens, August 4, 1789	32
October 5 and 6, 1789	33
The King and Royal Family taken to Paris from Versailles	35
Growing power of the rabble of Paris	35

CHAPTER III.

THE CONSTITUTION OF 1790—I.

Character of the period from the autumn of 1789 to the summer of 1791	36
The National Assembly begins to frame the Constitution	38
Useful reforms	38
Wild and precipitate innovations	39
The Rights of Man	39
Confiscation of Church and corporate property. Abolition of tithes	39
Equality	39
Provinces transformed into Departments	39
Character of the new Constitution; its glaring defects	40
Administrative measures	41
Assignats	42
False system of taxation	42
Undue favor shown to Paris	42

Contents. xi

PAGE

1790 The feast of the Federation, July 14, 1790. Enthusiasm
in Europe 43
Evil consequences of innovation; signs of disorder and
anarchy 44
The Jacobin and other clubs 45
Weakness of Conservative elements in the Assembly . 46
Attempts of Mirabeau to check the disorganization of
the State 48
His death 49
Threatening attitude of Foreign Powers . . 49
Dangerous projects of the King and Queen . . 49
The flight to Varennes, June 20, 1791 . . . 50
Consequences of this event 51

CHAPTER IV.

THE LEGISLATIVE ASSEMBLY.

1791 Character of the period from the summer of 1791 to
August 10, 1792 54
Deceptive calm. Meeting of the new Legislative Assembly 55
Character of this Body 55
The Gironde 56
Dissensions between the King and the Assembly . 56
Disorders in the Provinces 57
Religious and social troubles 57
Massacre at Avignon (Oct. 16—20, 1791) . . 57
Louis directly opposes the Assembly . . . 58
Nov. 1791 58
Indignation of the Assembly 59
Attitude of the Commune of Paris. The Clubs and
demagogues 59
Menaces of Foreign Powers 60
Declaration of Pilnitz, August, 1791 . . . 60
Projects of King and Queen 61
Divisions in the Assembly 61
It declares war against Austria. Prussia joins Austria 61

xii   *Contents.*

	1791	PAGE
	French failures in Belgium. April, May, 1792	61
	Indignation in France	61
	Insensate conduct of Louis	62
1792	He resists the decrees of the Assembly, and dismisses the Gironde ministry and Dumouriez	63
	Outbreak of June 20, 1792	63
1792	Encouraged by the popular leaders in the Assembly and by the Commune of Paris	64
	Reaction in favor of Louis	65
	New efforts of the Demagogues and the Commune	66
	Proclamation of Brunswick	67
	Invasion of France by the Prussians and Austrians, July and August, 1792	67
	The Assembly paralyzed; power passes to the Demagogues	68
	Preparations for a rising. Danton	68
	Paris on the night of August 9, 1792	69
	Attitude of the King and the Court	70
	August 10, 1792	70
	The armed populace at the Tuileries	71
	The King and Royal Family take refuge in the Assembly	72
	The Tuileries attacked and pillaged. Massacre of the Swiss	72
	Reflections on the rising of August 10	73

CHAPTER V.

THE CONVENTION, TO THE FALL OF THE MODERATES.

Effects of August 10	75
The Convention summoned	75
The King and Royal Family imprisoned in the Temple	75
Violent measures of the Commune of Paris	76
Lafayette throws up his command; advance of the German armies to Verdun	77
Massacre of September	77
September 2 to 6, 1792	78

Contents. xiii

		PAGE
1792	Frightful scenes in Paris 78	
	The Assembly indignant at the massacre . . 79	
	Battle of Valmy. Its great results; retreat of the Prussians and Austrians 80	
	Meeting of the Convention, September 22, 1792 . 80	
	Parties in it 81	
	France declared a Republic, September 22, 1792 . 81	
	Offer of liberty to foreign nations, November 19 . 81	
	Dissension renewed between the Moderates and Jacobins 82	
	Trial of Louis XVI. December 11, 1792 . . 82	
	Sentence of death pronounced by a majority of one . 83	
	Execution of Louis XVI. January 21, 1793 . . 84	
1793	Reflections on this event 86	
	Character and conduct of the King . . . 86	
	Coalition of Europe against France . . . 87	
	Battle of Jemmapes and early successes of the French, November—December 1792, January–February 1793 87	
	Fierce struggle of parties in France . . . 90	
	The Gironde denounced by the Jacobins and Demagogues 90	
	Distress and social disorders 91	
	Advance of the Coalition 91	
	Battle of Neerwinden, March 18, 1793 . . . 92	
	Flight of Dumouriez. He throws up his command . 92	
	Increasing power of the Jacobins. Danton. His energy 92	
	Formation of the Committee of Public Safety, April 6, 1793 93	
	Violent measures proposed by Danton . . . 93	
	And decreed by Convention 93	
	Propositions of the Commune of Paris . . 94	
	The party of violence generally prevails . . 94	
	The Gironde and Moderates denounce extreme measures 94	
	The Commission of Twelve 95	
	The forces of Anarchy become supreme . . 95	
	Danton tries in vain to reconcile the contending parties 95	

	PAGE
1793 Death-struggle between the Moderates and Jacobins	95
Rising of May 31 and June 2, 1793	96
Fall of the Moderates	96
Reflections on this event	97

CHAPTER VI.

THE REIGN OF TERROR. WAR. FALL OF ROBESPIERRE.

1793 Triumph of the party of violence in the Convention	97
Risings against in the Provinces. Civil war	98
Beginning of the war of La Vendee	98
Energetic measures of Danton and the leaders in power	99
The levee en masse	99
The Constitution of 1793	100
The maximum. The Revolutionary Tribunal	100
The risings in part of France quelled	100
Feebleness of the Coalition	101
Waste of time, in action and dissensions	101
Sept. 8, 1793	102
The Republic successful at home and abroad	102
Carnot. Hoche	102
Battle of Wattignies, October 16, 1793	103
Fall of Lyons, October 9, 1793,	104
Great defeat of the Vendeans at Savenay, December 23, 1793	104
Siege and fall of Toulon, December 19, 1793	104
First appearance on the scene of Napoleon Bonaparte.	105
The Reign of Terror	105
The Convention, a mere instrument of the Jacobin leaders	106
The Committee of Public Safety all powerful	106
Its tyranny and terrible expedients	106
Wild social changes	107
Atheism declared truth by the Commune of Paris	107
Appearance of Paris during the Reign of Terror	107
The levies hurried to the frontier	108
Appearance of the Convention	108
Dissolution of society and of morality	109

Contents.

		PAGE
1793	Cruelty and suspicions of populace	110
	General licentiousness	110
	The Goddess of Reason at Notre-Dame	110
	Scenes in the prisons	111
	The Revolutionary Tribunal and its work	112
	Trial and execution of Marie Antoinette, October 14-16, 1793	113
	Her character and conduct	115
	Divisions among the Jacobin rulers	115
	Three factions form themselves	115
	Growing ascendency of Robespierre	116
	He becomes supreme in the State	117
1794	Destruction of Hebert and the leaders of the Commune, of Danton and his followers, March 24, April 3, 1794	117
	Character of Danton	117
	Dictatorship of Robespierre	118
	His measures to secure his power	118
	The worship of the Supreme	118
	Terror at its height	118
	Frightful state of Paris	119
	Massacres in the Provinces	119
	The Republic obtains fresh successes in the campaign of 1794	121
	English naval victories of June 1	121
	The Allies defeated on all other points of the theatre	121
	Battle of Fleurus, June 26, 1794	121
	Reaction against the Reign of Terror	122
	Fall of Robespierre, July 27, 1794	122
	Execution of Robespierre, St. Just, Couthon and others, July 28, 1794	123
	Reflections on this event	123
	The Terrorists were not able men	124
	Notwithstanding the efforts of the French, the Allies could have put down the Revolution	125

CHAPTER VII.

THERMIDOR. FRENCH CONQUESTS.

		PAGE
1794	Reaction of Thermidor	126
	The prisons opened	126
	Punishment of several of the Terrorists	126
	Abolition of the Revolutionary Tribunal, and of the maximum	126
	The forcing of the value of assignats discontinued	127
	The populace of Paris kept down. The Jacobin Club suppressed	127
	Violence of the Reaction	128
	Revolution in manners	128
	The Jeunesse Dorée	129
	Renewed troubles	129
	Scarcity and distress	130
	The Jacobin party tries to rally	131
1795	Outbreaks of 12th Germinal (April 1)	131
	And of 1st Prairial (May) 1795	131
	Put down and suppressed	132
	The power of Jacobinism finally broken	132
	Measures of the Government against the Royalists	133
	Weakness of the State. Tendency to the rule of the sword	133
	Great successes of French against the Allies	133
	Conquest of Belgium and Holland, September 1794, January 1795	134
	Failure of English descent from Quiberon Bay, July 15—20, 1795	134
	The Coalition dissolved. Prussia and Spain make peace, April, June 1795	134
	Causes of this astonishing success of the Republic	135
	Continuing weakness of the Republic at home	136
	Extreme distress of the great cities	137
	Exhaustion of the Revolutionary spirit	137
	Desire for repose and a settled government. Reaction towards Monarchy	137

		PAGE
1795	Constitution of the year III	138
	The Constitution generally well received . .	139
	Opposition to the re-election of two-thirds of the Convention	139
	Rising of the reactionary sections of Paris, 13th Vendémiaire (October 4, 1795), put down by Bonaparte .	140
	The authority of the Convention restored . .	140
	The military power becomes stronger . . .	141
	Reflections on the course of the Revolution after Thermidor	141

CHAPTER VIII.

THE DIRECTORY. BONAPARTE.

	Character of this period	142
	State of the Republic after Vendémiaire . .	143
	Policy of the Directory	144
	National Bankruptcy virtually declared . .	144
1796	Preparations for the campaign of 1796 . .	145
	The campaign of Italy	146
	Bonaparte invades Piedmont from the seaboard .	146
	April 28, 1794	146
	May 9—30, 1796	146
	He marches to the Adige. Siege of Mantua . .	146
	The Austrians send an army to raise the siege of Mantua and to crush Bonaparte	147
	He defeats Wurmser in a series of engagements .	147
	August 3—6, September 1—13, 1796 . . .	147
	The Austrians send Alvinzi with a new army . .	148
	He is defeated at Arcola, November 14—17, 1796 .	148
1797	Decisive victory of Bonaparte at Rivoli, January 14, 1797	148
	Reflections on the campaign. Great skill of Bonaparte	148
	Character of his strategy	149
	State craft of Bonaparte	150
	Campaign of 1796 in Germany. Defeats of the French	150
	The Archduke Charles	150

A

xviii   *Contents.*

		PAGE
1797	Ability displayed by him	150
	Internal state of the Republic; revival of factions	152
	Royalist and reactionary schemes	152
	Coup d'état of the 18th Fructidor (September 4, 1797)	153
	Conclusion of the campaign of Italy	153
	Conciliatory policy of Bonaparte; his anti-revolutionary views	154
	He marches on Vienna from Italy	154
	Treaty of Campo Formio, October 17, 1797	155
	Gains of France	155
	Sacrifice of Venice	155
	Reflections on the conduct of Bonaparte	156
	Enthusiasm in France at his successes	156
	Admiration felt for him in Europe	156
	He returns to France, and is received with acclamation December, 1797	157 157

CHAPTER IX.

EGYPT AND THE 18TH BRUMAIRE.

1798	The Directory jealous of Bonaparte	158
	They engage him to attempt a descent on England	159
	He proposes to invade Egypt	159
	Expedition to Egypt	159
	Congress of Rastadt	160
	Renewal of causes of discord in Europe	160
	Formation of the Ligurian, Helvetian, and Roman Republics	160
	Bonaparte lands in Egypt July 1, 1798	161
	Battle of the Nile, August 1, 1798, and destruction of the French fleet	161
	Renewal of the war in Europe	162
1799	Murder of the French plenipotentiaries at Rastadt, April 28, 1799	162
	The Conscription	162
	Character of the campaign of 1799	163
	Defeats of the French	163
	Formation of the Parthenopæan Republic	163

Contents. xix

		PAGE
1798	Battle of Stochach, March 25, 1799	163
	Battles of the Trebbia and Novi, June 17, 18, and 19, and August 15, 1799	164
	The French driven from Italy	164
	Failure of English descent on Holland	164
	Battle of Zurich, September 25—28, 1789	164
	It saves France from invasion	165
	Lamentable internal state of the Republic	165
	Strife of factions	165
	The reverses of 1799 cause all parties to combine against the Directory	166
	Weakness and ruin of the State	166
	Desire for a strong Government	166
	Siéyès	166
	Fortunes of Bonaparte in Egypt	167
	He fails at Acre, March to May, 1799	167
	On hearing the news of the state of France, he leaves Egypt	168
	Enthusiasm with which he is received on his way to and in Paris	168
	He at once becomes the real centre of power	168
	He prepares a *coup d'état* to change the Government	169
1799	The 18th Brumaire (November 9), 1799	169
	Scene in Assembly at St. Cloud	170
	Formation of a provisional government. Bonaparte First Consul	170
	Character of the Revolution of 18th Brumaire	170
	Reflections on the conduct of Bonaparte, and on the march of events	170
	The *coup d'état* was not a crime	171

CHAPTER X.

MARENGO. LUNEVILLE. AMIENS.

1800	Wise and healing policy of the First Consul	172
	Financial reforms	172
	Fortunate position of Bonaparte as a mediator between factions	174

		PAGE
1800	Laws against clergy and émigrés repealed or mitigated	174
	Pacification of La Vendée	175
	Rapid recovery of France	175
	Constitution of the year VIII.	175
	The institutions founded by it	176
	Objects of Siéyès	176
	Bonaparte First Consul for ten years	176
	His Despotism is established, surrounded by merely nominal restraints	177
	Reorganization of the French armies	177
	Plans of the First Consul	177
	The campaign of 1800	178
	Operations of Melas in Italy, and of Moreau in Bavaria	178
	The First Consul crosses the Alps May 16–19, 1800	179
	The French army enters Milan, June 2	179
	Melas falls back	180
	Battle of Marengo, June 14, 1800	180
	The French recover Italy	181
	Campaign in Germany	181
	Advance of Moreau. Ability of Kray	181
	Battle of Hohenlinden, December 3, 1800	182
1801	Treaty of Luneville, February 9, 1801	182
	Great advantages gained by France	182
	Dictatorial tone of Bonaparte	183
1802	Treaty of Amiens, March 27, 1802	184
	Great results obtained by the First Consul	184

CHAPTER XI.

THE CONSULATE. RENEWAL OF WAR.

Internal Government of the First Consul	185
The time favorable for reconstructing society in France	186
Reforms in the State	187
The Judicial system	187
The Code	188
Centralization of local powers	188
Prefects and sub-prefects	189

Contents. xxi

		PAGE
1802	The Concordat	189
	Its effects	191
	Public Instruction	191
	General results of these reforms	191
	Changes in the army	191
	Creation of a new aristocracy	192
	The Legion of Honor. Restoration of Titles	192
	Bonaparte made Consul for life	192
	Modification, in a despotic sense, of the Constitution of the year VIII.	193
	Partial resemblance of the new Government to that of the Monarchy	193
	Its evils	193
	Its merits	193
	Wise Administration of the First Consul	194
	He encourages the movement towards Monarchy	194
	Change of manners in France	195
	Foreign Policy of the First Consul	196
	Its craft and ambition	196
	French intervention in Germany	197
1803	Great extension of French power and influence	197
	Disputes with England. March to May, 1803	198
	Renewal of war with England, May 18, 1803	198

CHAPTER XII.

THE EMPIRE TO TILSIT.

	The First Consul plans a descent on England	199
	The flotilla and camp of Boulogne	200
	Project of covering the descent by a large fleet in the Channel	200
	Conspiracy of the *émigrés* against the First Consul	201
1804	Execution of the Duke of Enghien, March 21, 1804	202
	This event hastens the movement in favor of Monarchy	203
	The First Consul proclaimed Emperor of the French, May 18, 1804	203
	Coronation of Napoleon, December 2, 1804	204
1805	New coalition against France	205

Contents.

		PAGE
1805	Plan of the attack of the Allies	206
	Campaign of 1805	206
	Napoleon quits Boulogne, and surrounds and captures an Austrian army at Ulm, October 19, 1805	206
	Battle of Trafalgar and destruction of the French and Spanish fleets, October 21, 1805	207
	The project of the descent might have succeeded	208
	Napoleon marches on Vienna	209
	The Grand Army	209
	Vienna occupied, November 13, 1805	209
	Battle of Austerlitz, December 2, 1805. Ruin of the allied army	210
	Peace of Presburg, December 15, 1805	210
	Changes effected by it	211
	Austria ceases to be Head of the German Empire	211
	The Confederation of the Rhine	211
	Isolation of Prussia	211
	Conduct of that power	211
	It declares war against France	212
	Campaign of 1806	212
	Battles of Jena and Auerstadt, October 14, 1806	212
1807	Ruin of the Prussian army and Monarchy	212
	Napoleon marches against the Russians	213
	Winter campaign in Poland	213
	Campaign of 1807	213
	Indecisive battle of Eylau, February 8, 1807	214
	Peril of Napoleon	214
	Reorganization of the Grand Army	214
	Decisive victory of the French at Friedland, June 14, 1807	214
	Characteristics of these campaigns	215
	Changes in the art of war	215
	Meeting of Alexander and Napoleon on the Niemen, June 25, 1807	215
	Treaty of Tilsit, July 7 and 9, 1807	216
	Alliance between France and Russia, and dismemberment of Prussia	216

Contents. xxiii

		PAGE
1807	Objects of Napoleon in making the treaty	216
	His power at its height	217
	Extent of the French Empire	217
	Vassal kingdoms	217
	Allied and subject States	218
	The Empire promoted civilization in some respects	218
	Prosperity of France	218
	Public works of Napoleon	219
	Character of his Government	219
	Elements of weakness and decay in the Empire	220
	Indignation of conquered nations	220
	Tendency of Germany to unite through common suffering	220
	Jealousy of Russia	221
	Decline of the Grand Army in strength	221
	The resources of France unduly strained	221
	Moral evils of the rule of Napoleon	222
	Insecurity of his power, which depended mainly on himself	223

CHAPTER XIII.

THE EMPIRE TO 1813.

Retrospect of the policy of Napoleon	224
It changes for the worse after Tilsit	225
The Continental system, 1807-8	226
Its mischievous effects upon the Empire	227
It urges Napoleon to make conquests	227
Project of invading Spain and Portugal	228
Napoleon dethrones the House of Braganza, November, December, 1807	228
The Royal Family of Spain enticed to Bayonne, and induced to abdicate the throne, May, 1808	228
General rising in Spain, May, June, 1808	229
Capitulation of Baylen, July 19, 20, 1808	229
First appearance of Sir A. Wellesley on the scene. Convention of Cintra, August 30, 1808	229

		PAGE
1808	Great reverses of the French	229
	Napoleon invades Spain and enters Madrid, December 2, 1808	230
	He leaves the Peninsula at the news that Austria was arming	230
	Campaign of 1809 in Germany	230
	Defeat of the Archduke Charles in Bavaria, April 18, 22, 1809	230
	Reverse of Napoleon on the Danube at Aspern, May 21, 22, 1809	231
	Battle of Wagram and victory of French, July 6, 1809	231
	Treaty of Vienna, October 14, 1809	231
1810	Napoleon divorces Josephine and marries the Archduchess Maria Louisa, March 11, 1810	232
	Successes of Sir Arthur Wellesley in 1809, in Portugal and Spain	232
	His profound insight and military skill	232
	Memorable campaign of Torres Vedras. and complete defeat of the French, June, 1810, May, 1811	233
	Great results of this campaign, and its influence on Europe	233
	Agitation in Germany and Holland	234
1811	Murmurs in France	234
	Birth of a son to Napoleon, March 20, 1811	235
	Jealousy of the Czar, and disputes with Russia	235
	Napoleon prepares to invade Russia, November, 1811, May, 1812	235
	Campaign of 1812	236
	The Grand Army crosses the Niemen, June 24, 1812	236
	Retreat of the Russians	236
	Political mistake of Napoleon in not restoring Poland	236
	He pursues the Russians	237
	Difficulties of the Grand Army	237
	Precautions taken by Napoleon	237
	He marches into the interior of Russia	238
	Battle of Borodino, September 7, 1812	238
	The Grand Army enters Moscow, September 15, 1812	238

Contents. xxv

		PAGE
1811	The Russian Governor of Moscow sets fire to the city	238
	Napoleon delays in the hope of peace . . .	238
	Beginning of the retreat from Moscow, October 19, 1812	239
	Horrors of the retreat	239
	Imminent peril of Napoleon and the remains of the army	239
	Passage of the Beresina, November 25–28, 1812 .	239
	Napoleon leaves the army for France, December 5, 1812	240
	Destruction of the Grand Army . . .	240
	Reflections on this catastrophe	240
	Causes of the ruin of the French . . .	240

CHAPTER XIV.

FALL OF NAPOLEON.

	Return of Napoleon to Paris	241
	Conspiracy of Malet	242
	Defection of York, December 30, 1812 . .	242
	Rising of Germany, January–March, 1813 . .	242
1813	Retreat of the French, February–March, 1813. Energy of Napoleon	243
	His immense preparations to repair his fortunes .	243
	Bad condition of the French levies . . .	243
	Campaign of 1813	244
	Battle of Lützen, May 2, 1813	244
	Battle of Baützen, May 20–21, 1813 . . .	244
	Success of Napoleon	244
	Armistice of Pleistwitz, June 4, 1813 . .	245
	Austria proposes terms to Napoleon which he unwisely rejects	245
	The successes of Wellington in Spain decide Austria to join the Coalition	246
	Battle of Vittoria, June 21, 1813 . . .	246
	The French driven from Spain . . .	246
	Europe in arms against Napoleon . . .	246
	His views and objects in the contest . .	246

		PAGE
1813	Plan of the Allies	247
	Battle of Dresden, August 27, 1813	247
	Battle of Culm, August 30, 1813	248
	Battles on the Katzbach, at Grossbeeren, and at Dennewitz, August 23 to September 5, 1813	248
	Great battles of Leipsic, October 16 and 18, 1813	249
	The French driven to the Rhine	249
	Defeats of the French in Italy. Wellington invades France	249
	Revolt of the Allied and subject states	250
	Desperate condition of the Empire	250
	Napoleon thinks only of a death-struggle	251
	His preparations	251
	The Allies invade France, December 20-26	251
	The military situation of Napoleon seems hopeless	252
	Prostration of France	252
	Campaign of 1814	252
	Battles of Brienne and La Rothière, January 29 and February 1, 1814	252
	Napoleon interposes between the Allies	253
	Battles of Champaubert, Montmirail, Vauchamps, and Nangis, February 10-18, 1814	253
	Astonishing success of Napoleon	253
	Success of the Allies on other parts of the theatre	254
	Fresh forces raised against Napoleon	254
	Battle of Laon, March 9 and 10, 1814	254
1814	Napoleon falls back on Lorraine to rally his garrisons, and strike the rear of the Allies	255
	The Allies march on Paris, March 25, 1814	255
	State of opinion in the capital	256
	Capitulation of Paris, March 30, 1814	256
	Napoleon dethroned. The Bourbons restored	256
	Napoleon hastily retraces his steps	257
	He abdicates April 4, 1814	257
	Character of Napoleon	258
	Reflections on his fall	259

Contents. xxvii

CHAPTER XV.
THE HUNDRED DAYS AND WATERLOO.

		PAGE
1814	Peace of Paris, May 30, 1814	261
	Congress of Vienna, September, 1814, March, 1815 .	261
	Unpopularity of the Government of Louis XVIII. .	261
	Conduct of the *émigrés*	262
1815	Napoleon leaves Elba, February 26, 1815 . .	263
	He lands in France, March 1, 1815 . . .	263
	His triumphant march to Paris . . .	263
	Pacific overtures of Napoleon	264
	The Allied Powers declare war, March 25, 1815 .	264
	Great efforts of Napoleon to restore the French army	265
	Campaign of 1815	265
	Two plans of operation open to Napoleon . .	265
	He resolves to attack Blücher and Wellington in Belgium	265
	Concentration of the French army on the frontier .	266
	It advances on June 15, 1815	266
	Battle of Ligny, June 16, 1816 . . .	267
	Battle of Quatre Bras, June 15, 1815 . . .	267
	Result of the operations of June 16 . . .	267
	Blücher rallies the Prussians, and moves to join Wellington on a second line	268
	Movements of Napoleon and Wellington on June 17, 1815	269
	Miscalculations of Napoleon . . .	269
	Results of the operations of June 17 . . .	269
	Great battle of Waterloo, June 18, 1815 . .	270
	Defeat and rout of the French army . .	271
	Reflections on the campaign . . .	271
	Conclusion	273
	Appendix	275

LIST OF MAPS.

EUROPE IN 1789, . . : . . *to face page* 19
EUROPE IN 1812, ... " " 234

THE
FRENCH REVOLUTION.

CHAPTER I.

STATE OF FRANCE BEFORE THE REVOLUTION.

THE FRENCH REVOLUTION marks the beginning of a new era in the History of the World. A rising in one of the great States of Europe against a long-settled order of things, it overthrew society in France, and wrought violent changes in the Continent; and, at last, directed by military genius, it culminated in domination and conquest, followed ultimately by a terrible retribution. During the progress of this wonderful movement ancient landmarks of reason, of thought, and of faith, were suddenly set aside or effaced; the birth of a new age was ushered in by atrocious deeds of disorder and blood; and in the gigantic strife which ensued the boundaries of Empires were wildly shifted and war was seen in unparalleled grandeur. We are, perhaps even now, too near these events to pronounce with confidence a judgment upon them; yet some of the results may be rapidly glanced at. The Revolution has destroyed a great deal that was worth-

[margin: General character and results of the French Revolution.]

less and in decay in France; it has stimulated the industry and promoted the material progress and wealth of the nation; and it has given better institutions to a large part of the Continent, and removed a number of ancient abuses. Yet, it may be questioned whether, as regards the permanent interests of mankind, this period of confusion, and the rule of the sword, has not led to as much evil as good. At present it seems impossible to form anything like an enduring government in France; faith and loyalty have lost their former power in the land of Coligny, Bayard, and Turenne. Europe, in Napoleon's remarkable phrase, appears destined, from the Tagus to the Volga, to become half Republican and half Cossack. Though wild theories of freedom disturb society in vast tracts of the Continent, true liberty and order have not been reconciled, and Despotism and Democracy are at sullen feud; whole nations have been turned into armed camps, preparing for an internecine struggle; at no period have international rights and the claims and privileges of weak States been so openly held in little respect; and those ominous phenomena may, in different degrees, be all ascribed to the world from 1789 to 1815.

It exhibited vividly the peculiar features of the French national character. In the peculiar features of the French Revolution we trace plainly the characteristics of the remarkable people in which it had its origin. No other community in Europe, perhaps, would, after a protracted period of torpor, have so suddenly awakened to agitated life, or so hastily rushed along the path of innovation. In no other community would attempts at reform have been marked by such rash extravagance united to many generous aspirations; in none would theories of Government and Law have been carried out with equal recklessness and so grave a contempt of existing facts, and yet have been presented to the world in such alluring colors. Hardly any other European nation would have exhibited such vehement outbursts of passion; would, in all that relates to political life, have passed so rapidly to opposite extremes, and oscillated with such uncertain quickness; would with such apparent readiness have cowered under a ferocious tyranny of which the crimes cast a deep stain on the French name; would have welcomed with such general acclaim a despotism of the sword as the best mode of government; would so eagerly have given up the brilliant visions of a few years before, to follow the phantom of military glory; or would so carelessly have abandoned its idol when it seemed to have lost its magical influence. Yet, on the other hand, few communities indeed, have displayed the noble though unreflecting ardor seen occasionally in the movement of 1789; have in defending the natal soil against apparently irresistible odds, given proof of the energy of 1793—4, overrated as that energy has been; have inscribed on their annals such a roll of victories as Rivoli, Arcola, Jena, Austerlitz, Hohenlinden, Friedland, and a hundred more; have made efforts that will compare with those made by France from 1792 to 1815. It should be remembered, moreover, that for evil or good, all these manifestations of French nature were largely due to circumstances of an extraordinary kind; and, probably, but for influences alien to it, the Revolution would have run a less terrible course. In one particular France was true to her general history during this period. Her influence over adjoining countries has at all times been distinct and immense; and it never was so great as when it swept away thrones, dominations, princedoms, and powers, in a pretended crusade for the

Rights of Man, and placed the Continent under the feet of Napoleon.

.The Monarchy of France before the Revolution; abuses in the system of Government.

But though the qualities of Frenchmen mark the Revolution throughout its progress, we must not suppose that a great change was not inevitable before that event. The institutions of France had ceased long previously to be in accord with the wants of the nation, and the frame of society seemed out of joint, and falling into decay and weakness.* The Government was an ancient Despotism, which gave no scope to political life, or guarantee for rational freedom, and under which the mass of the people were considered as serfs to be ruled

* It has been obviously impossible, in a sketch like this, to comment at length on the state of France before the Revolution, or to describe in detail the institutions of the Bourbon Monarchy, and their working. The number of valuable works on these subjects is so great, that it is difficult to make a selection for the reader. Perhaps the best general account of the political condition of old France will be found in M. de Tocqueville's *L'Ancien Régime et la Revolution*—see the translation by Henry Reeve, D.C.L., edition of 1873; though I venture to think the picture of abuses and evils somewhat too lightly colored. Professor Von Sybel's *History of the French Revolution*, though as a narrative dull and one-sided, contains also a valuable chapter on the France of Louis XV. and XVI.; and the whole subject is ably treated in the sixteenth and last volume of M. Henri Martin's *Histoire de France*. The political and social life of the time has been painted with extraordinary force by Mr. Carlyle in his well-known work; and with less justice but with great skill by MM. Michelet and Louis Blanc in their Histories of the French Revolution. Arthur Young's *Travels in France* in 1787-9 contain much valuable information on the economic state of the country; and the *résumé* of the Cahiers or instructions of the deputies to the States-General of 1789 bring out in clear and full relief the innumerable grievances of the nation.

CH. I.   *France before the Revolution.*   5

at pleasure. Here and there, indeed, the shadows survived of Estates which had controlled the Monarchy, and the Parliament of Paris still retained the semblance of an august authority; but practically, in the greater part of France, the only checks on the will of the Sovereign were either inadequate or simply vexatious. In most of the Provinces the edicts of the King, however oppressive, had the force of law; the Crown generally could impose taxes, imprison the subject without hope of redress, and interfere with the course of justice; and its powers were asserted and carried home everywhere by a system of administration highly centralized, and not seldom corrupt and iniquitous. Under this scheme of arbitrary rule true national liberty could not grow up; securities for public and private rights, long enjoyed in England, had no existence; and acts of violence and of cruel wrong were by no means of uncommon occurrence. It would, in truth, be easy to show that the Monarchy supplied, in many respects, too faithful precedents to the Reign of Terror; and wholesale massacres, ruthless deportations, robbery in the shape of forced contributions, arrests, and detentions without trial, confiscations, and frauds on the debts of the State, were known in France before 1793, though Jacobinism exaggerated in a few months misdeeds previously spread over centuries. Nor had the Monarchy, since the time of Louis XIV., exhibited that regard for the common weal, and that munificence in the national interests, which have so often veiled the evils of despotism in the eyes of the unthinking millions, and are sometimes of real benefit to them. More then one of the noble creations of Colbert* had been allowed to fall into decay; the great

---

* Jean Baptiste Colbert, one of the greatest ministers of Louis

highways and canals of France were in several districts in a state of ruin; and, while gorgeous luxury revelled in the palace, the public service was starved and neglected. Louis XV. probably spent more money on his harem than on any department of the State, and even in his successor's reign it was thought a marvel that during a struggle with England the king should have devoted to the fleet a mere fraction of his princely revenue.

The Church and the Nobility. Why these orders had become generally disliked. Beside the Monarchy, yet not giving the throne solid and useful support, were two great Orders which, at one time, had been supreme in France, and still held a high place in the State. The Church raised its front in feudal magnificence, enriched lavishly with the wealth of centuries, and possessing immense estates and a large jurisdiction; and its dignitaries formed a kind of nobility, drawn generally from the great Houses of France, and still invested with many privileges. These patrician prelates and lordly abbots were marked off by a broad line of distinction from the body of the inferior clergy; and their haughty demeanor and pretentious pride made them generally objects of fear and dislike. Beside them, spread over the whole of France, was the numerous Order of the lay Nobles, who formed one of the most unpopular and worthless castes that had grown out of the decay of the Middle Ages. The French Seigneurie of this period still possessed many of the most odious privileges of Feudalism in the sixteenth century; they were

XIV., born 1619, died 1683. In addition to the extraordinary impulse he gave to commerce and manufactures in France, he founded the dockyards of Brest, Teulon, and Rochefort, almost created the French navy, and constructed many of the great roads and canals of the country.

largely exempted from State Taxation, and enjoyed rights of the most oppressive kind over their vassals' property and even persons; and yet they were not linked by the more kindly ties of feudalism to their humble dependents; for, with many and honorable exceptions, they very seldom lived on their lands, and squandered their rents at Versailles or in Paris, They were, too, to a great extent, composed of new men and needy adventurers, who would have thrown discredit on any class; and they boasted but few historic names, illustrious for their services to the State, and justifying by their past or recent achievements the rank and position of the whole Order. Can we wonder that such a body as this, at once tyrannical and ignoble, was viewed in France with general dislike, and that the eighty thousand families of which it was composed, which held in thraldom, perhaps, two-thirds of the peasantry and the soil of the country, and locust-like preyed upon its resources, were in most instances dreaded and abhorred? The cause, however, has yet to be noted which perhaps contributed most to expose the Seigneurie to universal odium. It was easy enough to become a noble in France by honorable or dishonorable means; but the Nobles stood apart, as a class divided from all below them by the harshest distinctions; and the result was that they displayed an arrogance, an insolence, and a contempt of others, not readily understood in our time. It was quite usual for the young noblesse of that day to run down the canaille of the streets, and to insult the wives of the bourgeois to their husbands' faces; and, not fifty years previously, a distinguished seigneur had made it a grievance that Louis XV. should have administered to him a mild rebuke for following the pastime of shooting peasants. Undoubtedly many of the nobility of France were men of a very different kind; but in the large majority exclusive privilege had developed its ordinary consequences.

<small>The power of the ruling orders was divided and decayed and consequently weak.</small> Yet, however august the Monarchy seemed, and high the state of the Church and the Nobles, their powers, nevertheless, were weak and divided. The Sovereign of France had not full control over the ultimate support of all authority, for the Army was, to a considerable extent, in the hands of princes and great seigneurs independent of the Crown in different degrees; and the soldiery, shut out from promotion and reward, and subjected to a cruel and degrading discipline, had long been filled with elements of disaffection. The power of the Monarchy, too, was crossed and thwarted by the decaying remains of feudal institutions no longer capable of doing good; and it had lost a great share of the patronage of the State, and of the administration of the public service, through the ruinous practice of selling offices which had gone on for several generations. Thus while the prerogatives of the King were immense, and were often exercised with extreme harshness, the Monarchy was deficient in essential strength; its action was impeded in many spheres in which its influence should have been absolute; and it was, in a great and dangerous degree, deprived of the right of an Executive Government to select and dispose of its own instruments. As for the Church, virtue had gone out of it, and it was enfeebled by imbecility and discord. The hierarchy might boast of their sounding titles, and walk in purple and fine linen, but their moral influence had become nought; and though they could still torture oppressed Huguenots, and condemn heretical books to the flames, they were unable to stem the tide

of thought that was sweeping away their proud pretensions. Besides, little sympathy existed between these potentates and the lower clergy, divided from them by a broad barrier; and while in the high places of the Church no Bossuet stepped out to do battle with Voltaire, in many dioceses the village curés were secret enemies of their superiors, and hated the ecclesiastical system around them. The condition of the nobility, too, was one of weakness and internal dissension. In a State ruled as France long had been, the Order had little political power; and though it possessed most unjust privileges, and extravagant and oppressive local rights, its authority was exceedingly small in all that related to the central Government. The Nobles were not a great aristocracy with a potent voice in the national councils; they had no part in the work of legislation; and their influence was scanty and jealously curtailed in many departments of the public service, and even in the administration of the country districts. A tacit feud, too, existed between the more distinguished and inferior nobility: the Montmorencies and La Tremouilles despised the crowd of new and petty seigneurs whose pretensions seemed a disgrace to their own; and enlightened members of the Order condemned the insolence, tyranny, and greed, of the great mass of the men who called them fellows.

It should be observed, moreover, that the different Orders which embodied power and grandeur in France had been repeatedly in angry collision, and their representatives had largely incurred discredit. A quarrel between the Crown and the Nobles had come down from the days of Louis XIV., and had raged at intervals during the reign of his successors. The Parliament of

Dissensions between the Crown, the Church, and the Nobles, and discredit of all authority.

Paris, too, had, more than once, risen against royal assumptions or claims; and Louis XV., at the bidding of a harlot, had treated this body with odious severity. The Church, besides, had had many squabbles with what may be called the party of the Court nobles, and the Parliaments of the kingdom had often resisted its bigoted and intolerable-assumptions, though they had joined zealously in Huguenot persecutions, and, with the characteristic feelings of lawyers, had steadily refused to make changes in a barbarous scheme of criminal procedure. It is easy to estimate the effects of these open and public conflicts; the authorities of the State laid bare the weakness and vices of the institutions of France to the eyes of a nation deprived of its rights, and the growing contempt that was felt for them, and their unpopularity largely increased. As to the reputation of the higher Orders in France during the greater part of the eighteenth century, it is almost superfluous to refer to it. The orgies of the Regency can be only compared with those of the worst pagan Cæsars; and Louis XV. was a degraded being, a slave of coarse and unmanly vices, and a puppet of scheming priests and mistresses, all the more despicable because not their dupe. As for the nobility, whether in Church or State, some, doubtless, were blameless and illustrious men, but the great majority were only conspicuous for dissoluteness, extravagance, and frivolous luxury. The scandalous and not concealed debaucheries of cardinals and bishops had been common talk; and the ordinary life of the better of the class was a graceful round of refined amusement, of idleness, and of epicurean indulgence. Decline, however, was most apparent and beyond remedy in the lay nobility. Even among the historic families of France hardly a name of real eminence appeared; and the Richelieus and Condés, who had built up the realm, had degenerated into fops and courtiers. As for the great mass of the Nobles, they were different beings from the chivalry of Rocroi and Landen; very few had won honor in the field; their manhood was wasted in gambling and intrigues, in mere display and effeminate pursuits; and their ignorance and listlessness were on a par with their overweening arrogance and conceit. Not many of the young gallants of this time could write even a common letter; and pulling out the threads of silk tissue seemed to fine ladies the business of a day. Contrast in this, and in all other respects, the characteristics of the aristocracy of England trained under the discipline of public life, and taught to discharge high social duties by a vigilant and exacting general opinion.

Under this array of grandeur and state, iniquitous and oppressive, but really weak; with splendid traditions, but no vital strength; with lofty pretensions, but failing and decried, was marshalled the ill-governed Nation: the twenty-five millions of the French Commons, who, it was said, "counted as nothing in France." Discordant elements, however, lurked in the mass; and it is necessary to perceive this truth, or we shall never understand the events that ensued. A great Middle Class had grown up in France, especially in the principal towns; and the professional and mercantile Orders, reaping the fruits of ages of honorable toil, and not spoiled by luxurious idleness, had, in numberless instances, amassed wealth, and attained to a high degree of refinement. An aristocracy of riches and culture had been formed among the lawyers, the physicians, the manufacturers, and other traders; and though it had been trained in a bad school

State of the Commons of France. The middle classes; how they were cut off from the People, and the results.

of thought, and was wholly wanting in political knowledge, it really comprised what was most enlightened, most intelligent, and truly sound in the kingdom. This numerous and respectable class disapproved of the existing order of things, in which they were esteemed inferior beings, and especially regarded the Nobles with dislike, whose insolence was often directed against them. But, as regards the mass of the Nation, they too were isolated and stood apart; and a whole series of invidious distinctions cut them off from the People from which they sprung. In fact, Feudalism had left its stamp on this as on other Orders of the State, and a policy of distinction had made the mark deeper. The professions, the trades, and the industries of France, were organized on a system of exclusive privilege, and of grasping and close monopoly; and they formed everywhere a number of Corporations, of guilds, and of separate castes, with distinctive rights and peculiar immunities. The Bourgeoisie, as they were contemptuously called, were thus led to look down with scorn on the bulk of the community around; and though eminent men were among their ranks, they had little sympathy with the great body of the People, and they were viewed, as a general rule, with envy and ill-feeling by their poorer dependents. One of the cardinal facts of this period is the alienation that existed between the great employers of labor in France and the workmen and artisans of the towns, and it marked many phases of the Revolution.

In France, therefore, deep lines of distinction divided the Upper and Middle Orders, and separated both alike from the People. In no country were differences of class more offensively marked, and yet more unpopular; and Feudalism, which had knit society, in one of its stages, in close dependence, now broke it up into

CH. I.   *France before the Revolution.*   13

disunited fragments. We turn to consider the mass of the Nation, which may be viewed in its two chief parts, the inhabitants of the country, and those of the towns. The occupiers of the soil, as a general rule, were subjected to heavy and vexatious taxation, from which the owners, if noble, were exempt; and, in the distribution of the imposts of the State, were frequently treated with harsh injustice. Yet these grievances were small compared to the burdens their lords imposed upon them, and to the usage they had often to endure. Condition of In a very considerable part of France the the Peasantry. peasantry held the land by a permanent right; and in some of the Provinces, especially in the North, large farms were cultivated under long leases. Though the peasant estates were greatly subdivided, these districts were comparatively thriving; and they were easily distinguished by the signs of comfort and of agricultural progress evident in them. Yet the cultivators even of these favored regions were liable to numberless petty vexations, to iniquitous restrictions upon their industry, to services sometimes degrading and mean; and their very prosperity caused them to resent the imperious harshness and neglect of duty of their generally absentee superiors. In other parts of France the land was held, over most of its breadth, by precarious tenures; and, except in a few Provinces, where the relations between the lord and vassal were still not unkindly, the occupiers were a race of serfs, ground down by rack-rents and feudal oppression, kept in abject dependence, exposed to wrong, and often struggling on the verge of destitution. The districts held on these wretched conditions seemed, in spots, smitten as it were with barrenness; and an experienced eye-witness* wrote that, ex-

* Arthur Young.

cept in Ireland—at that time in her very worst state—he had never beheld such squalor and misery. In these tracts the food of the peasant was not seldom nettles and pulse; and it was in these that, a few years afterwards, rose the troops of half-clad and ferocious savages, who, at the first whisper that deliverance was near, burned the chateaux of the abhorred seigneurs, on whom they laid the charge of their sufferings. The condition of the lowest tillers of the soil must have been pitiable in this state of things; and there is reason to believe that the wages of the agricultural laborer in France before the Revolution were not half (in some places) what they have since become. As for the population of the towns, it had been allowed to multiply densely in ignorance and want; and the large cities swarmed with dangerous classes—poor, discontented, and enemies of the rich, who stood selfishly aloof from them—and blindly eager for any change. It was from these orders that Jacobinism recruited its armies of devastation and crime—the murderers who crowded the prisons with corpses—the furies who shrieked round the guillotine.

Of the population of the towns.

It should be remembered, too, that while the whole frame of Society in France was thus ill-ordered, and its component parts were weakened and diseased, a spirit of wild innovation had grown up, which fiercely assailed the tottering structure. Thought, at least among the privileged classes, had long been comparatively free; and it had embodied itself in a brilliant literature, audacious, sceptical, yet unreflecting, which held up almost every institution, and even the existing order of things, to universal contempt and ridicule. The movement, doubtless, originating in the inexperience in political life of

Destructive and sceptical tone of contemporary French Literature.

CH. I. *France before the Revolution.* 15

French men of letters, like all other Frenchmen, received a definite character from two men of genius; and while Voltaire sapped away the throne, the altar, and the privileges of the great by keen satire and malignant wit, the more profound Rousseau constructed theories for the regeneration and happiness of mankind, which bade defiance to all social arrangements. Thus intellect, which, in a healthy State, is always upon the side of order, and aims only at temperate reforms, became destructive and anarchic in France; and though it would be a mistake to think that it caused the Revolution, the causes of which lay much deeper, it accelerated that event, and left its mark upon it. Strange to say, too, so little were the signs of the coming time understood in France, this godless, false, and spurious philosophy found high favor among the classes destined to suffer most cruelly from it. It had become the custom before the Revolution, to scoff at faith, to decry the past, to relish attacks on people in high places, to complain of the absurdities of class distinctions, to see in the complication of old laws and customs a mass of rubbish to be swept away, to put together pretty and ingenious systems for making the world a scene of pleasure; and lettered marquises and brocaded dames babbled of the philosophic dictionary, and the *contrat social*, as though doctrines fatal to their pretensions at least were the very perfection of truth and wisdom. Of all the phenomena of this period, none is more instructive than this curious spectacle of the natural supporters of social order playing with the instruments that were to hasten its ruin.

This sketch of France before the Revolution may seem overcharged with dark colors as respects the immediately preceding period. But the sympathy which the appalling fate of thousands

The progress of evil continued down to the Revolution.

of unhappy victims evokes, ought not to blind us to the fact, that the worst evils of which we have given a brief account, were never more apparent and active than during the reign of Louis XVI. The King was certainly well-meaning; but the Monarchy was seldom guilty of acts more arbitrary, violent, and iniquitous than those sanctioned by Brienne* and Calonne.† At no time were the imbecility of the State and the dissensions between the privileged Orders more plainly evident than when Louis was twice compelled to dismiss his minister, at the bidding of an insolent party of the Noblesse, and when the Sovereign, the Notables, and the Parliament of Paris, were in angry collision on such subjects as the Public Debt and national bankruptcy. At no time, too, was the throne more weak than when Princes of the Blood were conspiring against it, or when the unjust reforms of St. Germain ‡ had increased the growing discontent of the Army. Nor at any period were the high ecclesiastics and Nobles of France more widely unpopular than when they clamored against Necker and Turgot,§

* Loménie de Brienne, Archbishop of Toulouse and Sens, born 1727, died 1794. As minister of Louis XVI. he exiled the Parliament of Paris to Troyes in 1787, and compelled it to register edicts of the King which it had opposed.

† Charles Alexandre Calonne, Minister of Louis XVI., born 1734, died 1802. He wasted recklessly the finances of the State, quarrelled with the Notables whom he had convened in 1786, and is believed to have promoted the policy afterwards followed.

‡ Claude Louis St. Germain, born 1707, died 1778. As minister of war to Louis XVI. he introduced a harsh and degrading discipline in the French army; and by his advice commissions were afterwards more restricted than they had ever been before to the class of the nobles.

§ For an account of the policy of Necker and Turgot, and of their plans of reform, see M. Henri Martin's *Histoire de France*,

CH. I. *France before the Revolution.* 17

and, at a season of national distress, refused to submit to equal taxation; nor had the lives of the class mended, though vice was, doubtless, less gross and cynical than in the days of Louis XV., and the arrogance of the great was sometimes tempered by a condescension not less insolent. Never, too, were the distinctions of class more sharply defined than at this juncture, and felt with more bitter resentment; and at no time had the poorer classes, in consequence of numerous bad harvests, suffered more hardships or been worse treated. Nor was the spirit even of the central Government patriotic, or in the general interest: its feeble attempts at superficial reforms were, for the most part, purely selfish expedients;. and, even when judicious, they were abandoned at the first symptom of class opposition. The King and Queen, too, did not escape the discredit which had fallen on all dignities; the weak character and awkward demeanor of Louis XVI. provoked contempt; and though the life of Marie Antoinette was pure, foul scandal had gathered around her name. The period, it is unnecessary to say, was especially one of wild speculations and of shallow schemes of universal change; and, in a word, all the elements of ill which had been gradually collecting in France had lost none of their fatal power.

Such, then, briefly was the condition of France before the crisis of 1789. English statesmen* trained in political life had long Brilliant anticipations of the future in France.

vol. xvi. Speaking generally, the measures they advocated were the abolition of the monopolies that sapped French industry, an equitable distribution of taxes instead of the injustice that prevailed, retrenchment, the publication of the finances of the State, decentralization, and something like representative assemblies. Turgot, however, was a much abler man than Necker.

* As far back as 1753 Lord Chesterfield had written: "All the

C

before seen that a change was at hand but no minister of Louis XVI.—few, as far as we know, among thinkers in France—had the least apprehension of coming danger. Many in high places, as we have seen, were intent on sweeping abuses away, and had planned magnificent schemes of reform; and the announcement that the States-General would meet seemed the dawn of a new and golden age to thousands foredoomed to death or exile, Even the agitation which followed that event—the disturbances which broke out in several provinces, the blind stirrings of the unenfranchised millions, dull, unintelligible, and yet ominous, and the clamorous exultation of the middle classes, who thought their time of hope had arrived—did not dissipate these illusions; for it was believed that the genius of a polite age would not allow popular excesses or passions. With these shallow and idle visions—the growth of ignorance, and of the false sentiment which pervaded a society in an unhealthy state—was mingled much that was truly noble, many generous and high aspirations; and a glowing rainbow of deceitful hope shone brilliantly over the dark torrent that was carrying old France to the depths below.

symptoms which I have ever met with in history, previous to great changes and revolutions in government, now exist and daily increase in France."

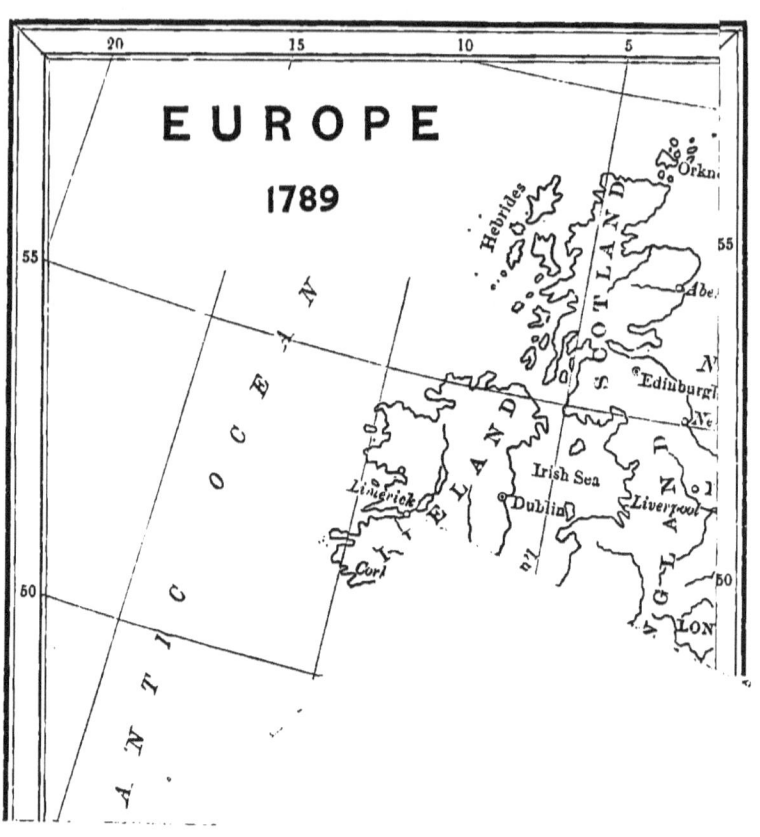

CHAPTER II.

THE STATES-GENERAL AND NATIONAL ASSEMBLY.

ON May 5, 1789, the States General met for the first time at Versailles. More than a hundred and seventy years had passed since, in the youth of the Bourbon Monarchy, this ancient Assembly of the Estates of the Realm had consulted upon the common weal; and they were now convened for the same purpose when that Monarchy was in decline and peril. The spectacle formed an imposing sight, and it seemed for a moment as if the elements of the long discordant community of France had blended in happy and auspicious union through the representatives of its different Orders. A great hall had been laid out in the palace, and prepared in stately and magnificent pomp; and royalty welcomed the National Estates, composed of more than twelve hundred deputies, with a splendor worthy of the solemn occasion. The King, with the ministers of State, in front, and the Queen and Princes of the blood at his side, sate on a throne brilliant with purple and gold; below, arrayed in separate processions, spread the ranks of the Nobles, all plumes and lace; of the Commons, in homely and simple garb; of the Clergy, the superb robes of the prelates mingling strangely with the cassocks of the village priests; and from galleries above a throng of courtiers, of jewelled dames, and of foreign envoys, contemplated curiously the interesting scene. Outside, crowds of eager spectators filled the balconies and covered the roofs of Versailles, decked out gaily for a brilliant holi-

Meeting of the States General.

old-out
ceholder

ng digitized, and will be inserted at future date.

day; and the groups extended as far as the capital, already stirring with passionate excitement. All seemed deference, good-will, and hope, when the King announced that he had called together the wisdom of France to assist at his counsels; and even a declaration that his chief object was to provide for the pressing wants of the State did not weaken the prevailing sentiment. Yet it was observed with regret that the face of the Queen seemed overclouded with settled care; and jealousy had been aroused in more than one breast by the distinctions drawn by the officials of the Court, and by the contrast between the feudal magnificence of the nobility and the lordly hierarchy, and the plebeian aspect of the meanly-attired Commons.

The Commons declare themselves the National Assembly. On the following day the Estates were invited, their first sitting having been merely formal, to meet again for the despatch of business. The intention of Necker, the chief minister, had been to convene them for the object mainly of procuring supplies for an exhausted treasury—an increasing deficit had for many years been one symptom of the ills of the State—but it had long been arranged that they were to advise on the administration and general affairs of the kingdom. A preliminary question, however, arose, which brought out distinctly the deep-seated differences already existing in this Assembly. According to ancient precedent, the separate Orders of the States-General gave their votes apart; and the Nobles and Clergy, if they coalesced, could easily neutralize the will of the Commons, voting being by orders and not by persons, and the votes of two orders being thus decisive. Trusting to this usage, the Court had consented, in the elections, which had lately taken place, that the number of the representa-

CH. II. *States-General and National Assembly.* 21

tives of the people should be double what it had been formerly; for it was thought no danger could possibly arise, and the concession was a popular measure. The Commons, however, had made up their minds not to be reduced to ciphers by ancient forms; and they insisted, accordingly, that the three Orders should hold their deliberations apart, and that votes should be given by head; that is, be determined by the majority of individuals in the collective Assembly. The Nobles protested against this scheme, being but three against more than six hundred Commons; and they resisted an invitation to a fusion in which their influence might be diminished, the three hundred clergy, though divided in mind, siding with them at the command of the bishops. During several weeks the separate Orders stood sullenly aloof and almost hostile, and nothing in the nature of business was done, to the mortification of a minister and a Court exceedingly in need of a supply of money. The Commons, however, held firm, backed by messages from the provinces, and by the attitude of the great neighboring city, already effervescing with agitation; and at last they adopted a decided course. On June 17, it being known that some Liberal nobles were on their side, and several of the inferior clergy having come to them, they declared themselves the National Assembly of France; and, while they invited their fellow-members to join them, announced that nothing should prevent their proceeding "to begin the work of national regeneration."

Three days after this important event, the Commons found, to their extreme surprise, the great hall at Versailles, in which they had sate, shut up; and the Grand Master of the Ceremonies curtly told Bailly—a distinguished member whom they had chosen president—that the place was wanted for the royal convenience. Alarm was seen in many faces, for a sudden act of violence was feared; but, at the instance of one or two courageous men, the whole body betook itself to an old Tennis Court at a short distance, and, amidst a scene of passionate excitement, swore a solemn oath "that it would never separate until it had set the constitution on a sure foundation." (June 20.) Meanwhile the Court had been forming schemes for dealing with these extraordinary proceedings, and for putting an end to a state of things which appeared to it the wildest presumption. Necker, timid and cautious, proposed a compromise, to which it is said the King inclined; but the counsels of an extreme party prevailed, and it was resolved to make a display of vigor. On June 23, having been kept standing by official insolence for some time under rain, the Commons were summoned again to the great hall; and the King read them a lecture, which had been put into his mouth, to the effect that it was his pleasure that the three Orders should, as in old times, deliberate and vote apart, and that, if further resistance were made, "he would do by himself alone what was meet for his people." This foolish harangue was met in silence; but when the Grand Master of the Ceremonies, following, it is said, the etiquette of the ancient despotism, commanded the Assembly to depart, he was told by Mirabeau *—a man whose

margin: The oath of the Tennis Court, June 20.

---

* Honoré Gabriel Riquetti, Count of Mirabeau, born in 1749, was the grandest and most striking figure of the first part of the Revolution. This extraordinary man was a noble by birth, but, like many other French nobles, had joined the party of innovation. This attitude was in part caused by the antecedents of a career of vice and recklessness, marked, however, by evidences of real genius, in which he had quarrelled with his family, and been perse-

pen and voice were already a power in France—that "they were met there by the will of the people, and that bayonets alone should drive them from the spot." In a few moments a vote was passed by acclamation, which declared the persons of members of the Assembly sacred, and made it a capital crime to molest them.

These bold measures, supported as they were by popular demonstrations in Paris, intimidated the Court, which thought that the Commons would be silenced with as much ease as the old Parliaments had been by Beds of Justice, the coups d'état of the Bourbon Monarchy, by which the Sovereign had often put down opposition in these feudal Assemblies. The King, when apprised of what had taken place, remarked, it is said, only, "Let them stay if they please." With his usual weakness, he allowed himself to float passively on the tide of events. Before this time a considerable number of the minor clergy had joined the Commons; and they were soon followed by the party in the Nobles which wished for reform, and even longed for change. The rest of the Order, however, still held aloof; but at last, at the request of Louis himself, they gave up an opposition that was becoming fruitless, and fell into the ranks of what had now been fully recognized as the National Assembly. This step, however, had been taken in order mainly to conceal arrangements by which the extreme Court party thought they would triumph and overawe the Commons they feared, yet despised. On July 11, Necker, whose advice to convene the States-General

cuted at Court. His powers as an orator were commanding; and though he stooped to become a demagogue, he had true political sagacity and insight, and many of the highest qualities of a statesman. Many of the most serious charges of contemporaries against him seem to be without foundation.

had made him very popular, whatever his motives were, was dismissed; a ministry of soldiers and of reactionary nobles, either unknown or disliked, was set up; and the Assembly saw, not without alarm, that batteries were being constructed at Versailles, and heard that troops were approaching in thousands, and that an armed force of irresistible strength was being directed upon the capital. Rumor spread, too, that it had been said in the palace "that the best place for a mutinous Assembly was a garrison town where it could be kept under," and that the Queen had shown her children to noble officers, and had asked, "Could she rely on their swords?" and there was a report of what was described as "an orgie" in which ladies of honor had done strange things to enthral youthful dragoons and hussars.

Dismission of Necker, and formation of a reactionary Ministry.

This intelligence, magnified by a thousand tongues, quickened the already fiery excitement of Paris, and the flame soon rose into a conflagration. On July 12 proclamation was made "on the part of the King" to keep the peace; and, presently, soldiery with strange faces—the half-foreign German and Swiss regiments, of which there were several in the royal army—were seen occupying the central streets and chief squares of the great city. The sight caused terror and indignation; angry meetings were harangued in the gardens of the Palais Royal by passionate speakers; and a procession was formed carrying at its head busts of Necker and of the Duke of Orleans,* whose largesses and opposition to the Court

Rising in Paris.

---

* Philippe, Duke of Orleans, born in 1745, was one of the most infamous personages of the Revolution. This Prince combined in himself all that most depraved and bad in the old noblesse, and all that was most odious in the ambitious mob leaders. Having

made him one of the idols of the low populace. In a charge made to disperse this assemblage, the Germans cut down one or two men of the French Guards with a few unarmed persons; and the foreign uniforms were ere long seen in the avenues of the Tuileries driving before them a scattering collection of citizens in flight. These incidents, not in themselves momentous, proved the spark that reached the combustible mass, and fired it in a wide-spread explosion. A spirit of disaffection— the natural result of a brutal discipline, and of harsh treatment—had shown itself in the French Guards, as, indeed, in other parts of the Army; and as it was very apparent in a body exposed to the allurements and mob speeches of Paris—for the Guards were part of the city garrison—the men had been lately confined to barracks. When the news arrived of the fate of their comrades, the Guards broke out and fired at the Germans; and the first example of military insubordination caused the dissolution of all military authority. Shouts of " Long live the Nation !" were heard from the quarters of regiments usually stationed in the capital; even the foreign troops were affected by the general contagion in a few hours,

Mutiny of the French Guards and insubordination in the Army.

become out of favor at Court, in part on account of his personal cowardice, he revenged himself by circulating slanders against the Queen, joined the party of reforming nobles, and laid himself out to gain popularity in Paris by flattering the populace and by a display of extravagance. He became afterwards one of the noisiest of the Jacobin leaders; and between 1789 and 1791 combined more than once, for his own selfish ends, against the throne, and even the life of Louis XVI. His complicity, however, with the crimes of the Revolution did not atone for his royal birth; and though he paraded the name of Egalité which he had assumed, he perished during the tyranny of Robespierre.

and sullenly declared they would not shed blood; and the only resource left to the indignant officers was to withdraw the demoralized mass, and to beat a retreat. A thrill of exultation ran through Paris at the disappearance of the strange invaders; and power once dreaded having proved worthless, disorder and violence were let loose. During the night the city was wildly astir; the dark swarms of poverty and vice, which became afterwards the legions of the Reign of Terror, emerged in thousands from their wretched haunts, mingled here and there with less hideous groups; and shops were sacked, and the great Town Hall invaded by these mobs to the cry of " Arms !" Next morning a provisional committee, composed of the chief men of the sixty districts into which Paris had been divided, took the rule of the capital into their hands, the old authorities having proved powerless; and an endeavor was made to give a kind of organization to the movement, and in some measure to direct and control it. The citizens were encouraged to form themselves into a militia of volunteers drawn from the districts; these bands were to wear in their cockades the Parisian colors of blue and red; and they were not only to find arms as best they could, but arms were liberally supplied to them. M. de Flesseles, head of the old town Council, was made president of this board; and, though the objects of the members varied, a general intention certainly prevailed to keep the insurrection within bounds. Such was the origin of the world-renowned Commune of Paris, and of the National Guard, names of deep significance in the Revolution.

The Commune, the National Guard.

Although partly controlled by these means, the revolutionary movement went on throughout the day with terrible energy. The levies of the district started into life, and were enrolled into the new civic army; the streets bristled with forests of pikes; arms were violently seized wherever they were found; and mobs were seen trailing antique cannon, and tossing about pieces of feudal armor, torn recklessly from arsenals, with swords and muskets. On the whole, however, the better class of citizens predominated in the National Guard, and checked the excesses of the lowest populace; and though it was accelerated by such events, the time had not yet come when the violent elements of society were to overpower all others. The presence of this better order of men in the ranks is strong proof of the general indignation felt at the late demonstration made by the Court; and the rising was anything but the mere work of a mob set on by a few designing leaders. In the afternoon the French Guards, to a man, went over to the popular side, their terrified officers protesting in vain; and, amidst wild shouts of passionate exultation, they were made grenadiers of the National Guard, and played an important part in the events that followed. On the 14th a great crowd entered the court-yard of the Hospital of the Invalides—a noble establishment like our own Woolwich—and the governor was obliged to allow them to take the vast store of arms laid up in the arsenal, for the inmates passively seconded their efforts. By this time nearly 80,000 men had been marshalled more or less regularly; and as no signs of resistance appeared, they were encouraged to acts of more open daring. On the verge of the quarter of Saint Antoine rose the celebrated fortress of the Bastille; and it was resolved to attack this dreaded place, the very emblem of ancient despotism, and infamous for its mysterious horrors. An armed mass poured down to the spot, and after an ineffectual attempt at a parley, the drawbridge

Siege and storming of the Bastille, July 14th, 1789. was passed, and the inner court reached, close to the eight frowning towers of the hated dungeon. A discharge of musketry drove the assailants back; but cannon were brought up by the late French Guards and a white flag before long was waved from the ramparts, the commandant, Delaunay, having been compelled by the garrison (alarmed or ill-disposed) to surrender. The victors rushed into the ancient den, amazed at the feat they had accomplished, and carrying out many of the arcana of the place—old instruments of torture, and prison records; but their victory was not unstained by cruelty. The greater part, indeed, of the garrison were set free; but Delaunay and several of his men were murdered, and their heads were borne on high on pikes—the first of many subsequent scenes of the kind. De Flesseles, too, was attacked and shot, for a tale spread that he had deceived the people; and several other deeds of blood were committed. As yet, however, the better part of the National Guards maintained comparative order; and the extraordinary and rapid changes which had occurred had rather proved the weakness of the royal authority than brought out anarchy in its most frightful aspect.

Such was the end of this sorry attempt to work a violent change in the State, to intimidate the Assembly, and to overawe Paris. The result had been to hand the capital over to unknown and revolutionary forces, and to prove that no trust could be placed in the Army, the chief and, usually, the sure instrument of power. The extreme Court party stood furious and aghast; and the Count of Artois, the younger brother of the King, and the Charles X. of a later age, with two other magnates of a like stamp, declared that these things were not to be borne, and hastened indignantly over the frontier. This was the beginning of the emigration—that desertion of the King by his natural supporters which was one of the many evil features of the time, though the circumstance will not be surprising to those who know what little genuine sympathy existed between the nobles and the Crown. Meanwhile the Assembly had loudly condemned the violent measures attempted by the Court; and Mirabeau alluded, in no ambiguous terms, to the part, said to have been taken by the Queen in a project "worthy of St. Bartholomew." The King, shifting in the usual way, hastened to make peace with the stronger side, dismissed the ministerial cabal, and recalled Necker: and the Assembly listened with sincere good-will to the explanations of an amiable being whose principal fault was weak simplicity. Soon afterwards a deputation from Paris invited him to pay the city a visit: and the Monarch assented, though Marie Antoinette, indignant at the affronts given to royal authority, and knowing how unpopular she was herself, entreated him with tears not to make the attempt. The citizens, however, proud of their triumph, received their Sovereign with acclamations: and a hint in an address that he had been " conquered" was treated graciously by Louis as a joke. All that had lately occurred was sanctioned by him; the provisional committee received the name of the Commune of Paris, with immense powers; and Bailly, the president of the Commons, was appointed mayor; while the young Marquis of Lafayette, one of the enthusiastic reforming nobles, was appointed commander-in-chief of the National Guard. In sign of reconciliation,

Beginning of the emigration of the Nobles.

Recall of Necker.

The King sanctions what had been done in Paris.

The Tri-color Flag. the white colors of the House of Bourbon were added to the blue and red of the capital on the ensigns of this force; and thus originated the Tricolor Flag, which Lafayette, with conceit or foresight, exclaimed "would soon make the round of Europe." Though two or three bad instances of violence followed, tranquillity seemed established in Paris for a time; the king returned well pleased to Versailles; but, between impotent threats and feeble concessions, how much of the divinity remained that hedged round the Monarchy?

Rising in the Provinces. Notwithstanding this quiescence, however, the events which had taken place in Paris went like an electric shock through the kingdom. The influence of the capital of France over the provinces has always been very great, and it acquired additional power at this juncture. The sudden collapse of the majesty of the throne, the successful triumph over ancient authority, and, above all, the revolt of the troops, stirred the minds of men to their very depths, and long pent up elements of hate and confusion broke out in many places in appalling strength. In the southern, midland, and south-eastern districts, wherever Feudalism was most oppressive, wherever misery was most keen, the peasantry rose against their lords; and from the Rhone to the Loire there was a great blaze of châteaux, the infuriated vassals tossing into the flames the charter-chests and muniments which contained the records of privileges no longer tolerable. A few murders of seigneurs also took place; even in the north the payment of rents and the customary services were generally resisted; and, wretchedness adding force to the movement, bands of squalid savages in some provinces "descended from the hills, destroying the

1789. States-General and National Assembly. 31

corn, plundering orchards, and doing all kinds of mischief." Many of the towns, too, showed signs of insurrection, clamoring for an extension of municipal rights, and for an abolition of old monopolies; and violent bread and meal riots were frequent, for the year was one of peculiar scarcity, and the sufferings of the poorer classes were extreme. Nor was the capital itself free from causes of disturbance and trouble. Order was, indeed, maintained by Lafayette; Bailly, the mayor, labored to please the citizens by civic pomp and gay exhibitions emblematic of their newly-acquired liberties; and the Commune, now formed into a body of three hundred members, made efforts to supply the wants of the poor, to find employment for artizans out of work, to cope with the difficulty of increasing poverty. But, as always happens on such occasions, the new powers were decried by envious demagogues, the more bitterly because they were new; and of what avail were displays of fireworks, enthusiastic "festivals of the Bastille," "trees of liberty" rising in gardens and avenues—nay, even doles, offerings, and all the expedients of a merely improvised system of relief—to thousands of hungry men and women? Between agitation and the presence of want, Paris was soon fermenting with elements of disorder, all the more dangerous because as yet suppressed.

These tidings of evil came to interrupt the consultations of the National Assembly. It had been engaged in economic discussions as to the best means of meeting the deficit, and as to framing a new constitution for France; and high-sounding principles of reform, conceived in the spirit of the new philosophy, had been already hailed with applause; the measures it adopted to remove or pal-

Legislative measures of the Assembly.

liate the stern practical ills it had now to face were, in part, conceived in a generous spirit, but were characteristic of the national temperament, and too plainly revealed the political ignorance and passion for change that widely prevailed. As for the towns, the Commune of Paris was encouraged in doing whatever it pleased; and Bailly and Lafayette were thanked for their well-meant and patriotic efforts. Little was attempted in the case of other towns, except to give "promises of free trade;" but the middle classes were allowed, or invited, to put down disorders, by themselves, by force; and in this manner an armed organization of National Guards was spontaneously formed in almost all the great cities of France, self-elected and independent of the State.

Sudden abolition of the feudal burdens, August 4, 1789. A great and sudden revolution, however, was effected in the social relations of the whole rural community in the kingdom; and the imposing edifice of antique Feudalism was thrown down in a moment, and laid in the dust. One or two nobles, on the Liberal side, having drawn a frightful picture of feudal abuses, the Assembly, in spite of a few protests, started to its feet and declared, almost to a man, that this state of abominations should cease; and resolutions were passed, in a single night, abolishing claims that had been the growth of centuries, and involving in a common extinction the most barbarous remnants of cruel serfdom, with tithes, quit-rents, and similar dues. The sitting closed with enthusiastic shouts, a Te Deum mingling in strange accompaniment; and though distinctions were afterwards drawn between such privileges as that of the lord bathing his feet, when cold, in the blood of his vassals, and others of a more modern kind, an opposition formed by the nobles was overborne by an increasing majority, the Commons and lower

1789. States-General and National Assembly. 33

clergy ruling the Assembly; and a clean sweep was made of many just rights of property, as well as of much that was bad and obsolete. The ultimate fruits of the liberation of the soil were great and beneficial in the highest degree, but the immediate results may be easily guessed. The excesses of the peasantry were not lessened by the sudden annihilation of the bonds of ages; and they were only put down or checked at last by the efforts of the middle classes in the country districts, alarmed at the evident progress of anarchy. These, too, thus found themselves with arms in their hands, and almost independent of any kind of rule.

Such was France in August and September, 1789, old authority falling on all sides, power being transferred into new hands, and want and disorder felt everywhere, although for the moment restrained. The Court party meanwhile, scotched, but not killed, had been rearing its head at Versailles; and rumor spread that a band of loyal nobles were about to take the King to Metz, and to liberate him from "rebellious subjects." Troops, too, were gradually moved from the frontier; and the new National Guard at Versailles—for such a body had been organized—was treated with scorn and contempt at the palace. A sentiment had been growing up in Paris, and found favor in the Assembly, that the King should be removed to the capital; and the feelings of the masses, irritated by want, had become ready for any sudden outbreak. A scene, which occurred in the first days of October, became the signal for a new explosion of passion. A party of young officers, at a banquet in the palace, dashed down the Tricolor from their helmets in the presence of the King and of his Court, at the sound of a well-known royalist air; and, heated with wine, and

October 5 and 6, 1789.

D

lured by the glances of courtly beauty and syren grace, vowed that they, at least, would not abandon the Throne. This second "orgie" gave rise to a remarkable demonstration from Paris, though it is not easy to say who were its chief designers. On the morning of the 5th a procession of women, stung with hunger, burst into the great Town Hall, and thence streamed over the short space which separates the city from Versailles, followed by savage and menacing crowds, and ultimately by Lafayette and his National Guard. The procession forced its way into the National Assembly, then discussing an unfavorable message from the throne, and a party of these strange visitors was allowed to enter the courts of the palace and parley with the King. Order was restored when Lafayette arrived, and the assemblage dispersed, to find exit as it could, most of the soldiers having given it a welcome, and the Body-guard of the King alone, a select detachment, having provoked ill-will. Early next morning a few chance shots, which struck down, unhappily, one or two of the people, became a forerunner of a general rising; and a furious mob fell on the Body-guards, and penetrated the interior of the palace. Dread faces of passion, hunger, and crime, appeared in the sanctuary of the State: the Queen, half-clad, was driven from her chamber amid the shrieks of affrighted attendants; and a terrible massacre would have taken place but for the interposition of the late French Guards, who shouting "We do not forget Fontenoy," rescued the Body-guards and the royal family. A seeming reconciliation took place afterwards; the King presented himself from the balconies; the Queen gave her hand to Lafayette to kiss, and the Tricolor shone on every armed crest; but the floors of the palace were drenched with blood, and two ghastly heads, borne aloft on pikes, attested the presence of still unslaked passions. At the request of a deputation, peremptory though bland, Louis consented readily to go to Paris; and the royal carriages, with the King and Queen, their children, and Madame Elizabeth, the fair and pious sister of the King, slowly trailed to the city escorted by a roaring chaos of armed bands, of women astride on patriotic cannon, of savagery in its hideous or grotesque aspects. The shout, "We have now the baker to ourselves, the baker's wife, and the baker's boy," significantly told what thoughts were uppermost in the hearts of the poorer mass of the multitude—by some conspiracy they had been deprived of bread by "aristocrats at Versailles." It was evening before the motley procession made its entry into the gates of the Tuileries; and when the royal party reached the palace, uninhabited by the House of Bourbon for years, they saw themselves surrounded by National Guards, and were told that regular soldiers could not approach.

The King and Royal Family taken to Paris from Versailles.

The events of these momentous days, known emphatically as the 5th and 6th of October, have been attributed to different persons; but it is superfluous to inquire whether Mirabeau,* the Duke of Orleans, or Lafayette, had any part in preparing the movement. What is to be noted is, that the rabble of Paris, though still controlled by the middle classes, had gained a great and marvellous victory; royalty had, as usual, shown itself ignoble, va-

Growing power of the rabble of Paris.

---

* It is now tolerably well ascertained that the Duke of Orleans instigated the mob to leave Paris, and attack the Palace. In a letter discovered after his death he directed a banker not to pay the money which had been agreed on as the price of the blood of the King. " L'argent," so he wrote, "n'est point gagné, le marmot vit encore." Mirabeau and Lafayette seem to have been innocent.

cillating, and amiably weak; and the illusions of power, once feared and august, had been dissipated like the idlest of dreams. Since that day Versailles has been a national museum, and for a time a ruin; it has sheltered legions of German invaders, and heard the wailing cry of a conquered Nation; but never again has it been the abode of a Prince wielding the sovereignty of France.

CHAPTER III.

THE CONSTITUTION OF 1790-1.

Character of the period from the autumn of 1789 to the summer of 1791.

THE next phase of the French Revolution may be fitly compared to the watery space, comparatively level, yet broken and tossed, and agitated by uncertain currents, which is seen occasionally between mountainous waves during the pauses of a tremendous storm. From the autumn of 1789 to the summer of 1791—a period of nearly two years—no events occurred of such obvious significance as the rising of Paris, the siege of the Bastille, the insurrection in the Provinces, and the 5th and 6th of October; and though elements of trouble gathered and grew apparent to a discerning eye, they did not yet form into a general outbreak. Some terrible crimes were, indeed, perpetrated under the influence of local passion or revenge; one or two conspiracies, real or feigned, were attempted by partisans of the Court; the emigration of the Nobles increased; all along the frontier rumors were heard of counter-revolution and even of invasion; the attitude of foreign Powers became doubtful; and throughout France, from the Pyrenees to the Rhine, innovation showed itself in a thousand forms; the hearts of men throbbed with the desire for change, and knavery and ambition appealed too successfully to the hearts, the jealousies, and the fears of the multitude. Nevertheless, the surface of things at least appeared for a time less disturbed than before; some reforms were attended with permanent good, and others with benefits for the moment; the dangerous pressure of popular distress, so evident in 1789, lessened; and it seemed to thousands as if the Revolution was tending to happiness, peace, and progress. The King had been separated from the faction of the Court; the National Assembly was supreme; the removal of the feudal burdens from the soil improved agriculture as if by magic; France enjoyed such liberty as she had never enjoyed before; the Middle class and the National Guards seemed sufficient to keep mob violence down; signs of increasing opulence were not wanting; and though disorder was still abroad, and demagogues held formidable sway, and the echoes of strife and discord were heard, were not symptoms like these inevitable at a crisis of great and rapid change, and would they not before long disappear? The issue was to be otherwise; and this brief moment of comparative calm was to see France brought nearer to the abyss, to accelerate the dangers collecting around, and ultimately to give renewed force to revolutionary passion and suspicion. Yet History rejects the false creed of fatalism, though she admits the stupendous power of circumstance; and while large allowances must, in justice, be made for inexperience and the difficulties of the situation, it is not the less, in our judgment, true that had France found statesmen among her rulers, had her aristocracy been less spoiled by arrogance, and less morally worthless, had her Sovereign and those around him been less unwise, the course of events would have been very different.

The National Assembly begins to frame the Constitution.

After the scenes of the 5th and 6th of October, the National Assembly returned to the task of re-modelling the institutions of France, which had been, almost from the first, its mission. Much that it accomplished during the following months, although done with precipitate haste, was a great improvement on the old state of things, and has since had beneficent results.*

Useful reforms.

Old barbarous penalties were abolished; seignorial jurisdiction disappeared; internal trade, which had been crippled by mischievous restrictions, was set free; a project was formed to fuse into a Code the medley of written laws and customs, conflicting and obscure, which prevailed in the kingdom; the monopolies and exclusive guilds of the towns vanished with the feudal charges on the land; and, above all, religious toleration was proclaimed, the whole system of taxation was reformed, and the iniquitous exemptions of the privileged orders in this particular were removed. These measures, and many others of the kind, were salutary, and, for the most part, just; and Englishmen may, in these respects, agree with those Frenchmen who extol "the immortal principle of 1789." But the work of the Assembly, considered as a whole,

* A learned account of the Constitution of 1790-1 will be found in Professor Von Sybel's *History of the French Revolution.* Burke's *Reflections on the Revolution in France,* remain, however, the best and most profound commentary on the work of the National Assembly and its tendencies. Many of the observations of the great philosophic statesman have proved prophetic.

was marked by a passion for mere theory, and a perilous disregard of facts; and it displayed itself in wild innovations which irritated and exasperated many classes, made settled government at best precarious, and added strength to revolutionary tendencies. *Wild and precipitate innovations.* Instead of addressing itself simply to mitigating the political and social grievances of which such a multitude existed in France, it had begun its labors by a grand Declaration—at once imposing, dangerous, and untrue—of what it regarded as the Rights of Man; and it proceeded to carry out these principles, more or less faithfully, in its subsequent legislation. *The Rights of Man.* Like the feudal exactions, the immense property of the Church, and of a number of other corporations, was confiscated with a stroke of the pen; and though compensation was promised to existing interests, it was to a great extent illusory. Soon afterwards titles of honor were suppressed, however dignified or historical; places, offices, and privileges were abolished with little reflection, or even justice; and it was announced as an eternal truth that Frenchmen were essentially equal, notwithstanding the inequalities that must exist in an ancient, or indeed in any community. *Confiscation of Church and corporate property. Abolition of tithes.* *Equality.* In addition, an extraordinary change was made in the local constitution of the Kingdom; the old Provinces were effaced from the map, with their complex variety of rights and immunities; the local associations thus formed were destroyed, and the Kingdom was parcelled out into new divisions, ever since known by the name of Departments, each with a perfectly uniform organization and distribution of local authority. *Provinces transformed into Departments.*

Having thus levelled, in a few months, almost every

Character of the new Constitution; its glaring defects. institution of old France, the Assembly began the work of creating a new Constitution for the transformed Kingdom. The Monarchy was continued and liberally endowed; but it was shorn of most of its ancient prerogatives, and reduced to a very feeble Executive; and while it obtained a perilous veto on the resolutions and acts of the Legislature, it was separated from that power, and placed in opposition to it, by the exclusion of the Ministers of the Crown from seats and votes in the National Assembly. The Legislature was composed of a Legislative Assembly, formed of a single Chamber alone, in theory supreme, and almost absolute; but, as we have seen, it was liable to come in conflict with the Crown, and it had less authority than might be supposed, for it was elected by a vote not truly popular, and subordinate powers were allowed to possess a very large part of the rights of Sovereignty which it ought to have divided with the King. This last portion of the scheme was very striking, and was the one, too, that most caused alarm among distant political observers. Too great centralization having been one of the chief complaints against the ancient Monarchy, this evil was met by a radical reform, which also fell in with the new doctrines of equality and the supremacy of the people —two main tenets of the Rights of Man. The towns received extraordinary powers; their municipalities had complete control over the National Guards to be elected in them, and possessed many other functions of Government; and Paris, by these means, became almost a separate Commonwealth, independent of the State, and directing a vast military force. The same system was applied to the country; every Department was formed into petty divisions, each with its National Guards, and a considerable share of what is usually the power of the government; and in each Department a higher administration was entrusted with a kind of general superintendence. In every separate centre in town and country this immense authority was for the most part wielded by men chosen by a scarcely restricted suffrage; and Burke's saying was strictly correct, "that France was split into thousands of Republics, with Paris predominating and queen of all." With respect to other institutions of the State, the appointment of nearly all civil functionaries, judicial and otherwise, was taken from the Crown, and abandoned to a like popular election; and the same principle was also applied to the great and venerable institution of the Church, already deprived of its vast estates, though the election of bishops and priests by their flocks interfered directly with Roman Catholic discipline, and probably, too, with religious dogma. As for the Army, it was also in a great degree removed out of the hands of the King; and while unjust privileges were swept away, it was organized on a democratic model, commissions and similar rights being abolished.

Many acts, too, of the National Assembly administration of affairs were unwise and dangerous. Notwithstanding the opposition of Necker, who, though hardly a statesman, understood finance, it was resolved to sell the lands of the Church to procure funds for the necessities of the State; and the deficit, which was increasing rapidly, was met by an inconvertible currency of paper, secured on the lands to be sold. This expedient, borrowed to some extent, from precedents set by the old Monarchy, and indeed by other governments in distress, and not wholly mischievous under careful restrictions, was carried out with injudi-

Administrative measures.

Assignats. cious recklessness. The Assignats, as the new notes were called, seemed a mine of inexhaustible wealth, and they were issued in quantities which, from the first moment, disturbed the relations of life and commerce, though they created a show of brisk trade for a
False system of taxation. time. In matters of taxation the Assembly, too, exceeded the bounds of reason and justice; exemptions previously enjoyed by the rich were now indirectly extended to the poor; wealthy owners of land were too heavily burdened, while the populace of the towns went scot free; and though little wrong was as yet done, the example was set of future injustice. Very large sums also, belonging to the
Undue favor shown to Paris. State, were advanced to the Commune of Paris, now rising into formidable power, at an interest much below the market rate; and thus the Nation was made to minister to the needs of one favored portion of it—a perilous and iniquitous principle. With the assent of the Assembly, the funds so obtained were lavishly squandered in giving relief to the poor of the capital in the most improvident ways—in buying bread dear and reselling it cheap, and in finding fanciful employment for artizans out of work. The result, of course, was to attract to Paris many thousands of the lowest class of rabble, and to add them to the scum of the city; and, indeed,* not a few of the communistic theories which predominated during the Reign of Terror, and have ever since been a curse to France, may be traced, partly in operation, at this time.

It is easy to point out on what erroneous principles the Assembly founded a large part of its work, and

* Professor Von Sybel's *History*, book II., chapter iv., has brought out clearly the Communistic tendencies of part of the legislation of the National Assembly.

time was soon to show what a series of ills inevitably resulted from much that it had done. But the attractive nature of the doctrines it laid down, and the generous liberality of many of its speakers, created enthusiasm for the moment; and the declaration of the Rights of Man aroused feelings of exultation and delight, not only in France, but throughout Europe. On the first anniversary of the fall of the Bastille, and before the Constitution had been finished, Paris witnessed a scene which vividly expressed the sentiments with which millions welcomed what seemed the inauguration of a new age of gold. A great national holiday was kept; and, amidst multitudes of applauding spectators, deputations from every Department in France, headed by the authorities of the thronging capital, defiled in procession to the broad space known as the Field of Mars, along the banks of the Seine. An immense amphitheatre had been constructed, and decorated with extraordinary pomp; and here, in the presence of a splendid Court, of the National Assembly, and of the municipalities of the realm, and in the sight of a great assemblage surging to and fro with throbbing excitement, the King took an oath that he would faithfully respect the order of things that was being established, while incense streamed from high-raised altars, and the ranks of seventy thousand National Guards burst into loud cheers and triumphant music; and even the Queen, sharing in the passion of the hour, and radiant with beauty, lifted up in her arms the young child who was to be the future chief of a disenthralled and regenerate people—unconscious happily of the dark clouds that were gathering already over so many victims. The following week was gay with those brilliant displays which Paris knows how to arrange so

The Feast of the Federation, July 14, 1790. Enthusiasm in Europe.

well; flowery arches covered the site of the Bastille, fountains ran wine, and the night blazed with fire; and the far-extending influence of France was attested by enthusiastic deputations of "friends of liberty" from many parts of Europe, hailing the dawn of an era of freedom and peace.

Evil consequences of innovation; signs of disorder and anarchy. The work, however, of the National Assembly developed some of its effects ere long. The abolition of titles of honor filled up the measure of the anger of the Nobles; the confiscation of the property of the Church; above all, the law as to the election of priests, known as the Civil Constitution of the Clergy, shocked all religious or superstitious minds. The reduction of the old rights of the Crown, and the antagonism created by the absurd severance of the Legislative and Executive powers, enfeebled the State, and caused the King his Ministers, and the Assembly to clash; and Necker and all his associates but one were dismissed, and replaced by men of an inferior stamp. The extinction of privilege, too, in the Army, provoked discontent among the whole class of officers; and yet it did not much please the men, for no great immediate benefits followed, and their superiors stood more than ever aloof. Meanwhile the substance of power began to pass to the masses to an alarming extent, through the regulations as to the National Guards and the administrative services of the Kingdom; and though they did not yet know their strength, leaders were not wanting to teach the lesson. The ascendency of Paris, too, became more decided than it had ever been; and the dislocation of authority caused by the extreme weakening of the central government disintegrated France to a great degree, and gave a wide scope to low popular influence. It is easy to imagine the results in a country torn by deep divisions of class, where an ancient throne had been suddenly weakened, where nothing was permanent, fixed, and established, and where anarchy and license, though for the moment checked, had made themselves so perilously apparent. The emigration of the Nobles, which had become very general from the 5th and 6th of October, went on in daily augmenting numbers; and, in a short time, the frontiers were edged with bands of exiles breathing vengeance and hatred. In many districts the priests denounced as sacrilege what had been done to the Church, divided the peasantry, and preached a crusade against what they called the atheist towns; and angry mutinies broke out in the Army, which left behind savage and relentless feelings. The relations between the King and the Assembly, too, became strained, if not hostile, at every turn of affairs, to the detriment of anything like good government; and while Louis sunk into a mere puppet, the Assembly, controlled in a great measure by demagogues and the pampered mobs of Paris, felt authority gradually slipping from it. Thus anarchy was not restrained from above, while, so to speak, it was organized from below; and the rein was thrown on the necks of a people long misgoverned, and whose excitable nature had been aroused by every kind of stimulant. As yet, however, the mere popular forces did not break out in general disorder; but their increasing influence was plainly seen in the ascendency gained by brawling demagogues, in an immense diffusion of cheap and bad journals, and in the multiplying of associations of an extreme type in politics. One of these societies, sprung from a small beginning, had established itself in an old convent in Paris; and here, growing into larger num-

The Jacobin and other clubs.

bers, it held frequent sittings, at which the members discussed the acts of the National Assembly, or made vehement addresses to the people. The most ardent reformers of the Commune were prominent in it, and were wont to report to the populace, in the forty-eight sections into which the capital had been divided, whatever had been decided or done; and the society had affiliated to it a great number of bodies of the same character throughout the principal cities of France. Such was the origin of the famous Jacobin Club—a dread name in the drama of the Revolution.

Weakness of Conservative elements in the Assembly. It may appear strange that the powerful interests which were represented in the National Assembly did not contend better against these immense changes; and that the Commons, of whom very few had genuine sympathy with the lowest classes, should have given such free scope to anarchic disorder. But the Crown and the Nobles were divided from each other; the Nobles were divided among themselves; the prelates and lower clergy were not friends; and many of the lay and clerical aristocracy were unwise enough to join the ranks of the emigrants. Of the Conservative Nobles and prelates who remained in the Assembly, few had anything like talent; and the chief defenders of the ancient rites of the throne of Henry IV., and of the Rohans and Mortemarts, were a young dragoon officer and a simple abbé, the impetuous Cazalés,*

---

* Cazalés, the brilliant military champion of Conservatism in the Assembly, was born in 1752. He has been well described as a " chivalrous soldier, sans peur et reproche ;" and Mirabeau said of him that " if the knowledge of Cazalés equalled the charms of his elocution, all efforts would be ineffectual against him." But he was rash to a fault, and seems to have had as little judgment as information.

the subtle Maury.* As for the reforming Nobles, among whom were several men of fine parts, many doubtless went further than they wished; but some were carried away by the false philosophy in fashion; others bid against each other for popular support, and they never united in a rational policy of what might have been called constitutional reform. The Commons, too, were mere tyros in politics, though many were apt at the tongue and pen; they were also full of the new doctrines, and could not see what innovations were unsafe; and they were largely influenced by a strong dislike of the old institutions and the privileged orders. Add the characteristics of the French intellect, addicted to system, and to carry out ideas, without regard to facts, to their extreme consequences; add the impetuous and ardent French temperament, often wildly generous and sentimental; and we shall see how the Assembly, without any intention, prepared the way for a part, at least, of what followed. Yet what contributed most, perhaps, to the annihilation of the noble classes, and encouraged measures of a revolutionary tendency, was the pitiful conduct of those best known by the still dishonorable name of *émigrés*. In a few months the great majority of the aristocracy of France had fled the kingdom, abandoning the throne around which they had stood, breathing maledictions against a contemptuous Nation, as arrogant as ever in the impotence of want, and thinking only of a counter-revolution that

* The Abbé Maury was born in 1746. He had been versed in ecclesiastical and political affairs before the Revolution, and defended with skill and eloquence the cause of the Monarchy, the Church, and the Nobles in the National Assembly. He became afterwards an Archbishop and a Cardinal, and died in 1817, having witnessed the Bourbon Restoration.

would cover the natal soil with blood. History makes allowances for these men; for they were the victims of an evil order of things; but France could not make allowances for them at a crisis of agitation and passion; and their utter want of patriotism and of sound feeling made thousands believe that the state of society which had bred such creatures ought to be swept away.

Attempts of Mirabeau to check the disorganization of the State. One man, however, in the National Assembly, saw distinctly whither events were tending. The life of Mirabeau was stained with vices; and his public career was deeply marked by reckless ambition and perhaps crime. But he added keen insight and strong common sense to eloquence of extraordinary force; he was not the dupe of deceptive theories, and he perceived that France was falling into confusion. He had protested against the destruction of the Church and Nobles as leading to civil war; he had declared that it was dangerous and unwise to refuse the ministers of the Crown a seat in the Assembly; and he summed up a great truth in the words that what France required was a firm Executive to keep anarchy down and to maintain order. We cannot affirm whether he had thought out a scheme of Constitutional Monarchy for France; but as early as 1790 he made overtures to the Court, and he had more than one interview with the Queen, to whose "force of character" he did admiring homage. His projects were to remove the King to a town in the interior of France, to rally around him the loyal part of the Army, and to summon a new Assembly, which would undo what was most mischievous in the work of the old; and he promised that he would answer for thirty-six Departments, and expressed a strong hope that the middle classes, alarmed at the prospect of mob rule, would throw their weight on the side of the Monarchy. The Court, however, vacillating and suspicious, would not trust the proud man of genius; and Mirabeau could not obtain the adhesion of Bouillé, the most popular chief of the Army, and of Lafayette, all powerful with the National Guards, whose co-operation he deemed necessary. Death came to put an end to his hopes and fears; he expired in April, 1791, and with him perished the best chance of arresting the Revolution already at hand. *His death.*

Meanwhile, the attitude of neighboring States had become uncertain, if not threatening, and sounds of counter-revolution, and even of war, had begun to gather definite shape. The old Monarchies and Aristocracies of Europe were naturally alarmed at what they called French principles; and Prussia and Austria suddenly composed their feuds, while, in England, the House of Commons rang with cheers at Burke's invectives against the Assembly. The *émigrés*, too, were in every Court, soliciting aid and making empty noise; and a little Army of Seigneurs formed along the Rhine, which they boasted was only the advanced guard of a crusade in their holy cause. The death of Mirabeau at this conjuncture made the King and Queen despair of obtaining deliverance through French help alone; and they began wistfully to look abroad, and to dabble in those foreign intrigues which were to end in the destruction of both.* Both, indeed, feared and disliked the *émigrés;* nor did either, as yet at least, think of restoring the Mon- *Threatening attitude of Foreign Powers.*

Dangerous projects of the King and Queen.

* A complete picture of the dealings of Louis XVI. and Marie Antoinette with Foreign Powers during the Revolution, and indeed of the life and conduct of the Royal Family at this crisis, will be found in the collection of *Letters of Louis XVI., Marie Antoinette,*

E

archy by foreign bayonets. But, not to speak of many other grievances, the conscience of Louis was wounded to the quick by what he thought was sacrilege done to the Church; Marie Antoinette resenting the eclipse of the throne, and slights offered to her consort and herself; and the condition of France appeared to both alike something unintelligible and beyond endurance. A project was formed that the King should escape, should place himself in the hands of an Austrian detachment, to be marched quietly within the frontier, and should make an appeal to all loyal Frenchmen; and no doubt can remain but that a violent change in the Constitution was in contemplation to be effected by the " friends of the Monarchy." The idea of calling in Austrian troops shows that the Queen, a daughter of the House of Austria, was the chief author of this perilous scheme; and Bouillé, who was in command in Lorraine, was let into the secret, and promised assistance. On the night of June 20, 1791, the Royal Family set off, eluding the guard at the gates of the Tuileries, the King having left a declaration behind, in which he disavowed all that had been done in his name, and with his assent, since " he had been in durance in Paris," and denounced the constitution he had sworn to maintain. The carriage arrived safely next day at Châlons, but was stopped at last at the little town of Varennes, a postmaster called

The flight to Varennes, June 20, 1791.

et Madame Elizabeth, edited by M. Feuillet de Conches. Some of these documents may be apocryphal, but enough of undoubted genuineness remains to show that the suspicions entertained by the popular leaders of the King and Queen were in part justified. The collection throws also much light on the policy of the Continental Courts from 1790 to 1793, and the dissertations and notes of the editor are valuable and interesting.

Drouet having recognized the King, and given the municipality a hasty warning. A parley took place, the ill-fated Monarch, as usual, showing ignoble weakness: but the party would have escaped had not a detachment sent by Bouillé shouted " the Nation for ever," and refused to obey their officers' orders. Meanwhile, at the news of the flight of the King, the Assembly decreed the recall of the fugitives, and assumed the functions of complete sovereignty, and commissioners were despatched to enforce its mandates. On the arrival of the delegates at Varennes, Louis instantly yielded, in spite of the entreaties of the Queen : he seemed, it is said, " to have been most anxious about finishing his morning meal." The Royal captives were eight days returning, every village looking on at the sorry sight: and the procession threaded the streets of Paris amidst a multitude silent, and with covered heads. Pétion, one of the commissioners, had been rude and forward: another, Barnave, had been fascinated by the Queen, and had shown that his feelings had been deeply touched. Each of these men were to go different ways in the dark drama of future events, in consequence, perhaps, of this accident in their lives.

Napoleon said, many years afterwards, that this abortive attempt sealed the fate of the Monarchy; it at least caused general indignation and distrust. The Nation did not, indeed, know the whole truth; but the protest of the King against the constitution was read by many in the worst light, and what was really feebleness was thought treachery. The demagogues swarming in France made the most of the chance which had fallen to them; angry meetings were held in many places, and appealed to in threatening and

<small>Consequences of this event.</small>

wild language; the vile name of Marat* emerged from darkness, and those of Danton,† Robespierre,‡ and others,

* Jean Paul Marat, born in 1744, was bred a physician, and afterwards became a veterinary surgeon in the stables of the Count of Artois. Though unsuccessful in his profession, he was not without parts, and at the beginning of the Revolution he became editor of the *Ami du Peuple*, one of the most violent journals of the time. In this evil production he systematically advocated the destruction of the upper and middle classes, and the subversion of property. Though at first decried even by the demagogues, he by degrees emerged from obscurity, and became one of the most prominent and repulsive figures of the Reign of Terror. He was assassinated in 1793.

† George Jacques Danton was born in 1759. This remarkable man was brought up to be a lawyer, and plunged with characteristic energy into the vortex of the Revolution. Mirabeau soon discovered his talents, and he quickly became the most effective of the mob leaders of Paris. He rose to be the most conspicuous actor in the Revolution during the first part of the Reign of Terror; and though his crimes were many, his courage and patriotism plead for him. He labored also, at the risk of his life, to reconcile parties, and to stop the tyranny of the Committee of Public Safety, and was guillotined in 1793.

‡ François Maximilian Robespierre was, like Danton, born in 1759, and bred an advocate. He was one of the few extreme Revolutionists who obtained a seat in the States-General; and for some months he could not get a hearing when he attempted to speak, though Mirabeau predicted that his earnestness would raise him into notice. He became one of the chief of the Parisian demagogues, winning his way, not by eloquence or boldness, but by a reputation for integrity, and ultimately stood at the head of the most frightful Dictatorship Europe ever saw. Opinions are still divided whether he was a mere bloodthirsty tyrant or a merciless fanatic; I incline to the second view. Mr. Carlyle has thus graphically described Robespierre:—"Who of these Six Hundred may be the meanest? Shall we say that anxious, slight, ineffectual-looking man, under thirty, in spectacles, his eyes, were the glasses

soon to become by-words of universal terror, were repeatedly in the mouths of the populace, and even the word "republic" was heard in the Assembly. That body, besides, had pronounced itself the Government during the flight to Varennes; the King and Queen were so completely prisoners that they could hardly leave the courts of the Tuileries; and captive royalty seemed dead to the multitude. Nevertheless order was still maintained, at least to a considerable extent; some of the mob-leaders in Paris were silenced for a time; and an attempt at an outbreak was put down by Bailly and Lafayette, not without blood. Signs of returning consciousness, too, were now and then seen; Louis and his consort were more than once greeted with cheers when allowed to show themselves at the opera; and, notwithstanding all that had taken place, generous hearts felt for their fallen splendor. A kind of instinct, also, told the middle classes that an hour of trial and peril was near; and at the distant sound of the approaching tempest thousands turned their eyes towards that tottering throne, which, burdened as it was with evil memories, seemed at least a rallying point against anarchy.

off, troubled, careful; with upturned face, snuffing dimly the uncertain future times; complexion of multiplex atrabiliar color, the final shade of which may be the pale sea-green?"

CHAPTER IV.

THE LEGISLATIVE ASSEMBLY.

Character of the period from the summer of 1791 to August 10, 1792.

WE have now reached a period when the elements of disorder, comparatively quiescent for a time in France, were to burst out with a force never seen before; when the consequences of her ancient ills and discords, and the vices of her new made institutions, were to reveal themselves with portentous distinctness; and when popular passion, given sudden strength in the weakness of an ill-organized State, and quickened by the most powerful incitements, was to overthrow the already unstable Monarchy, and to lead ere long to a terrific catastrophe. These events, fraught with momentous issues, were again to give proof how deep-seated were many of the mischiefs afflicting the kingdom, were again to bear witness to the want of wisdom of the higher orders and the unhappy Sovereign, were to bring out again in too clear relief the faults of the work of the National Assembly, and the numberless resulting perils and evils; and were, too, to show by a fresh awful example how power may suddenly fall away from classes which seemed in possession of it; and how, in France especially, perhaps, a vehement, reckless, and daring minority, may, in certain circumstances, overbear opposition, and rise into powerful and commanding authority. The causes, however, of these phenomena were not to be sought within France alone; they were largely due to the influences external to her; and but for elements alien from it in the main, and arousing national excitement to frenzy, the course of the Revolution would, we think, have been different.

A few weeks after the flight to Varennes the National Assembly dissolved itself, having declared that its great work was done, and that it left "France, as it hoped, regenerate." The King, having with apparent readiness accepted the Constitution he had labored to subvert, and a general amnesty having been proclaimed, the political sky seemed for the moment brightening; and the royal family were seen in Paris in splendor, and what it was assured was liberty. The new Legislative Assembly met in October; and, as the elections had been tolerably quiet, many began to hope that "the glorious gains" of the two preceding years were at last realized, and that what had been done was finally established. One circumstance, however, was not in favor of the political experience of the fresh made Legislature. The National Assembly, by a self-denying ordinance, had excluded its members from its successors' ranks; and thus the Representative Body of 1791 was as ill-trained as the States-General had been. The Legislative Assembly, of course, contained very few members of the late Noble Order, and was chiefly composed from the Middle classes; but its prevailing wish was, at first at least, to uphold the constitution of 1790–1, though a republican party existed in it, and it was desirous of trying its hand at reform. It numbered 750 deputies, divided into a Right, a Centre, and a Left party; the first conservative, the last radical, and the second, which was very numerous, wavering between them. The Left, in the political slang of the day, became known as the Mountain, and the Cen-

Deceptive calm; meeting of the new Legislative Assembly.

Character of this Body.

tre as the Plain; and these odd nick-names were, before long, to acquire a strange and world-wide celebrity. Taken altogether, the Legislative Assembly was inferior in brilliancy to its predecessor; and it had no member of the powers of Mirabeau. It was not, however, without men of fine parts; and one knot of deputies, known afterwards by the name of the Department from which many of them came—the Gironde, part of the old Province of Guyenne—became conspicuous for their persuasive eloquence, and their ardent, if not very wise enthusiasm.

The Gironde.

Dissensions between the King and the Assembly. For a brief space the Assembly and the King made a sincere effort to work well together. Louis composed his ministry of moderate men, known as Feuillants, from a club of that name, set up to counteract the power of the Jacobins; and some of the reformers in the National Assembly, among whom Barnave was conspicuous, endeavored to aid the Court with their counsels. From the first moment, however, the King had been vexed by slights put on him by some deputies in return for want of courtesy on his part; irritation was aroused by what was thought an extravagant augmentation of the military force allowed the Sovereign by the Constitution, and by the refusal of Court lords and ladies to accept places in the newly-arranged household; and causes of dissension quickly multiplied, and were aggravated by the absurd provision which, by excluding them from seats in it, made the Ministers of the Crown appear dictators and strangers to the Assembly. Meanwhile the acceptance of the Constitution had stirred the *émigrés* to increased wrath; and though their army as yet made no signs of life—for noble officers could get few soldiers, and would not stoop to serve in the ranks—the brothers of the

King uttered vehement protests against the acts of the National Assembly, and their emissaries swarmed across the Rhine, preaching discord and trying to excite trouble. The movement was largely se- *Disorders in* conded by the priests, who had very gene- *the Provinces.* rally refused to take an oath to respect the new order of things in the Church ; and it created not a little disturbance, ancient sympathies and religious feelings coming into collision, in many Departments with the sentiments and instincts of the Revolution. *Religious and* Some frightful disorders, too, broke out at *social troubles. Massa-* Avignon, for ages a fief of the Pope, but an- *cre at Avignon (Oct. 16–20,* nexed by the National Assembly to France. *1791.)* The French and papal parties rose against each other, and a foul and hideous massacre took place ; several towns in the South and South-east were convulsed by the strife of angry factions already approaching a civil war ; and bands of armed and houseless vagrants prowled about the kingdom in many districts. levying black mail, and doing all kinds of outrage. A feeling of general discontent, besides, grew visible ere long in the great cities, and the populace was occasionally on the verge of insurrection. The assignats had quickened trade at first, but the reckless use of paper money produced before long the inevitable results ; and the prices of everything rose rapidly, while, in the unsettled position of affairs, employers became alarmed and cautious. The millions of artizans and workmen felt the necessaries of life grow dearer and dearer, while their wages did not increase in proportion, and there were many to tell them that this was caused by the selfishness of the rich and of jobbing speculators. Besides, the Revolution, it was said, was over; yet, after all, what had it done for the poor, how had it realized the fair visions held before the multitude by specious orators? The Middle classes were, no doubt, better off; but the Middle classes were as hard as the nobles; and was the end to be a mere change of masters? These dangerous sentiments were fanned and excited by the Jacobins in Paris and kindred societies; and the fires of agitation spread far and wide, at first smouldering and irregular, but gradually gathering volume and force.

Louis directly opposes the Assembly. These disorders were not calculated to better the relations of the Assembly and the King, or to give repose to the national mind; and the elements of mischief soon became more active. The Assembly, at different times in the winter, passed severe decrees against *émigrés* and priests; and although these may have been unnecessarily harsh, the occasion justified strict precautions. Louis, however, possibly with a kindly sentiment,

Nov. 1791. but certainly with extreme imprudence, affixed his veto to these measures, and thus directly opposed the will of the Legislature, although expressed in a decisive manner, and that, too, on a most important occasion. The grievance was aggravated by the fact that the King was continually in communication with his brothers, at least, in the *émigré* camp; and that, parading his dislike of the new settlement of the Church, he had chosen his chaplains and confessors from priests who had refused to take the constitutional oath. We can readily conceive the results of this folly—which Englishmen would not have borne for a day, though trained for centuries in political life—in the case of a Legislature without experience, and exceedingly jealous of its new rights, and of a nation vehement, ignorant, and distracted. The Assembly, hitherto inclined to act with the King, became full of anger and suspicious

1791. *The Legislative Assembly.* 59

fears; many moderate men fell off from the Court; and the Legislature being for the time baffled, the general indignation found vent in passionate outbreaks of popular wrath. The Commune of Paris besieged the Assembly with petitions signed by its united sections; the Jacobin Club, and one even more violent, the Cordeliers, grew into increased importance; and the Jacobins regularly usurped the functions of a great deliberate body, and despatched emissaries to stir up the people in every part of the kingdom. By these means, aided by the affiliated clubs, and by a Press growing in rabid license, existing elements of discontent and anger were made intense, and a general outburst of passion was organized against the King, the Court, and even the Constitution, which it was asserted had proved worse than useless. Meanwhile the masses were everywhere taught to seize and make use of their immense power; the machinery of government and of administration fell more and more into the hands of the populace, under the superintendence and control of demagogues; and the National Guards become more and more filled with what were called patriots, or were debauched by them. This was more especially the case in Paris, where, Lafayette having resigned his command, the National Guard had been remodelled, and where Bailly 'had been replaced by Pétion, a false and artful popularity seeker, though the Court, with hardly intelligible silliness and spite, had thrown its influence into the scale on his side for the office of mayor against Lafayette. By this time the National Guard of Paris had been largely recruited from the lower ranks; its officers had been in some degree changed; and it was divided in mind and general senti-

Indignation of the Assembly.

Attitude of the Commune of Paris. The Clubs and demagogues.

ment. It was still, on the whole, on the side of order; but its discipline had been much relaxed; and in the contest between the Assembly and the King its sympathies were with the popular cause.

<small>Menaces of Foreign Powers.</small> It was thus faring ill with regenerate France, by reason of crime, misrule, and bad institutions. Meanwhile an influence was drawing near from without which was to give sudden and appalling strength to the elements of disturbance in the State, and to stamp a character on the Revolution more terrible than any it had yet shown. Not long after the flight to Varennes, the Sovereigns of Austria and Prussia had met; and, at an interview at <small>Declaration of Pilnitz, August, 1791.</small> the little town of Pilnitz, had laid down a plan for a Coalition against France, with a solemn protestation that the cause of Louis XVI. was that of all the Monarchies of Europe. German writers,* whose mission it has been of late to deny the possibility of German ambition, may say that this League was a mere pretence; but it could not have so appeared to Frenchmen, and it was followed by demonstrations of force, and by fair words at least to the collection of *émigrés* who were menacing France from German territory. Prussia, too, at this time was hankering after Alsace; the Count of Artois had been base enough to hint at concessions in Lorraine as the price of aid to the good cause; and Russia, Sweden, Piedmont, and Spain, held an attitude more or less threatening. It is certain, moreover, that for months afterwards the

---

* Professor Von Sybel is the most eminent of these apologists, but his arguments are mere special pleading; and the very fact that the Sovereigns of Austria and Prussia, hitherto hostile, issued the manifesto of Pilnitz, was more than enough to provoke France.

King and Queen were in regular correspondence with the Emperor of Austria and other Sovereigns; and though they still repudiated foreign war, Marie Antoinette urged the necessity of an armed Congress upon the frontier, which would place the Monarchy on a new footing, and of course lead to a counter-revolution. These intrigues, however, were not fully known, though a kind of instinct apprehended part of the truth; and the Legislative Assembly was for a considerable time divided on the question of peace or war, the Moderates and the Gironde being for hostilities, the extreme Left condemning an appeal to arms as tending to a dictatorship and the rule of the sword. After an envenomed controversy with his opponents, the Austrian Minister, Cobentzel, at last indicated an intention on the part of his master to intervene directly in the affairs of France, and to put down the Revolution by force, and this precipitated the impending crisis. The Assembly declared war against Austria in April, 1792, the King assenting with seeming readiness. Prussia eagerly coalesced with her Austrian rival; and thus commenced a tremendous conflict, which was to shake the world for twenty-three years, in which France, we think, was not the first aggressor. Three French armies were despatched to the frontier; but the soldiers, spoiled by long neglect of discipline, were unable to look in the faces of their foes, and they were driven out of Belgium after a severe skirmish, slaughtering in their fury one of their chief officers. Before long, too, it became evident that the whole forces of the Kingdom were demoralized, and wanting in almost every appliance of war; and Lafayette, who commanded one

Projects of the King and Queen.

Divisions in the Assembly.

It declares war against Austria. Prussia joins Austria.

French failures in Belgium. April, May, 1792.

of the three armies, and in whom confidence was generally placed, made no secret of the danger of the situation.

Indignation in France. These tidings spread consternation through France, and exasperated the passions that stirred the capital. The war party in the Assembly, swayed by the Gironde, at once acquired a decisive ascendency; the leaders of the populace shouted treason, and vociferated that the troops had been sold; and dark suspicions accumulated against the Court, the King, and especially the Queen. Even in the Assembly it was openly said that an Austrian committee sat in the palace, betraying the dearest interest of France; and fierce threats were uttered that an Austrian woman should not be allowed to stand in the way of the Nation. Ere long the insensate conduct of Louis added fresh fuel to the kindling excitement.

Insensate conduct of Louis. He had been compelled, before hostilities began, to part with his Feuillant administration, one of the members of which had been impeached for pusillanimity in the negotiations with Austria; and he had formed a ministry mainly composed from the Gironde and popular party, but of which the real chief was Dumouriez,* an able and brilliant soldier of fortune. This cabinet had proposed a new law against the non-juring and half-rebellious priests, and the Assembly had voted it with acclamation; and soon after the defeats on the frontier one of the ministers brought forward a measure for creating a camp of twenty thousand volunteers near Paris, which would become

* Dumouriez, born 1745. This able general and brilliant diplomatist had served and intrigued with distinction before the Revolution. His character is drawn with skill and fidelity by M. Thiers, *Histoire de la Revolution Française*, vol. ii. p. 58, ed. 1842.

the nucleus of a national army to be drawn together from all parts of the kingdom. An enthusiastic vote welcomed this scheme also; and it deserves notice that although Dumouriez expressed at first his dissent from the project, and made use of the opportunity to intrigue against three of his Gironde colleagues, he recurred to it almost immediately, however worthless and dangerous, besides, such a force must have seemed to an experienced soldier. The King, however, even at this crisis, directly thwarted the vote of the Legislature; refused to sanction the double decree; dismissed first the three Gironde ministers, and Dumouriez himself a few days afterwards; and chose a new Cabinet from the unpopular Feuillants, suspected, in part at least, of weakness, and discredited in the eye of the Assembly and the Nation. *He resists the decrees of the Assembly and dismisses the Gironde ministry and Dumouriez.*

History justly condemns the excesses that followed, and the bad use that was made of popular passion; but neither ought she to forget the provocation, or the circumstances that led to the triumph of anarchy. The leaders of the Assembly, once more brought into collision with a Sovereign and a Court believed to be leagued with the national enemy, at a crisis of sudden national peril, turned to the capital for support; and while they denounced openly the conduct of the King, they sought the aid of the demagogues and mobs of Paris as instruments against the intrigues of the palace. This course was unwise, and in part selfish, but motives of patriotism concurred; nor is it perhaps surprising that these men made this wild appeal to revolutionary forces. Pétion, the Mayor of Paris, gladly organized the powers of the Commons to stir up agitation; the Jacobins and Corde- *Outbreak of June 20, 1792.*

liers called on all patriots to take up arms to resist oppression; and the galleries of the Assembly were nightly thrown open to swarms of ferocious and squalid spectators, who clamored down attempts to oppose the majority. In a very short time the streets of the city were once more dense with masses of pikemen, who overawed or won over the National Guards, and this growing army of savagery was largely recruited from the desperadoes who for some months had been congregating into the dens of the capital. An occasion for an outbreak soon arose, and there can be no doubt that it was at least connived at by many in the Assembly and by the municipal authorities. On June 20, the anniversary of the oath of the Tennis Court, a great crowd collected to commemorate that event, and it burst armed into the hall of the Legislature, waving banners with murderous or grotesque emblems, and calling on the deputies to act with energy. The mass, unchecked and even welcomed, next broke through the gates of the Tuileries, and the courts of the palace were soon filled with an excited multitude, crying, " Down with the veto," " The Nation and the patriot ministers forever." Several thousand National Guards were present, but they looked on with indifference or had no orders; and one battalion, it is said, shouted "that it knew who was its real enemy." The chambers of the royal family were quickly reached, and at the sight of Madame Elizabeth yells arose fiercely against the "Austrian woman," the princess being taken for the Queen, while the King was assailed with epithets of "Monsieur Veto," and "the Constitution or death." The impassive attitude of Louis, however, had some effect in calming the crowd, and no hand was lifted up against him, though a cap of liberty

Marginal note: Encouraged by the popular leaders in the assembly and by the Commune of Paris.

was thrust upon his head, and he remained in this humiliating position for hours, surrounded by execration and ribaldry. The Queen, meanwhile, had been happily rescued by the efforts of a few courageous men; and awestruck, it is said, by her majesty and grace, her intending murderers turned aside their weapons, while a few kindly words from her lips melted into tears some of the female furies who had hung on the skirts of the hideous procession. Towards evening Pétion, who had at least offered no opposition to the demonstration, persuaded the multitude to disperse; but the secret of the defenceless state of the palace had been discovered, and was not forgotten; and royalty seemed, as it were, trailed in the dust.

The disgraceful scene of June 20, caused a slight reaction in favor of the King. The patience of Louis excited compassion; the Assembly began to dread the forces which its leaders had rashly called to their aid; and the Gironde party, appalled at the prospect, made overtures for the recall of the three Gironde ministers. Lafayette, too, hastened from the frontier to condemn the violence of the Commune and the Jacobins. Pétion was prosecuted for his conduct on the 20th, and the moderate citizens, still the majority, were sincerely desirous of seeing order restored. But the movement ere long made renewed progress, precipitated by the intelligence of fresh defeats, by passion, and by the obstinacy of the Court. On June 30 the Assembly passed a resolution that all existing authorities should be in permanent session, and thus the organization of democratic forces which had been created all over France, and had fallen under the control of demagogues, was kept in motion to excite the people. Petitions began to pour in from the provinces; the towns fermented with

F

Reaction in favor of Louis.

angry agitation; the municipal assemblies, and those of the Departments, were mastered by low and reckless mobs, all more or less with arms in their hands, and Paris formed the centre from which this machinery was worked by those who managed those turbulent masses. Meanwhile an attempt was made to create the very armed force which the King had opposed; volunteers were invited to flock to Paris for the approaching commemoration of the fall of the Bastille; the Constitutional Guard of Louis was disbanded; and the staff of the National Guard was changed and filled with men of a revolutionary type. At the same time the ferocious bands who had shown their power on June 20 were held in the leash by their desperate leaders, and vile incitements were not wanting to urge all "patriotic men" to join them. The

<small>New efforts of the Demagogues and the Commune.</small> Commune of Paris, almost independent and Sovereign within its own limits, was, in the main, responsible for those measures; but the majority of the Assembly concurred, and they were attended with the desired results. On the day of the festival Louis found himself in the presence of a host of armed men—many came from distant parts of the kingdom—who either maintained an ominous silence, or shouted, "The Nation," "Pétion," or "Death;" and even the National Guards were wild and unsteady. By this time the state of the capital had become so alarming that the King was implored by ministers and trusty friends to fly; two high-souled noblemen, faithful among the faithless, placed their wealth at his feet; and even Lafayette promised to come to his aid and to take him in safety to the army. But irresolution and evil councils prevailed; the unhappy monarch refused to move; and Marie Antoinette exclaimed, in a burst of passion, "that she would rather perish than trust such a hypocrite as

Lafayette." Nor were other motives, as we now know, wanting: the King and Queen had been kept informed of the intended march of the German armies; and she had boasted exultingly that her deliverance was at hand. Pity as we may an august victim, that deliverance would have been wrought in blood and fire, even if this result had been against her will; and truth requires us to note the circumstance.

France and Paris were in this critical state when a memorable incident suddenly removed the last checks on the revolutionary forces. At the end of July the Prussian army, under the Duke of Brunswick, was set in motion, two Austrian divisions being on either wing; and the invading host, headed by bands of *émigrés*, wild with delight, and thirsting for revenge, advanced from the Rhine to the Moselle and the Meuse. Brunswick issued a proclamation, ever to be condemned by those to whom national freedom is dear, and which years afterwards met its fitting reward. This manifesto, among other outrages, summoned Paris instantly to "submit to its King," declared that it would be "razed to the earth" if any insult were offered to the royal family; and, after announcing that the "Legislative Assembly, the National Guards, and the municipal authorities would be held answerable for whatever occurred, to military courts-martial, without a hope of pardon," kindly added that "their Austrian and Prussian Majesties would do their good offices with his most Christian Majesty to obtain forgiveness for his rebellious subjects." This infamous document caused a thrill of fury and wrath to shoot through the capital; and though Louis, no doubt sincerely, disavowed what the Allies had done, the mischief, unhappily, was beyond

Proclamation of Brunswick.

Invasion of France by the Prussians and Austrians, July and August, 1792.

recall. In the outburst of indignation which stirred the citizens, the first thought was of safety and vengeance; and as the Assembly, at this crisis, did little but applaud the orators of the Gironde, and had no resolute and practical policy, power passed quickly to the more reckless demagogues, and there was hardly anything to oppose the most desperate projects, though the party of order was still the most numerous. An insurrection was regularly planned, its object being to dethrone the King, and to keep him a hostage with the rest of his family; and, as we have seen, means to work on the populace, and formidable armed power, were not wanting, while all other authorities were weak and doubtful. Revolutionary committees, as they were styled, were formed in the Jacobin Club and in the Commune; and delegates from these harangued the sections, called upon them to organize themselves and rise, and laid the train for a general explosion. Danton shone eminent among these leaders; and his terrible aspect, fierce earnestness, and rude, savage, but genuine eloquence, had already gained him the name of the "Patriot Mirabeau." By this time thousands of volunteers had arrived to swell the bands of Parisian pikemen; and among them the contingent from Marseilles, "six hundred men who could do or die," were conspicuous for their audacious bearing. The rising was fixed for August 9; and as some of the members of the Commune were not willing to go the necessary lengths, it was resolved to replace this body suddenly by men of the true patriot stamp from the sections. Pétion, treacherous and timid, assented to the scheme, so that his hand in it should not be seen; and it was veiled under a show of legality, an immense petition from the forty-eight sections

The assembly paralyzed; power passes to the Demagogues.

Preparations for a rising. Danton.

for the immediate setting aside of the king having been presented to the Assembly.

On August 9, when darkness had fallen, the note of preparation began to sound. The summer moon was calm in the heavens; and all those who in a great city love quiet, whatever the passions of the hour, were sunk in sleep, unconscious of what was to come. Many, too, though by nature friends of order, also half knew that wild schemes were abroad, and were not sorry that a stern lesson was to be given to what they thought a perfidious Court; and timidity, selfishness, and dull indifference, combined to make thousands tame and passive. But the more agitated parts of the capital were alive with a fierce tumultuary stir; and dark figures flitted through streets and lanes to reach the appointed places of meeting, while bells clanged forth from Town Hall and steeple, as ages before they had rung out a challenge to invading Teutonic hordes, as they had ushered in that hour of horror and death when the kennels ran thick with Huguenot blood. Here vehement and gesticulating groups were seen hanging on the lips of a fiery orator; there conspirators sate in secluded conclave receiving tidings from thronging messengers; in other places loud cheers greeted the gatherings of the mustering bands, and the quick rattle of the drum beat a wild assembly. Meanwhile all that was most daring had met in the sections; the form and voice of Danton rose high and bold, though other mob leaders had slunk off in silence; and at a given signal a body of delegates, elected by the sections with vociferous applause, made their way into the council chamber of the Commune, and seizing on the Government of the capital, accelerated and directed the outbreak. The forces of anarchy now

Paris on the night of Aug. 9, 1792.

developed themselves; the tramp of armed columns in the streets grew dense; the sullen clank of cannon was heard; and deep masses, headed by desperate men of hideous aspect, in military garb, collected in the broad squares and ways, fringed at the edges by insurgent multitudes. Yet signs of hesitation were not wanting; more than one tongue-valiant leader was driven on by exasperated followers threatening him with death; and the fear of Brunswick, want of mutual confidence, and the consciousness of a dangerous purpose, made many pause and turn weakly away. Hours passed before the rising attained anything like really formidable strength; and it was daylight before the forest of pikes, here and there bristling with deadlier weapons, and skirted by yelling and enthusiastic crowds, advanced along the banks of the Seine to the thick labyrinth of enclosures and streets, from which, at that time, the broad front of the Tuileries rose in antique magnificence.

Attitude of the King and the Court.

The King and the Court had during these hours been kept informed of the peril at hand. Terror and anxiety reigned in the palace; though at a report that the rising had failed, fine gentlemen jeered at the "cowardice of the canaille," and fine ladies joined in pretty disdain. Preparations were hastily made for defence; National Guards were collected from the most loyal quarters; and Pétion, Judas-like, was in attendance to screen himself and utter smooth words of hope. A hand-

August 10, 1792.

ful of Nobles and their domestics, too, flocked in to strike a last blow for the throne; though the main trust of the Court lay in a few hundred Swiss, a remnant of the old Body-guard, who still lingered in the royal service. A lamentable incident, however, lessened whatever prospect of success existed. The

1792.   *The Legislative Assembly.*   71

commander-in-chief of the National Guards, a brave soldier of the name of Mandat, had prepared an able plan of resistance; and as his influence on his men was great, they might possibly not have fallen away from him. But, doubtless with the connivance of Pétion, he was lured away and murdered by the conspiring Commune; and his death left the palace without a head or leader. At the first appearance of the insurgent columns Louis went out to address the National Guards, and had he spoken and looked as became a King he might have found a way to their hearts. But the downcast bearing and hesitating gestures of the unhappy Monarch made the appeal useless; and the contempt of the crowd grew into anger when Marie Antoinette, pointing, it is said, to the few Nobles standing haughtily aloof, exclaimed, "These are men who will show you your duty." By this time the assailants had reached the palace, swarming round the approaches on every side; and, far as it could gaze, the eye rested on a wild chaos of passionate wrath, of tossing steel, of menacing faces, of revengeful clamor, of hideous revelry. *The armed populace at the Tuileries.* The weapons of the National Guards fell from their hands at the sight; and the miserable spectable of distrust and mutiny of which so many proofs had been given was fearfully repeated at this supreme crisis. A well-meaning officer of the old Commune—Pétion had got away, his work being done—implored the King to avoid bloodshed, and to seek refuge within the Assembly, the chamber of which was a hall close by, and the ill-fated Louis quietly assented. The royal family passed in sad procession along the gardens of the Tuileries, amidst the yells of ferocious mobs, baulked, for the moment, of their intended prey; and in a few minutes they were in a place of safety. The King was received with cold respect, and, indeed, many of the alarmed Assembly would have even now turned to him again if they dared; but he was soon made to feel that he was a mere captive. A deputy having made the remark that the debates of the Assembly must be free, the royal family were huddled away into a box at the back of the reporters' gallery, and not a voice was raised of loyalty or pity. The eyes of Marie Antoinette dropped bitter tears, but the heavy features of Louis looked dull indifference; and the chief of the illustrious race of Bourbon, in sight of the falling throne of his sires, ate, it is said, with seeming content, a dish of peaches!*

The King and Royal Family take refuge in the Assembly.

Before long the irregular sounds of disorder were lost in the din and roar of battle. The mob had forced the gates of the palace soon after the departure of the royal family; and it seemed as if the outbreak would cease, the triumph of the populace being complete. But a shot or two fired on either side caused passion to flame up more fiercely than ever; and the insurgents, headed by the men of Marseilles, made a wild dash at the inner doors of the palace. Then was seen what military worth can do against undisciplined numbers; the Swiss Guard fired and charged home, and in an instant the assailants were yelling in flight, and the refluent multitudes surged heavily backwards. At this moment, however, an order came from the unfortunate King to cease firing; and as the obedient soldiery reluctantly fell back, the revolutionary forces again pressed forward, in the exultation of unhoped-for victory. A murderous and horrible scene ensued;

The Tuileries attacked and pillaged. Massacre of the Swiss.

* *Souvenirs de la Terreur*, per George Duval, quoted by M. Feuillet de Conches, vol. vi. p. 285.

the Swiss were hemmed in and at last overpowered; and the popular fury wreaked itself on the bodies of the dead in hideous outrage, while fiendish women danced round the mangled corpses. The palace was now stormed by the triumphant multitude; and while bands of cut-throats plied the work of murder, all that was disorderly and vile in a great city revelled in the deserted abode of royalty. In a few moments the treasures of ages were destroyed; the costly floors were strewn with the wrecks of pictures in tatters and broken statues, and troops of harlots, shrieking for the "Austrian woman"—Court gossip had proclaimed she was as bad as themselves, and the infamous falsehood had reached the streets—were seen bedizened in the finery of the Court. Yet signs of humanity were not wanting even in these foul saturnalia of license; the ladies and women of the Court were spared, amidst shouts of "Do not disgrace the Nation;" and a kind of principle controlled the excesses of passion, for vulgar pillage was generally forbidden, and more than one thief was caught and hanged. The lowest depths of anarchy had not yet been reached, when wickedness riots without restraint.

Such was the terrible outbreak of August 10, 1792, leading to the immediate overthrow of the Bourbon Monarchy. The causes of disorder which had agitated France, undermined the throne, and destroyed authority, had been made more active by various events; and foreign aggression came to give a new and extraordinary impulse to them. In the effervescence of passion which ensued, the representatives of the nation, contending against a Sovereign and Court believed to be false, had turned for aid to revolutionary Paris; and this power, organized by mob

Reflection on the rising of August 10.

leaders, had overborne open and secret opposition, and displayed great and appalling strength. Authority was ere long to pass away from the classes which had so lately seized it; and the reign of license and terror was soon to prevail, with results which history will never forget. Yet many of the deeds we have briefly described were condemned by the majority of Frenchmen; and, even in Paris, the greater part of the citizens lamented the horrors of August 10. But the Constitution of 1790 gave scope to revolutionary forces; the different parties on the side of order were divided or suspicious of each other; above all, the cause of National independence and of the new interests created in 1789 seemed identified with that of the so-called patriots in circumstances which gave them extraordinary strength; and the result was that the anarchists triumphed, although really a minority in the State. It is a peculiarity, too, in the French national character, to yield easily to daring leaders; and this contributed to the fearful issue, though general causes may account for it. We shall now see how the revolutionary powers which had become ascendant went along their course, in the agony of a Nation distracted at home, and struggling to hold foreign invaders at bay.

CHAPTER V.

THE CONVENTION.

THE immediate effect of August 10 was to give the Legislative Assembly comparative freedom.* It might secretly dread the mobs of the capital ; but it was no longer fettered by the veto and the Court ; and whatever sympathy it felt for the unhappy King, it was restored, so to speak, to life by the outbreak. While the Tuileries was still in the power of the multitude, Vergniaud, the most brilliant orator of the Gironde, moved that Louis XVI., should be deposed for the present, and that a National Convention should be at once summoned to pronounce on the future destiny of France ; and the vote passed amidst thunders of applause. Before long the ill-fated royal family was imprisoned in the Temple, an old fortress, so called from the famous Order of that name, and was placed in the hands of the city authorities, who claimed the charge as their lawful right ; and the three Gironde ministers who had been dismissed were recalled, the ministry of justice, at the same time, being bestowed on Danton, to please the

Effects of August 10.

The Convention summoned.

The King and Royal Family imprisoned in the Temple.

* The internal history of France, just before and during the Reign of Terror, has been described by many writers. some of them eloquent and picturesque. As an accurate and clear analysis of the events of the time, and of the working of the revolutionary institutions and press, M. Mortimer Terneaux's *Histoire de la Terreur* seems to me to deserve special notice. The notes, too, of M. Feuillet de Conches, in his sixth volume, are often valuable.

populace. Simultaneously, energetic attempts were made to strengthen the national defences; the camp near Paris, which had been the subject of such fierce contention, was hastily armed; and commissioners were despatched to announce the events which had taken place to the chiefs of the armies, and to make preparations for the new elections. Meanwhile, the usurping Commune of Paris left nothing undone to consolidate its powers and to make the triumph of the 10th complete. With the assent of the half-willing Assembly, the delegates of the sections annulled the existing magistracy of the capital, and seized on its internal police; and the National Guards were wholly changed, their numbers being trebled, and their ranks crowded with the huge bands of insurrectionary pikemen. By these means the government of the city was secured to the demagogues and their dependents, supported by an immense armed force; and though an attempt at opposition was made by the citizens in the more wealthy sections, it was silenced at the cry that France was in danger. By this time the vile mob leaders who had skulked away during the struggle of the 10th had come back to their wonted haunts; and the Jacobins, the Cordeliers, and other places, rang with vehement exhortations to the people to make use of their newly-won liberties, and to exact a terrible vengeance "for the deaths of their children" from the aristocratic and Court factions, who, with the assistance of the approaching enemy, were "planning the extermination of all patriots." By the orders of the Commune, and probably of Danton, suspected houses were, accordingly, searched, and the prisons were crowded with hundreds of captives, who, it was openly boasted, were detained as hostages, and marked out, in

Violent measures of the Commune of Paris.

certain events, for destruction. Pétion, who, in return for the base part he had played, had been nominally made mayor again, but whose influence had altogether waned, was obliged to sanction these fearful proceedings, though he had already began to tremble at them.

At this crisis a terrible incentive was suddenly applied to this collection of passions. On receiving the news of the deposition of the King, Lafayette refused to obey the Assembly; and after a fruitless attempt to influence his troops, threw up his command, and fled across the frontier. *Lafayette throws up his command; advance of the German armies to Verdun.* Meanwhile, the Austrian and Prussian armies had advanced into the interior of France; and having rolled past the great stronghold of Metz, were making directly, by Verdun, for the capital, their light cavalry scouring the plains of Champagne. All seemed lost; and though the awestruck Assembly made passionate appeals to French patriotism, several of its leaders, especially the Gironde orators, proposed that Paris should be abandoned, and the seat of government transferred to the Loire, Danton came, however, conspicuously to the front, and declared that such cowardice was not to be thought of; and, at the same time, with a ferocious threat, certainly not understood by the other ministers, exclaimed that the real danger was from within, and that a guilty faction must be taught to tremble. Daring and unscrupulous, though less cruel than more than one of the mob leaders, he perhaps gave the signal of blood to the Commune; and, in the fury of the moment, a committee of that body proceeded to carry out the scheme of revenge which had been held out to the popular imagination. Bands of assassins were hired to force open the prisons; and, hideous mock trials added horror to the *Massacre of September.*

scene, their unhappy victims were ruthlessly butchered, and thrown out in heaps to crowds swarming around, amidst shouts of exulting frenzy. The execrable work of slaughter went on for days; fear, anger, wickedness, and fiendish hate, uniting in a dreadful carnival of crime; and the complicity of the Commune is proved by the fact that it baffled several attempts to stop the triumph of blood, and its revolutionary army of National Guards was never called out to restore order, and was allowed to join or not, as it pleased, in the massacres. In this way, much that was noble and fair in a once splendid Court was ruthlessly destroyed, intermingled with numerous less known victims; and the frenzy of the murderers became so extreme that a band of State prisoners, being escorted from Orleans, was immolated with frightful cruelty at Versailles. Nor was it possible to check the deviltry of passion when carnage had ceased in the emptied prisons; the form of the lovely Princess of Lamballe,* one of the most intimate friends of the Queen, was dragged, hideously mutilated, through the streets, and exposed to the eyes of Marie Antoinette; and ghastly processions of heads on pikes were carried through the principal streets of the capital, to strike terror into the hearts of the "foes of the people." At the same time pillage was let loose; the mansions of the rich and many churches were sacked; the repository of the Crown jewels was rifled; and some quarters of the city seemed like a town abandoned to a

---

* Louisa of Savoy, Princess of Lamballe, was one of the purest and fairest ornaments of the Court of Versailles, and one of the few real friends of the unfortunate Queen. M. Thiers tells her death well, *Histoire de la Revolution Française*, vol. ii. p. 335, edit. 1842.

plundering enemy. Yet, as always happens, even when man appears in his most revolting aspect, faint gleams of humanity flickered here and there over these scenes of terror and dismay; noble examples of endurance and virtue were given; and many of the "patriots" refused to share in the spoil robbed by their baser fellows. The victims of the butchery seem to have reached the number of fourteen hundred persons.

Such was the "massacre of September," as it has ever since been called; and, though bloodier scenes occurred afterwards, no event perhaps in the French Revolution was more atrocious than this sanction of horrors by the authorities of a great capital. Terror and hatred account for the frightful crime, though no excuse for it can be offered; and it is missing the truth to ascribe it to mere party motives, or even to any special vice in the nature of Frenchmen. From this time the divisions between the Assembly and the mob rulers of Paris began to grow more and more deep; the Right, the Centre, and even the Jacobin Mountain, concurred in the expressions of anger and blame; and though the guilty committee of the Commune published an eulogy on the "justice of the people," hardly one even of the city demagogues recurred with approbation to these days of blood. In fact, the frenzy which provoked the massacre gave way ere long to different sentiments, for a time at least comparatively in the ascendant, in consequence of a sudden change of fortune. After the flight of Lafayette the chief command of the French armies was given to Dumouriez; and as the invaders began to hesitate at the critical moment when they reached the Meuse, that general was able to pluck safety from what appeared peril beyond remedy, though he must have failed against

The Assembly indignant at the massacre.

determined foes. Drawing together all his available forces, and summoning Kellermann from Louvain to his aid, Dumouriez retreated behind the long hill range, known by the name of the Ardennes and the Argonne, which crosses Champagne just west of the Meuse; and, having seized the passes through this intricate region, he waited steadily the attack of the allies, while thousands of recruits were sent off to his camp from the capital and the adjoining Provinces. He succeeded in making a stand for a time, though driven from his positions with little difficulty; and when, at last, on September 20, the Prussians had forced his line of defence, a misdirected manœuvre of Brunswick enabled the French, bad troops as they were, to defeat an attempt to dislodge them from the heights of Valmy.* This trifling advantage had wonderful results; the King of Prussia, Brunswick, and the Austrian generals began to disagree, and to feel alarm; and the extreme wetness of an inclement season caused the invading army to perish by thousands. Before many days had passed the proud hosts which had advanced near Châlons was in full retreat; and France and Paris were rescued from an invasion which, if properly directed, must have crushed all resistance.

<small>Battle of Valmy. Its great results; retreat of the Prussians and Austrians.</small>

Meanwhile the National Convention had met, and before long was installed in the Tuileries, the forsaken abode of captive royalty. This Body, elected under the influence of August 10 and of foreign invasion, was more revolutionary than its immediate predecessor, but it was largely composed of the same men, and the majority

<small>Meeting of the Convention, September 22, 1792.</small>

* New and interesting details about the Battle of Valmy will be found in Feuillet de Conches, vol. vi. p. 338.

were opposed to anarchy. The party of the Mountain in it, however, was more powerful than in the Legislative Assembly; the Plain or Centre was even more uncertain; and it was observed that several of the most distinguished deputies, who had formerly sate on the Radical Left, were now seen on the Conservative Right. The orators of the Gironde were again returned, and became the chiefs of what were called the Moderates; and the Assembly, if eager for political changes, was, on the whole, on the side of social order, though the representatives of Paris—of whom Marat, Robespierre, and Danton were the most conspicuous— were taken generally from the class of demagogues. The first measures of the Convention showed what really were its natural tendencies. A committee was appointed to inquire into the charges against Louis XVI.; and Monarchy was abolished and a Republic proclaimed with hardly a single dissentient voice, the conduct of the Court during the preceding year, especially since the declaration of war, having excited general indignation and distrust. Efforts, too, were made to strengthen the armies, now pursuing the enemy across the frontier; and in reply to the manifesto of Brunswick, and the not-forgotten declaration of Pilnitz, the cause of Nations was arrayed against that of Kings, and liberty was offered, in the name of France, to any people who would put down its despots. If, however, this revolutionary creed was aggressive and even destructive abroad—and the provocation must be borne in mind—the majority of the Convention sincerely wished to curb anarchy and license at home; and it viewed with alarm the terrible events which had lately disgraced the capital. The Moderates, led by the brilliant Gironde, denounced

G

Parties in it.

France declared a Republic, Sept. 22, 1792.

Offer of liberty to foreign nations, Nov. 19.

the atrocities of September; asserted openly that the Commune of Paris was assuming a power fatal to the State; and declared that Robespierre and men of his stamp were aiming at the worst of all tyrannies. These accusations were generally well heard, and though fierce recriminations were uttered, though the Commune challenged inquiry into its acts, and the clubs of the anarchists echoed with threats, the party of mere disorder was at first comparatively powerless in the Convention.

Dissensions renewed between the Moderates and Jacobins. Savage passions, however, had been aroused; the mobs of the capital made angry demonstrations, and the demagogues within and outside the Assembly—known now generally by the name of Jacobins, from the society which was the centre of their power—began to view with deadly hatred and jealousy the Moderates, and especially the leaders of the Gironde, whose eloquence and culture provoked their resentment.

Trial of Louis XVI. Dec. 11, 1792. The Convention was in this disturbed state when the report of the conduct of the King was brought up. After an attempt on the part of the Jacobin leaders to obtain a summary sentence of death, it was resolved to put Louis upon his trial, and to proceed by a regular impeachment. On December 11 the ill-fated monarch, taken from his prison to his former palace, appeared at the bar of his republican judges, was received in silence and with covered heads, and answered interrogatories addressed to him as " Louis Capet," though with an air of deference. His passive constancy touched many hearts; and such is the sympathy that is always felt for fallen greatness when before the eye, that an immediate decision would have perhaps saved him, though the suspicions of the Assembly had been lately renewed by the discovery of papers of a questionable kind secreted in an iron chest by his orders. On the 26th the advocates of the King made an eloquent defence for their discrowned client, and Louis added, in a few simple words, that the "blood of the 10th of August should not be laid to his charge." The debates in the Assembly now began, and it soon became evident that the Jacobin faction were making the question the means to further their objects, and to hold up their opponents to popular hatred. They clamored for immediate vengeance on the tyrant, declared that the Republic could not be safe until the Court was smitten on its head, and a great example had been given to Europe, and denounced as reactionary and as concealed royalists all who resisted the demands of patriotism. These ferocious invectives were aided by the expedients so often employed with success, and the capital and its mobs were arrayed to intimidate any deputies who hesitated in the "cause of the Nation." The Moderates, on the other hand, were divided in mind; a majority, perhaps, condemning the King, but also wishing to spare his life: and the Gironde leaders, halting between their convictions, their feelings, their desires, and their fears, shrank from a courageous and resolute course. The result was such as usually follows when energy and will encounter indecision. On January 14, 1793, the Convention declared Louis XVI. guilty, and on the following day sentence of immediate death was pronounced by a majority of one, proposals for a respite and an appeal to the people having been rejected at the critical moment. The votes had been taken after a solemn call of the deputies at a sitting protracted for days; and the spectacle of the vast dim hall, of the shadowy figures of the awestruck judges meting out the fate of their

Sentence of death pronounced by a majority of one.

former Sovereign, and tier upon tier of half-seen faces, looking, as in a theatre, on the drama below, and breaking out into discordant clamor, made a fearful impression on many eye-witnesses. One vote excited a sensation of disgust even among the most ruthless chiefs of the Mountain, though it was remarked that many of the abandoned women who crowded the galleries shrieked approbation. The Duke of Orleans, whose Jacobin professions had caused him to be returned for Paris, with a voice in which effrontery mingled with terror, pronounced for the immediate execution of his kinsman.

Execution of Louis XVI. Jan. 21, 1793. The minister of justice—Danton had resigned—announced on the 20th the sentence to the King. The captive received the message calmly, asked for three days to get ready to die (a request, however, at once refused), and prayed that he might see his family and have a confessor. A few hours afterwards the doors of his room were opened by the officers of the Commune, who stood looking on without saying a word; and the Queen, Madame Elizabeth, and the two royal children, were locked in the arms of the doomed monarch. Why raise the veil on the agony of that scene; why note too curiously the mute resignation, the passionate tears, the heart-wrung grief, of that tragic and woful parting? Early next morning, after a tranquil night, Louis rose and gave his single attendant a wedding-ring as a token for his wife. He had promised to see his family again, but he wished to spare them the pangs of the interview. Soon afterwards he received the sacrament from the Abbé Edgeworth, a non-juring priest, who did his holy office at the peril of his life; and he remained for some time in fervent prayer, undisturbed by the sounds that rolled around the prison. At about eight the municipal officers announced curtly that the hour had come; and the King obeyed, after a few words of request that care would be taken of a will that he had made, and that a sum of money should be repaid to his counsel. He then quietly stepped into a carriage drawn up in the midst of a dense mass of bayonets, and with his faithful confessor by his side, repeated the solemn prayers for the dying, apparently unconscious of surrounding objects. The melancholy procession threaded its way through long-drawn lines of National Guards ranged on either side of the streets; and though a few sounds of anger or compassion were heard, the bystanders were rare, and for the most part silent, and shops were shut and windows closed along the course of that sad journey. For the moment pity and fear were in the minds of men; and, in the presence of the terrible fate about to reach the descendant of a hundred Kings, even revolutionary frenzy was hushed, and the tongues of the most reckless were dumb. At ten the carriage reached a square space in view of the high front of the Tuileries; and here, near a broken statue of Louis XV., rose the guillotine, a new instrument of death. Around were deep rows of horsemen and cannon, their sabres drawn and their matches lit; a vast multitude had collected too; and amidst the rabble of the streets was seen the familiar face of the Duke of Orleans, come again to confess his Jacobin faith. After an ineffectual attempt to address the people, drowned by the rattle of a hundred drums, the victim was placed beneath the high-raised axe; and, as the head fell, shouts of exultation burst from the lips of the vile populace, charmed hitherto as it were by a palsying spell, and a weight seemed lifted from the breasts of all.

The execution of Louis XVI. was one of those poli-

Reflections on this event. tical faults which are worse than crimes. It caused profound indignation in Europe, promoted anarchy and license, and enlisted universal sympathy for the discrowned martyr who had borne himself so meekly in death. Those who wield power ought not to forget that a policy of bloodshed is always dangerous; and, when an august victim is selected to fall, the reaction of sentiment is sometimes wonderful. The trial, too—a mere party struggle before a popular Assembly—was a mockery of justice; and the King was innocent of the greater part of the heinous accusations made against him. But if the question be whether Louis XVI. had kept faith with the French people, and had acted in the spirit of the institutions which he had sworn to respect and uphold, History cannot record a verdict for him; and though he deprecated foreign invasion, he encouraged and dealt with the national enemy in an audacious attack on national rights.

Character and conduct of the King. Undoubtedly, unlike our Charles I., he was not, as it were, false on principle; he was not able enough to show kingcraft, and in his private life he was a good man, though wanting in moral and social dignity. But he repeatedly crossed the will of his subjects in a manner that looked like studied perfidy; and he appeared to betray the dearest interests of France at a crisis when her existence was at stake—a more fatal position than any in which Charles I. was placed by the hand of Fortune. That this tortuous conduct was due to weakness, amounting to imbecility, is no doubt true. His situation also was extremely difficult; and if we judge of his acts merely by their moral quality, we may admit that he was continually under the influence of unwise or evil counsellors. But Frenchmen, in a moment of national peril, could not draw, or trust to, distinctions like these; and had Louis been deposed when the war broke out, or even after the flight to Varennes, they would have been fully justified in the sight of posterity.

The death of the King proved the signal for a general coalition of Europe against France. Such a League, indeed, had been already gathering, for the crusade of liberty which the Convention preached had exasperated every settled government; and the progress, besides, of the French arms had been in the highest degree alarming. After his success at Valmy Dumouriez had carried the war boldly into the Low Countries, and had won a brilliant victory at Jemmapes, and by the early spring he had overrun Belgium, had advanced to the banks of the Lower Meuse, and had made an audacious raid into Holland. Another French army had seized Savoy and Nice; and a third, under Custine, had crossed the Palatinate, had taken possession of the great fortress of Mayence, and was even threatening Germany beyond the Rhine. It is not strange that the old Powers of the Continent should have viewed these invasions with hatred and fear; for the results, though caused to a certain extent by the renewed dissensions of Austria and Prussia, were evidently in the main due to the astonishing force of the new ideas which spread with the march of the French troops, and led everywhere to popular risings; and the Autocracy and Feudalism of the eighteenth century were almost necessarily led to combine against the principles of the French Revolution, which, overflowing its natural borders, was threatening with ruin their decaying authority. No definite alliances, however, had yet been made,

Coalition of Europe against France.

Battle of Jemmapes, and early successes of the French, Nov., Dec., 1792; Jan., Feb., 1793.

and all was mere hesitation and doubt, until the execution of Louis XVI, fused suddenly together these blending elements, and united the rulers of all the Continental States in what they called a holy war against regicide, undertaken in the cause of God and of order. The princes of Germany followed the example already set by her leading Sovereign; Spain joined Piedmont for some time in arms; the little governments of Italy denounced France; and even Russia and Sweden stirred in their frozen deserts against the common enemy. England, too, was swept into the general movement, for the attack on Belgium had added strength to royal and aristocratic passions, and the middle classes were shocked and disgusted at the scenes which had taken place in Paris; and, amidst the exultation of the Tory party, supported by the great Whig secession, Mr. Pitt was forced into a war which he had earnestly labored to avert.* By February and March, 1793, the allied

* Having reached the second year of the war, I must refer to a few authorities on the subject. A really scientific and yet popular history of the contest in a tolerably small compass is still, perhaps, a desideratum, though an approach to such a work has been made by Colonel Hamley in his *Operations of War*, in which some of the most important campaigns, from 1796 to 1815, have been reviewed with real insight and perfect fairness. The war, however, has been illustrated, in its minutest details, in numerous elaborate Histories and Memoirs, and few subjects have been treated with equal ability. Jomini has commented fully on the Revolutionary and Napoleonic campaigns; and M. Thiers, in his *Histoire de la Revolution Française*, has described the first in his usual perspicuous style, and with less partiality than he has shown in his second great work. As an account of the memorable campaigns of Italy and Germany in 1796, and of the campaigns of 1799 and 1800, Napoleon's *Commentaries* are, in many respects, unrivalled; but the Emperor is sometimes inaccurate and unjust, though incom-

armies were all in motion; and while France was threatened from the Alps and the Pyrenees, what seemed an overwhelming tide of invasion, extending from the

parable as a critic of military combinations. The *History of the Consulate and Empire*, by M. Thiers, is a magnificent monument to Napoleon as a warrior; but the narrative of his exploits and those of the Grand Army is generally one-sided and flattering, and should be continually checked by those of German and English writers. The campaign of 1805 is very well analyzed by Colonel von Bristow; Thiers, Alison, and Jomini may be compared for those of 1806 and 1807; and valuable papers on the operations round Ulm, and in Poland, will be found in the *Staff College Essays* by Lieutenant Baring. For the history of the war in Spain and Portugal, from 1808 to 1814, the English reader will, of course, turn to the brilliant and exhaustive work of Napier; and the campaign of 1809 in Austria is well described by Generals Pelet and Stutterheim. The Russian campaign has been admirably criticised by Clausewitz and Jomini, and delineated with more or less accuracy by Ségur and Chambray. For the great struggle of 1813 and 1814 see the work of Plotho, and the narratives of Müffling, Gneisenau, and Bulow; on the French side, besides Thiers, the Memoirs of Marshal Marmont will be found useful. As for the Waterloo campaign, the authorities are almost innumerable. Mr. Hooper's account is exceedingly able and concise, but it errs on the side of praise of Wellington. Colonel Chesney, in his *Lectures on the Campaign of 1815*, has done justice to the part played by the Prussians in deciding the issue; Clausewitz and Müffling have also brought out clearly this feature of the contest; and the treatise of General Shaw Kennedy contains many valuable remarks. On the French side the *Commentaries* of Napoleon, though very unjust to his adversaries, deserve careful study; and Jomini's Précis of the campaign of 1815 seems to me very judicious in its general conclusions. Of later French writers, Thiers and La Tour D'Auvergne should be read as apologists for Napoleon, and Charras and Quinet as professed detractors and censors; but the work of Charras, able as it is, seems to me unsound and unfair. For the all-important question of the operations of Grouchy, see the pamphlet of that general, and the

Scheldt to the Rhine, rolled towards her eastern and northern frontiers.

During these events the struggle between the parties and factions which divided France had been growing more and more fierce. The vacillation of the Moderates and the Gironde on the occasion of the trial of the King had increased the power of the mob leaders; and Robespierre, who was beginning to rise into influence by a fanatical parade of republican doctrines, and through a reputation of austere probity, found many opportunities to denounce what he called the "royalism of the Convention." Expressions, too, of the Gironde orators were tortured into charges that the whole party wished to divide France into a Federation of States; and this aroused intense indignation in Paris, more especially when it was artfully proclaimed that these fine talkers had proposed to desert the capital, a few months before, at the approach of danger. The Gironde recriminated by fierce invectives against the Jacobins and the Duke of Orleans, whom they accused of secretly aspiring to the throne; but, though in the Convention they were still supreme, the revolutionary forces acquired strength, and they suffered from the inevitable results of new and almost usurped authority. The strife of

Fierce struggle of parties in France.

The Gironde denounced by the Jacobins and Demagogues.

clear but somewhat too sanguine observations of Marshal Gerard. In addition to these and many other works on the war, the diligent reader should continually refer to the *Correspondence* of Napoleon, the *Despatches* of the Duke of Wellington, and the admirable military works of the Archduke Charles. The *Military Souvenirs* of the Duc de Fezensac are perhaps the best extant records of the characteristics and composition of the Grand Army. The naval operations of the period are set forth in the fullest detail in James's History.

which Paris was the centre appeared in a thousand forms throughout the rest of France, and usually with the same results ; the middle classes and wealthier orders being for the most part on the side of the Moderates; the poor, the reckless, and the discontented, taking part with the anarchists and growing in power. All the mischiefs, too, which had already arisen from the influence exercised by mere demagogues over the local authorities throughout the country ; from the issue of assignats, now more excessive than ever ; from the decline of trade which had progressed steadily, and from the pressure of poverty continually on the increase; began to tell with extraordinary force at this juncture against the upholders of social order. The rise of prices almost inevitably led to a demand that they should be fixed by the State; and measures of communism and of a maximum rate for all the principal necessaries of life were clamored for by the popular chiefs and by the masses who looked up to them. It was in vain that the leaders of the Convention condemned such expedients as worse than useless ; it is always difficult to argue with hungry men ; and when Marat, with the approbation of many in the Commune, declared "what the poor wanted was to hang the grocers," he found thousands to echo the frightful sentiment. *Distress and social disorders.*

Meanwhile the forces of the Coalition, though feebly directed and advancing slowly, had been make alarming progress. On the Rhine Custine had been driven into Alsace, and Mayence was besieged by the Prussians and Austrians, as a preliminary step to further movements. Before long Dumouriez lost a great battle, at Neerwinden, and fell back in disorder, through Belgium, upon the French frontier ; the young recruits, *Advance of the Coalition.*

Battle of Neerwinden, March 18, 1793.

who formed a part of his army, disbanding at the first reverse in thousands. The North of France was thus threatened with invasion again; and the peril was increased by a quarrel between Dumouriez and the Convention, which repeated disasters envenomed and brought to an ominous issue. Dumouriez had condemned the execution of Louis XVI. and the revolutionary address to foreign nations; he complained that Jacobin sentiments destroyed discipline, and that Belgium was pillaged by the Jacobin emissaries, who had already associated liberty and rapine; and, having been called to account for his conduct, he abandoned, like Lafayette, his command, and left his army without a leader. At the same time intelligence arrived of a royalist insurrection in the West; and in more than one of the cities of the South, especially where the influence of the Gironde was great, the long-standing feud between the rich and the poor broke out into open civil war, and the upper classes denounced angrily the Jacobins and the mobs of Paris. These reiterated misfortunes of course embittered the strife of parties in the Convention and outside it; and in the explosion of passion which ensued everything tended to weaken the power of the Moderates and to secure ultimate success to their foes. Danton, always prominent in the hour of danger, had, at the first news of the defeats in the North, brought forward a series of revolutionary schemes; and he now insisted that the one thought of Frenchmen ought to be to save and defend the Republic by any expedients, however desperate. The isolation of the ministry from the Legislature, which had been continued up to this time, being obviously injurious at a great crisis, he obtained a de-

Flight of Dumouriez. He throws up his command.

Increasing power of the Jacobins. Danton. His energy.

cree by which a small cabinet, chosen within the Convention, became invested with what was practically supreme authority; and thus began the Committee of Public Safety, the most terrible dictatorship, perhaps, which modern or ancient times ever witnessed. A second committee, called that of General Security, formed at his instance, obtained the superintendence of all the higher police of the country; and he procured decrees for the arrest of all suspected persons and the establishment of an extraordinary tribunal, free from most of the safeguards and checks of procedure, to coerce and terrify what he called the factions. By these means the foundations of a formidable power were laid, which might become a tremendous despotism; and, in order to provide for the national defence, Danton urged not only that energetic efforts should be at once made to recruit the armies, but that, if necessary, the whole youth of the country should be placed at the disposal of the State. To obtain the willing support of the masses, he advocated, besides, an excessive tax on the rich, violent measures to keep up the value of assignats, and, above all, the maximum of prices, the cherished scheme of the Parisian demagogues. "Blast my memory," he exclaimed, in one of those harangues which electrified the Convention with their rude force, "but stop at nothing to save your country."

Formation of the Committee of Public Safety, April 6, 1793.

Violent measures proposed by Danton,

These impassioned appeals, in which we trace a strange mixture of true insight, of absurdity, and of mere popularity-seeking, were of course supported by the Jacobin leaders; and, under the pressure of danger, a great part of the policy of Danton, as we have seen, received the

and decreed by Convention.

Propositions of the Commune of Paris. assent of the alarmed Convention. At the same time the Commune of Paris threw itself boldly into the general movement, and openly asserting its independence, prepared an armed force to be sent to the frontier, and called on the other cities of France to follow its example. Meanwhile, the machinery of agitation was plied with ever-increasing energy; the populace were told that now was the time for patriots, and that whoever opposed them were the foes of France; and while the Convention despatched commissioners to visit the armies and collect recruits, the revolutionary organization which overspread the country promoted whatever Jacobinism wished in the name of the national independence at stake. The general result was to give overwhelming strength to the rapidly growing insurrectionary forces; and even in the Convention the violent Mountain began ere long to become ascendant, and the uncertain and feeble Plain to gravitate by degrees to the more audacious party. This consummation was accelerated by the Moderates, and especially by the chiefs of the Gironde, at this great and terrible crisis. As patriotic as their opponents at least, but fearful of revolutionary projects; and with no hold on the popular masses, they had supported a part of Danton's policy; but they denounced as schemes of democratic tyranny the extraordinary tribunal and the Committee of Public Safety; and they resisted the maximum and the tax on the rich, as projects of robbery in the name of law, though precedents for communism were not wanting. Thus, at a moment of extraordinary peril, they thwarted what was passionately announced as necessary to the National Safety; and they crossed what its leaders took

The party of violence generally prevails.

The Girondes and Moderates denounce extreme measures.

care to proclaim was the declared will of the Sovereign People, and what certainly was the desire of the mob. Nor was even this the limit of what their adversaries called their crimes against the State. They had obtained a commission of twelve deputies to inquire into the arbitrary acts of the Commune; and this body had ordered two of the worst of the demagogues to be put on their trial.. They had, besides, insisted on impeaching Marat, had proposed to break up the Commune of Paris, and to surround the Convention with a guard from the Provinces; and one of their members had incautiously exclaimed that "if a hair on the head of a deputy were touched Paris would be blotted out of the list of cities." *The Commission of Twelve.*

Thus, at a crisis of national danger, the forces of anarchy, which had been merely held in check, and had long ceased to be under control, rose again, sustained by what seemed to be the patriotic sentiment of France; while the party of order appeared vacillating, incapable of a bold resolution, and opposed to the popular demands, and it lost weight even in the national representation. Danton, with a singleness of purpose which marks him off, stained with blood as he was, from the worse demagogues, endeavored to reconcile the contending factions and to unite the Jacobin and Gironde leaders; but his attempts were fruitless, for it was a death-struggle. The Marats and Robespierres hounded on the mob against what they stigmatized as a party in league for a long time to break up the Republic, and now openly plotting against France; and all patriots were adjured to support the cause of the people and of national right. The Gironde retaliated by de- *The forces of anarchy become supreme.* *Danton tries in vain to reconcile the contending parties.* *Death struggle between the Moderates and Jacobins.*

nouncing the assassins of September, and the fomenters of trouble; but their influence daily became more weak, and power, even in the Convention, shifted from the Moderates, while they had nothing to oppose to the Commune, the Jacobins, and the Parisian populace. In this state of things their fall was at hand, and the end was not slow to arrive. An insurrection very similar to that of August 10, was planned and organized; delegates from the sections of the popular type entered the Town Hall by a preconcerted arrangement, and suddenly usurped the powers of the Commune; and on May 31 a great armed force invaded the Convention, and obtained from the deputies a decree to extinguish the Commission of Twelve, amidst frantic shouts against "Moderates," "Federalists," "Gironde traitors," and "other enemies of France." On June 2 eighty thousand national guards hemmed in the Convention, with cannon in their front; and a demand was made by the now audacious Mountain, supported by a threatening multitude, that twenty-two of the Gironde leaders should be given up and impeached for their crimes. A few courageous men protested in vain; the Plain fell off from the losing side, and the Convention decreed what was sought from it, in a state of doubt, uncertainty, and terror. The twenty-two, with seven names added, were surrounded and placed under arrest, and, the chiefs of the Moderates being struck down, the triumph of Jacobinism was complete. Thenceforward hardly anything remained to check the forces of anarchy in their career; the Convention was to follow the impulse of the Commune, and to yield obedience to the same leaders, and the Revolution was to enter on its most appalling phase.

Rising of May 31 and June 2, 1793.

Fall of the Moderates.

The fall of the Moderates and the Gironde was in a great part due to the causes which had produced the previous outbreak of August 10. General alarm, the result of foreign invasion, made the elements of disorder and passion, already too powerful, completely ascendant; and a sentiment that the National cause and that of the extreme revolutionists was one, concurred with all the many incentives which acted on the discontented and poor to precipitate and assure the catastrophe. As for the defeated party, it was as attached to France and her interests as its opponents could be; and there is no reason to suppose that, had it continued in power, the Republic would have succumbed to the Allies. But the Moderates and the Gironde were wanting in the audacity and recklessness which almost always obtain a mastery in violent revolutions; and their fate illustrates a general law of History. *Reflections on this event.*

CHAPTER VI.

THE REIGN OF TERROR.

THE revolution of June 2 having given the party of violence power, its leaders proceeded to strengthen themselves in the position they had unscrupulously won. Commanding the Commune of Paris and most of the sections, and at last dominant in the Convention, they held the reins of government in their hands; and their influence was sustained throughout France by Jacobinism, by the wants of the masses, and, largely, by national interests and

Triumph of the party of violence in the Convention.

sentiments. Whatever portion of the policy of Danton remained incomplete was now put in force; and while efforts were made to resist the Coalition with renewed energy, it was sought to extend and confirm everywhere the authority of the victorious demagogues by th˙ devices so often tried with success. The forces of ˙hy were not, however, to triumph without prov˙˙

<small>Risings against it in the Provinces; civil war.</small> sistance anarchic as themselves, was for some time to be torn, in ˙ sence of her foes, by fierce civil disse.

Some of the Gironde leaders escaped arrest, and these, with other chiefs of the party, ˙ deavored to excite a general rising against what the, justly described as Jacobin tyranny. Before long symptoms of discontent appeared even in many of the Provinces attached to the principles of the Revolution; and, at the intelligence of the fall of the Moderates, the angry war of class in the cities of the South broke out into inexpressible fury. Within a month after the struggle of June 2, a large part of Normandy was in insurrection; threatening sounds were heard in Burgundy and Alsace, in Franche Comté, Dauphiny, and Languedoc; and the wealthier orders being for the moment in the ascendant, Marseilles, Bordeaux, Toulouse, and Grenoble, stood in open revolt against the central government, to be soon followed by Toulon and Lyons. Meanwhile the disturbances in the West, which had been menacing for some time, assumed suddenly immense proportions; and in Poitou, Anjou, and a part of Brittany, thousands of armed men rose up to defy an irreligious and regicide Republic, to the rallying cry of

<small>Beginning of the war of La Vendée.</small> "God and the King." In these secluded and remote districts the seigneurs had for the most part lived on their lands, and the

influence of the Church was kindly and great; and the peasantry, accordingly, had cared little even for the good which the Revolution had done them. But when that event had brought with it the spoliation of the landlords they revered, and terrible laws against their beloved priests, they had given proofs of angry irritation, and, at the news of the death of Louis XVI., they had expressed their indignation in passionate risings. The severe means by which the government forced their sons to fight for a detested cause filled up the measure of their discontent, and by the middle of 1793 they had formed great insurrectionary bands, which were to prove far from contemptible foes. Such was the beginning of the celebrated war of La Vendée—so called from a Department of that name—one of the darkest episodes in the revolutionary drama.

These perils, though added to those of foreign war, did not, however, prostrate the energies of the men who were now supreme in France. Vile and worthless as many of these leaders were, some were not wanting in daring and constancy; and Danton urged the Governing Powers to redoubled efforts. A levy of three hundred thousand men which had been voted was ordered to the frontier; and while preparations were made to enforce the decree for what was called "levée en masse," the Jacobin leaders turned against their domestic foes. The extraordinary force which had been set on foot in Paris, and which received the name of the revolutionary army, was marched against the insurgent districts, with as many National Guards as could be spared; the cities in revolt were summoned to yield; and emissaries were despatched to stir up the masses against the "enemies of France and the allies

Energetic measures of Danton and the leaders in power.

The levée en masse.

of the stranger." Meanwhile a Constitution of the most democratic type was offered as a rallying-point to the People; good patriots were commanded to form everywhere revolutionary committees to support their leaders; the maximum and the tax on the rich were announced as assuring universal comfort to the poor; and the extraordinary, now styled the Revolutionary Tribunal, began to send daily its victims to the guillotine, while the prisons were filled with suspected persons. These measures were attended with astonishing success, though, but for deeper causes, they would have certainly failed. Lyons and Toulon, indeed, long remained in arms; and the rising of La Vendée, sustained by a principle, and at first encountered only by levies of recruits, became in the highest degree formidable. But the insurrection in the North was quickly dissipated; most of the Provinces became soon quiescent; and before long nearly all the Southern cities were overawed or tamed into submission. This rapid collapse, as we have said, was due to causes beyond the mere acts of the Jacobins, though these unquestionably were not fruitless. The authority of the central government was immense; and when Jacobinism had laid hold of the capital it quickly triumphed in other parts of the country, already largely controlled by it. Besides, the feud which divided France was generally one between the needy and the well-off; and in the existing state of all institutions, the needy were certain to prevail, even apart from the tremendous stimulants supplied lavishly to the wildest passions. Moreover, strongest motive of all, the cause continued in full force which had made Jacobinism succeed at first; and it seemed treason to the State, and fatal to France, and to all that had been done since 1789, to oppose Danton and his supporters when they hurled defiance against the foreign invader.

From these causes the civil war in which France for a moment appeared engulfed was soon confined to a few narrowing centres. What, in the meantime, had been the achievements of the mighty Coalition of banded Europe? Success, that might have been great, was attained on the Alpine and Pyrenean frontiers; and had the Piedmontese and Spaniards been well led they could have overrun Provence and Rousillon, and made the insurrection of the South fatal. But here, as elsewhere, the Allies did little; and, though defeated in almost every encounter, the republican levies held their ground against enemies who nowhere advanced. It was, however, in the North and the North-east that the real prize of victory was placed; and no doubt can exist that had unanimity in the councils of the Coalition prevailed, or had a great commander been in its camp, Paris might have been captured without difficulty, and the Revolution been summarily put down. But the Austrians, the Prussians, and the English, were divided in mind; they had no General capable of rising above the most ordinary routine of war; and the result was that the allied armies advanced tardily on an immense front, each leader thinking of his own plans only, and no one venturing to press forward boldly, or to pass the fortresses on the hostile frontiers, though obstacles like these could be of little use without the aid of powerful forces in the field. In this manner half the summer was lost in besieging Mayence, Valenciennes, and Condé; and when, after the fall of these places, an attempt was made to invade Picardy, dissensions between the Allies broke out, and the British contingent was detached to besiege Dunkirk, while the Austrians lingered in French Flanders, intent on enlarging by conquest Belgium, at that period an Austrian Province. Time was thus gained for the French armies, which, though they had made an honorable resistance, had been obliged to fall back at all points, and were in no condition to oppose their enemy; and the French army in the North, though driven nearly to the Somme, within a few marches of the capital, was allowed an opportunity to recruit its strength, and was not, as it might have been easily, destroyed. A part of the hastily raised levies was now incorporated in its ranks; and as these were largely composed of seasoned men from the old army of the Bourbon Monarchy, and from the volunteers of Valmy and Jemmapes, a respectable force was before long mustered. At the peremptory command of the Jacobin Government, this was at once directed against the invaders, who did not know what an invasion meant. The Duke of York, assailed with vigor and skill, was compelled to raise the siege of Dunkirk; and, to the astonishment of Europe, the divided forces of the halting and irresolute Coalition began to recede before the enemies, who saw victory yielded to them, and who, feeble soldiers as they often were, were nevertheless fired by ardent patriotism.

Sep. 8, 1793.

The Republic successful at home and abroad.

As the autumn closed the trembling balance of fortune inclined decidedly on the side of the Republic. The French recruits, hurried to the frontiers in masses, became gradually better soldiers, under the influence of increasing success.

Carnot. Hoche.

Carnot,* a man of great but overrated powers, took the general direction of military

*Lazare Nicolas Marguerite Carnot was born in 1753, and

affairs; and though his strategy was not sound, it was much better than the imbecility of his foes. At the same time, the Generals of the fallen Monarchy having disappeared, or, for the most part, failed, brilliant names began to emerge from the ranks, and to lead the suddenly raised armies; and though worthless selections were not seldom made, more than one private and sergeant gave proof of capacity of no common order. Terror certainly added strength to patriotism, for thousands were driven to the camp by force, and death was the usual penalty of a defeated chief; but it was not the less a great national movement, and high honor is justly due to a people which, in a situation that might have seemed hopeless, made such heroic and noble efforts, even though it triumphed through the weakness of its foe. Owing to a happy inspiration of Carnot, a detachment was rapidly marched from the Rhine, where the Prussians remained in complete inaction; and with this reinforcement Jourdan gained a victory at Wattignies over the Austrians, and opened the way into the Low Countries. At the close of the year the youthful Hoche, once a corporal, but a man of genius, who had given studious hours to the theory

<small>Battle of Wattignies, October 16, 1793.</small>

brought up to be an engineer. He distinguished himself in his profession, and at the crisis of 1793 was made Minister of War, and became one of the Members of the Committee of Public Safety. His energy was above praise; but though it has been said of him that "he organized victory," his military schemes were often unsound. He was, however, the only member of the Committee whose hands were, in some degree, free from the stain of blood. In after life he was exiled, opposed the Empire, supported it in the hour of danger, distinguished himself for his defence of Antwerp, and served as Minister of the Interior during the Hundred Days. He outlived Waterloo several years.

of war, divided Brunswick from the Austrian Würmser by a daring and able march through the Vosges; and the baffled Allies were driven out of Alsace, the borders of which they had just invaded. By these operations the great Northern frontier, the really vulnerable part of France, was almost freed from the invaders' presence; and, though less was achieved on the Southern frontier, the enemies of the Republic began to lose courage. Meanwhile Lyons had fallen after a terrible siege; and though the struggle in La Vendée was not over, the cause of the royalists was rapidly declining. On this theatre the Catholic army, as it called itself, had won a series of triumphs; and the peasant bands, commanded by their seigneurs, and largely composed of excellent marksmen, proved more than a match, in an intricate country, for revolutionary recruits and generals chosen from the noisest spouters of the Commune of Paris. At last, however, the garrison of Mayence, and a real commander, Kleber, appeared on the scene; and science and skill inevitably prevailed, though the contest was protracted and desperate. After the loss of a great battle at Cholet, in Poitou, the Vendeans were driven north of the Loire; and before long the remains of their forces were well-nigh annihilated on the field of Savenay. The insurrection had been so formidable that a few months before they might not improbably have marched to Paris and seized the capital.

Fall of Lyons, October 9, 1793.

Great defeat of the Vendeans at Savenay, Dec. 23, 1793.

Siege and fall of Toulon, Dec. 19, 1793. Towards the end of December a memorable incident brought the eventful struggle of the year to a close. Toulon had, as we have seen, revolted; and the citizens of the upper and middle classes had unhappily called in the allies to aid them. An English and Spanish fleet, accordingly, had taken possession of the port and the arsenal; and though the town had been partly invested, the siege, conducted by incapable men, made no progress for several months. A plan of attack was at last despatched from Paris; but at a council of war a youthful artillery officer, as yet only in a subordinate rank, observed that regular approaches were useless, and that if a point were taken which commanded the roadstead, the allied fleets would certainly make off, and an immediate surrender be the consequence. Putting his finger on a promontory marked on a map, he said decidedly, "There is the key of Toulon;" and his audience was so struck with the evident truth that it ventured to neglect the government order, and allowed its young adviser to work out his project. After a sharp engagement the point was occupied; and the French batteries had no sooner crowned the heights than the allied squadrons made haste to depart, and Toulon was in a few days in the hands of the victors. This remarkable exploit was the prelude to a career at which the world grew pale. The young artillery officer was Napoleon Bonaparte,* the mightiest product of the French Revolution.

<small>First appearance on the scene of Napoleon Bonaparte.</small>

Meanwhile, under the double influence of foreign war and peril at home, the anarchic forces which had become ascendant had consolidated themselves into a fearful tyranny, and the period known by the ominous name of the Reign of Terror had opened on France. The Convention, after the fall of the Moderates, became a mere instrument

<small>The Reign of Terror.</small>

---

* The biographies of Napoleon are innumerable. A very able, but unfavorable, account of his early life and career, will be found in M. Lanfrey's *Histoire de Napoleon I.*

The Convention, a mere instrument of the Jacobin leaders.

of the Jacobin chiefs; seventy-three of its members were arrested for secret protest against the 2d of June; the Right, baffled and suspected, cease to struggle; and the Plain registered the decrees of the Mountain, itself bowing in passive subjection to the terrible Committee

The Committee of Public Safety all powerful.

of Public Security. That Body, formed of extreme Jacobins, drew to itself all the powers in the State; and, with the national representation in its hands, and controlling and directing the Committee of General Security, the Commune, the clubs, and the revolutionary committees which spread their network over the country, it exercised an

Its tyranny and terrible expedients.

appalling despotism. Under this extraordinary scheme of government the whole resources of France were grasped by a knot of audacious and desperate men; and the most violent effort ever beheld was made, not only to crush the enemies of the State, but to turn society upside down, to subvert all its ordinary relations, to change the usages, the habits, and the faith of the nation, and to overbear opposition by sheer terror. The *levée en masse* was rigorously enforced, and every man, woman, and child in France was ordered to aid in the national defence, while the whole products of the country were declared to be "in requisition" for the use of the Republic. The lands and goods of *émigrés* and of prisoners of State were confiscated by a summary process; and decrees of the most ferocious kind were levelled against the revolted cities. Measures of frightful severity were taken against the unhappy class now known by the name of "suspects;" an ampler and freer sweep was given to the guillotine; the Revolutionary Tribunal was made permanent; and expedients, such as were never heard of, were adopted to keep up the failing assignats, while the maximum was extended to almost all commodities ; attempts were made to regulate the consumption of the nation ; the National Debt was what was called republicanized, that is, to a great extent, wiped out ; and the systematic plunder of the rich became a regular device of government. Death was the normal penalty for the slightest complaint against this wide-spreading scheme of oppression ; nay, even for lukewarmness or "want of *civism ;*" and a failure in the field was usually followed by a mandate from the Republican commissioners, who attended the armies, for speedy execution. At the same time a complete revolution was made in dress, manners, and even modes of speech ; the very forms of language were violently changed ; the Calendar and the whole system of measures were transformed ; and though the Committee of Public Safety did not yet publicly proscribe the Christian faith, they regarded with aversion and distrust priests of all kinds, non-juring or otherwise ; atheism was proclaimed truth by the Commune of Paris— an example imitated by other cities ; and the churches were everywhere handed over to the municipalities and local authorities, to be shut up or destroyed at their pleasure. *Wild social changes.* *Atheism declared truth by the Commune of Paris.*

The scenes witnessed during this strange period of tyranny in union with popular license brought out human nature in its most stern, most terrible, and most ludicrous aspects. Paris seemed turned into a vast camp, hundreds of smithies and forges filling the squares, for the manufacture of arms and cannon, the streets barricaded and patrolled by the pikemen, houses lettered with the names of their inmates ; while young men were hastily *Appearance of Paris during the Reign of Terror.*

drilled in thousands, old men and women were told off in bands "to excite patriots to revolutionary work," and children scraped lint and made bandages, amidst mob oratory and wild airs of music. Long lines of faces were seen at the bread-shops, waiting for the supplies fixed and priced by the State; and government emissaries filled the establishments once dedicated to the splendor of Versailles, to enforce the maximum for "good citizens." Informers crowded the banks and the Exchange, to mark down any one who dared to cheapen assignats; and these pieces of paper, converted literally into tickets of plunder by the rule of terror, paid debts, and served to transfer commodities, at their nominal value, to some extent at least, although rapidly becoming worthless. Meanwhile commissioners, "in the name of the Republic," seized and piled in storehouses whatever was needed "for the armies of the patriotic poor;" and it fared badly with those who dared to look clean, to dress well, to wear a watch or a trinket; for if not hurried off to prison as "suspects," they were freely relieved of superfluous luxuries. Similar sights were seen in other great cities; and the chief roads swarmed with masses of recruits rolling to the frontier, in varying moods of fear, regret, and fiery exultation, while the crops, the stock, and the horses of the peasant, were numbered or taken by flocks of officials, their owners sometimes looking on in despair, but more often exclaiming that, after all, "France and the Revolution must be saved." The hall of the Convention, at the same time, echoed with strange debates, and still stranger reports, in which a jargon of pagan antiquity mingled with vulgar ribaldry and the slang of fish-wives, vociferously applauded by overflow-

The levies hurried to the frontier.

Appearance of the Convention.

ing galleries; and the same eloquence was heard in all other assemblies, but usually at a still lower level. The prisons, meanwhile, grew more and more full with ever-increasing lists of "suspects;" and even the fearful means by which they were cleared could not keep down the vast tale of victims. Nine or ten men, of whom the most conspicuous were Robespierre, St. Just, Couthon, Collot D'Herbois, Billaud Varennes, and Barère,* sate in a small closet in what had been the Tuileries palace, directing the immense organization of force by which France was moved and controlled.

In this ecstacy of revolutionary passions and overturn of social relations, whatever was most violent was sure to prevail; the long-standing vices and ills of the State provoked a retribution worse than themselves; and the popular frenzy displayed itself in excesses of license which knew no limits. As has been observed in similar movements, the very signification of words was changed; and pitilessness became Republican virtue, moderation culpable treason to France, inexorable severity patriotic devotion, atrocious cruelty irregular justice. Then, too, were seen in their worst aspect the ill-will and hatred engendered by the differences of class in the old Monarchy; to be an "aristocrat" was in itself a crime: the

sidenote: Dissolution of society and of morality.

---

* The leading Terrorists, as was the case too during the reign of the Commune of 1871, were for the most part men of low origin, and broken fortunes. St. Just, a fanatic like Robespierre, was an unknown student. Couthon was a cripple. Collot d'Herbois had been an actor hissed off the stage. Billaud Varennes had been expelled his father's house, and had been a tailor, an actor, and a dependent of the Jesuits. Barère, the "Anacreon of the Guillotine," began life an obscure man of letters, and ended it a traitor and a spy.

few Nobles and prelates who lingered in France were either condemned, or usually shrank out of sight; and the popular exasperation rose even fiercer against the professional and trading orders, the lawyers, the merchants, the employers of labor, the dependents of the Court, the old servants of the State, the horror-stricken reformers of 1789. In the jealousy against all eminence which prevailed, even the aristocracy of intellect was denounced; men of letters and science were largely proscribed, and art and learning were either degraded to mean uses or were declared dangerous. Licentiousness, too, broke through all bounds in the general collapse of old-social restraints; the increase of concubinage, of divorces, and of illegitimate births, alarmed even Jacobin politicians; and the vices of the great were wildly imitated, with reckless indecency, by the multitude. Perhaps, however, the most striking sign of the times was the manner in which religion was treated. Christianity, we have said, was not yet disavowed by the State; but in hundreds of places the churches were stripped of their ornaments by exulting mobs; and the profession of atheism by the Commune of Paris was celebrated by a ceremony in which a painted harlot was installed in the aisles of Nôtre-Dame, and hailed as the Goddess of Reason; while festivals, pagan in their character, commemorated the prolific powers of the seasons. Too often, besides, priests were found who denied the faith of which they were living witnesses; the mysteries of Christianity were profaned by one perjured bishop in a revolting parody; and much that was foul and hideous came out from under that august Church which had been long tainted by sin and

Cruelty and suspicions of populace.

General licentiousness.

The Goddess of Reason at Nôtre Dame.

corruption. Yet these blasphemies were by no means general; and thousands of the clergy, pursued as they were by Jacobin suspicion, continued to perform their holy offices to reverent congregations, who still adhered to the creed of their fathers. Nor was all evil even in this fearful season of national trial and social subversion; noble instances of fidelity and virtue were seen, apart from the patriotism, which inspired Frenchmen; and a kind of distempered public spirit may be traced in the scheme of Jacobin policy, extravagant and iniquitous as it was.

The march, however, of the Reign of Terror has yet to be viewed in its most tragic aspect. The prisons, we have said, were thronged with victims whom ferocious laws, or ruthless suspicion, or private malice, sent to their precincts; and, in Paris alone, the number of captives was usually from five to six thousand persons. In these dark and terrible abodes were packed in masses—without regard to distinctions of rank, of age, of sex—the noble, the beautiful, the highly refined, with the vile, the worthless, and the merely criminal; the seigneur, the court dame, the man of taste, chiefs of the National and Legislative Assemblies, unfortunate generals, discarded magistrates, priests, merchants, and caterers for the luxury of Versailles, confusedly mingled with forgers and thieves, and the most degraded refuse of the streets. Eye-witnesses have left vivid descriptions of what occurred in these frightful Assemblies; how human nature became desperate, or reckless, or callous, or even mirthful, under the influence of continued suffering; how social differences were jealously preserved or vanished in the presence of common peril; and how virtue asserted its natural authority in the disappearance of

Scenes in the prisons.

conventional forms; and the depraved treated the good with respect, while they persecuted the vicious, whatever their station. A collection of prisoners was almost daily consigned to the Revolutionary Tribunal; and though that murderous court was not yet at its worst, its ordinary process was swift and fearful. The condemned were hurried off to the guillotine, and, in the presence of revelling crowds of the most ruthless and cruel populace, were usually slaughtered in batches at a time, amidst clamorous shouts of "Long live the Republic." So perished, with numbers of less known victims, not a few of the most illustrious names of France, surviving ornaments of the old order of things, brilliant popular leaders of a few years before. Several of the Gironde deputies had died miserably in the rising of June 2, and Pétion, among them, had met a fate which History cannot call undeserved; but most of the arrested twenty-two were sacrificed, with Vergniaud, the most eloquent Frenchman of his time. Such, too, was the doom of the once famous Bailly, of the high-souled and chivalrous Barnave, of the infamous and recreant Duke of Orleans,* of Custine, and other distinguished officers, of Malesherbes, the great advocate of Louis XVI. But why dwell further on the appalling record? Two deaths, however, strikingly showed what was most noble in the social life which the Reign of Terror endeavored to destroy. The

The Revolutionary Tribunal and its work.

---

* The death of this disgrace to his name is thus described by Mr. Carlyle :—" Philippe's eyes flashed hell-fire for an instant; but the next it was gone, and he sate impassive, Brummellean polite. On the scaffold Samson was for drawing off his boots. 'Tush,' said Philippe, 'they will come better off *after*. Let us have done; dépêchez-vous.'"

fair and saintly Madame Elizabeth* drew tears even from Jacobin eyes, as, piety struggling with maiden shame, she bowed her head meekly to the fatal axe ; the sterner but heroic Madame Roland,† the celebrated wife of a minister of that name, went with a smile on her lip to the scaffold, exclaiming, "Liberty ! oh what crimes are done in thy name ?"

On October 14, 1793, Marie Antoinette was brought before the fatal tribunal. Her appearance filled for an instant with pity the hearts even of her hardened judges, and

<small>Trial and execution of Marie Antoinette, October 14–16, 1793.</small>

* "The only emotion she showed," says an eye-witness, "was when the executioner approached her to remove her shawl. 'For Heaven's sake, sir,' she exclaimed, 'spare me the exposure!'"— *Six Jours au Temple*, p. 75 ; F. de Conches, vi. p. 556.

ἡ δὲ καὶ θνήσκουσ' ὁμῶς
πολλὴν πρόνοιαν εἶχεν εὐσχήμως πεσεῖν,
κρύπτουσ' ἃ κρύπτειν ὄμματ' ἀρσένων χρεών.

† Marion Jeanne Phlipon, Madame Roland, one of the most celebrated characters of the Revolution, was born in 1754. She was the daughter of an engraver, and her Memoirs show how, even in early life, she resented the distinctions between the Noblesse and Bourgeoise. In her teens she gave proof of the energy, the fervor, and the sentimentalism of her mature years; but she grew up a sceptic, fed on the false literature and philosophy of the day. In 1780 she married M. Roland, then an inspector of manufactures at Rouen, and, soon after the beginning of the Revolution, repaired with her husband to Paris. There she became Queen of the Gironde party, and, when M. Roland was made Minister, his chief adviser. Her Memoirs illustrate the enthusiasm, the genius, and the unpractical conduct of the Gironde orators, and throw a vivid light on most of the events which led to the Reign of Terror. She was involved in the proscription of the Gironde, and perished on the scaffold in 1793. Her death had something grand and yet theatrical about it; and though her character was noble, it was hardly womanly, and was too artificial to charm.

I

of the barbarous audience which thronged the hall.
The hair of the Queen had turned white; grief had furrowed prematurely her noble countenance; she was
arrayed in a coarse, miserable garb, which hung loose on
her still stately form; and in the light which drew out her
figure from the dim benches and galleries around, she
looked a wreck of oppressed majesty. How different
from that vision of youth and grace that had once flitted
along the terraces of Versailles; how changed from that
princely yet winning presence so often greeted by
applauding multitudes, so long the centre of the homage
of chivalry! But the sentiment of compassion passed
away, for Marie Antoinette was abhorred and feared,
and the mockery of a trial quickly went on. More than
one personage of the late Court, willing to barter honor
for the chance of safety, bore witness against the doomed
captive; and a nameless and execrable charge was
made which received an answer of such pathetic truth
that even the foul-hearted accuser was silenced. Sentence was, of course, before long pronounced, and on
October 16 the victim was led to the guillotine. Forms
of decency had long ago disappeared; and Marie Antoinette was drawn to the place of execution, exposed to
the insolent gaze of the populace, in a common cart,
with her arms bound, in a prison dress, like the vilest
criminal. The calm dignity, however, which had more
than once abashed her judges a few hours before, did
not desert the Queen in her last moments; and it was
observed that several of the woman fiends who crowded
round to yell as she passed shrank from her steady and
serene gaze. On the fatal journey she seemed perfectly
composed, except when, in the words of an eye-witness,
"her face gave signs of lively emotion" at the sight of
what had been once the Tuileries; and she encountered

death without display or flinching. Her end was noble, and the foul slanders which gathered against her pure life were falsehoods; and we need not inquire what, in her case, was the iniquity of the Revolutionary Tribunal. But it is not the less true that Marie Antoinette, like Louis XVI., had wronged France; and the wrong she had done was the more grievous in that she was a chief counsellor of her imbecile husband, and he was mere clay in her proud hands. Still, in judging her conduct, the associations of her life and of her situation must be fairly weighed; and History, as it marks that stately figure, tossed, feebly resisting, over the abyss, may well muse on the tyranny of circumstance, and echo the truth that the Tower of Siloam may fall on those not the most guilty. *Her character and conduct.*

For several months few changes were made in this system of wide-spread tyranny; and the men who had seized on power in France forgot or sunk their differences under the stress of danger. When, however, the Republic emerged from its first trials, divisions sprung up among the Jacobin chiefs; and three parties gradually developed themselves, representing the conflicting views of their leaders. Danton, who, even as early as July, had quitted the Committee of Public Safety, inclined before long to the side of clemency; and his wishes were seconded by a large following, who looked up to him as the champion of the revolution. These men, turbulent and savage as they were, had nevertheless human sympathies and feelings; they were not maniacs of fanatical principles, and they aimed rather at enjoyment and influence than at any fixed Republican ideal; and though, like Danton, they were morally corrupt, they had desired to spare the Gironde victims, and *Divisions among the Jacobin rulers.* *Three factions form themselves.*

began to condemn the excesses of the Reign of Terror. The second faction, led by a wretch called Hébert,* was composed of the extreme anarchists of the Commune of Paris, who had preached atheism, and given the freest rein to license; and the political object of these miscreants was to make the capital supreme in the State, and to secure independence to the great cities, while their social creed was mere sensual indulgence. The third party was led by Robespierre, and by degrees it became the strongest, for the reputation of that singular being had gained for him a great moral ascendency; and the views he professed with a parade of virtue fell in largely with the popular sentiment, always gratified when its worst aspirations are flattered in the name of the public good. The hope of Robespierre and his immediate followers was to set up a Republic in accordance with the wild and mischievous notions of Rousseau; and as this end could not be approached without carrying out relentlessly the system of Terror, they condemned what they called the moderation of Danton, while they abhorred, as opposed to their theories, the godless licentiousness of the Commune demagogues. Robespierre, though possibly not cruel by nature, was, like all men of his type, pitiless when ruled by the ideas on which he had brooded; and this was the character of one or two of his chief subordinates, though

Growing ascendency of Robespierre.

* Jacques Réné Hébert, born in 1755, was a footman and a boxkeeper at a theatre, and had lost both places for dishonesty. When the Revolution broke out he became Editor of the *Père Duchesne*, the most indecent and ribald print probably that has ever seen the light, though an imitation of it appeared during the Jacobin saturnalia of 1871. This miscreant became one of the chief officers of the Commune of Paris, and it was he who made the unnatural and foul charge against the Queen alluded to above.

the great mass of the party were mere Jacobins, yielding to that impulse which always secures authority for a resolute faith, sustained by real or seeming probity.

Before 1793 had closed, the ascendency of Robespierre was complete. He was the especial favorite of the Jacobin Club; his influence in the Convention was supreme, and he was the dictator of the Committee of Public Safety. The dissensions between the hostile parties soon broke out into open discord, and personal antipathies deepened the feud. With the system of government which prevailed, the possessors of power could easily destroy their rivals; and Robespierre and his satellites turned without scruple the tremendous machinery in their grasp against their adversaries on either side. Under the pretence of conspiracies, of which proofs were always forthcoming in an atmosphere of preternatural suspicion and passion, Hébert and the leaders of the Commune were first swept away, and with their fall that famous organization which had been a main-spring of the Revolution, and had made Paris dominant in the State, lost a great deal of its immense influence. The turn of Danton and his chief friends came next; and though the struggle was perilous and long, they too passed before the Revolutionary Tribunal, and were immolated by means of a special decree obtained from the overawed Convention. With them perished what may be described as the Moderates of the Reign of Terror, and compassion must be felt for the fate of their leader. Danton was a man of great natural powers; courageous, resolute, with a genius for command, with an eloquence, rude, but of extraordinary force; and if the blood of September be on his head—

He becomes supreme in the State.

Destruction of Hébert and the leaders of the Commune, of Danton and his followers, March 24, April 3, 1794.

Character of Danton.

and he often played the demagogue for his own ends—
he had, nevertheless, a patriotic heart; he is entitled to
any merit which belongs to the Jacobin scheme of national defence; and it is to his lasting honor that he
risked and lost his life in the sacred cause of humanity.
After his death Robespierre and his creatures became
the absolute masters of France, and they lost no time in
strengthening their sway. The authority of the Committee of Public Safety was made more com-
Dictatorship of Robespierre. plete than it had ever been; and in order to
keep down the Commune of Paris, the revo-
lutionary army was disbanded, and the democracy of the
sections was in a great measure controlled, while the
chief magistrates were chosen from dependents of
His measures to secure his power. Robespierre. At the same time clubs and
popular societies, with the one exception of
the trusty Jacobins were suppressed by a
summary mandate; and, as if to show what a Republic
of virtue was to be, atheism was pronounced "an aristocratic falsehood," the worship of "the Supreme" was
declared the national faith, and Christianity
The worship of the Supreme. was proclaimed a base superstition, and its
ministers criminal dupes or impostors.

And now, mastered by Robespierre, the Reign of
Terror at its height. Terror quickened its march, and grew more
fearful in its murderous activity. A merci-
less fanatic swayed the small oligarchy of which the
powers had been just increased; and, as if to prove what
Jacobin "freedom" was, the worst deeds of which the
old Monarchy had been guilty in the course of ages
were infinitely surpassed in a few months, under a form
of government in many respects similar. A decree was
wrung from the oppressed Convention by which the
Revolutionary Tribunal was set free from all checks,

and "moral conviction" was made sufficient proof of crime ; and the energy of that instrument of slaughter became suddenly more than ever appalling. Prisoners were tried by forties and fifties at a time, and sent to their doom with summary glee at a nod or a wink of infamous accusers ; and—a fitting emblem of the revolting scene—the guillotine appeared in the place of judgment. "Suspects" were crammed, literally in thousands, in dens, in which vile informers glided about, making sure of the means to do them to death; and when other charges could not be made "conspiracies in the prisons" were feigned to serve the purpose. The dread and agony which had taken possession of all within the possible reach of this frightful tyranny proved often too much for nature to endure ; and suicides and madness awfully increased, while Paris bore the look of a city abandoned to a mere multitude of reckless barbarians, what was orderly and decent having cowered out of sight. Meanwhile, the system of spoliation inaugurated by the maximum and forced assignats was carried on more stringently than ever; and as authority had become fully concentrated, devices of escape grew more difficult. At the same time the most atrocious vengeance ever witnessed perhaps in western Europe was wreaked on the hapless revolted cities. Attempts were made to raze Lyons and Toulon to the earth ; and "floods of death," as it was said, "swept away traitors and moderates" in these devoted places. Similar horrors were seen at Bordeaux, Arras, and Marseilles ; and for miles below Nantes the Loire rolled to the sea hundreds of corpses twisted in ghastly embraces, the victims of what, with hellish mirth, were designated as "republican marriages," having been tied

Frightful state of Paris

Massacres in the Provinces.

together, and, crowded in barges, deliberately scuttled and then set adrift. Simultaneously La Vendée, still in part insurgent, was traversed throughout by "infernal columns;" and, notwithstanding a manly protest of Kleber, who foresaw the inevitable results, these bands everywhere marked their advance by murder, pillage, and widespread havoc. Commissioners, despatched with "full powers" from the capital, urged the populace, wherever they could, to these crimes ; and Robespierre was the sovereign head and absolute lord of this system of blood. If in the *chambres ardentes* of the Bourbon monarchy, in the frequent oppression of the old Parliaments, in the horrors of the Bastille and other State prisons, in the massacres of St. Bartholomew and at La Rochelle, in the centralized, cruel and suspicious governments of more than one of the Kings of France, we see a faint foreshadowing of this order of things, tyranny so rapid and deadly had never before been witnessed; and few probably will think that the execrable character of the last and worst phase of the Reign of Terror was mitigated by blasphemous festivals to " the Supreme," or even by empty and illusory projects to "abolish poverty" and other social evils.

Such was the fulfilment of the glowing hopes which had animated France four short years before ; such was the practical issue of the philosophy which had dazzled a generation by its glittering chimeras. The land was a land of mourning and carnage; and the Rights of Man terminated in a ruthless despotism sustained by the worst dregs of the masses. And what made this tyranny the more atrocious was that the impulse was failing which had first given the Jacobins overpowering force ; for, instead of being threatened with destruction, the Republic was entering on a career of victory. The discomfiture of 1793 had made the Allies more than ever divided; the long-standing jealousies of Austria and Prussia were aggravated by intrigues about Poland; and when the war was renewed in the spring of 1794, the Coalition was ill-prepared to encounter a daring and resolute enemy. Meanwhile, the gigantic efforts of France had been attended with great results, and fully half a million of men stood in arms on her frontiers to confront her adversaries. The consequences were such as usually follow a struggle between discordant weakness and earnest and enthusiastic strength, though other and potent causes concurred. The new French levies, indeed, were still often defeated, even with a large advantage of numbers on their side; and, without an admixture of trained soldiers, they still proved comparatively worthless. On the sea too, the hastily equipped fleets of the Republic met a crushing reverse; and the great victory of June 1 gave England the first of a long series of triumphs. But numerical force, union, and patriotism told; and they were aided by a direction at least always better than that existing in the hostile camps. The Spaniards were driven behind the Pyrenees; Savoy and Nice were brilliantly regained; and the young conqueror of Toulon, baffling the Piedmontese by one of those manœuvres which began to show his powers, beheld, Hannibal-like, from the tops of the Alps, the plains soon to be the scenes of his most splendid exploits. Meantime, after a protracted struggle, the Duke of York was beaten on the Belgian frontier; and while Pichegru and Moreau advanced into Flanders, Carnot repeated the operation of the preceding year, and, profiting by the remiss-

The Republic obtains fresh successes in the campaign of 1794.

English naval victory of June 1.

The allies defeated on all other points of the theatre. Battle of Fleurus, June 26, 1794.

ness of the enemy in the Vosges, moved a considerable force from the Meuse to the Sambre, which gave the French victory on the plains of Fleurus, and made them masters, in a few days, of Brussels.

<small>Reaction against the Reign of Terror.</small> By this time the horrible excesses of the Reign of Terror had begun to provoke the reaction certain at last to set in; and the triumphs of the Republic concurred in making the system of Jacobinism, at its worst, disliked. The conscience even of the populace of the towns revolted at the scenes of blood and despair which had made France miserable in the midst of her glories; and a growing sentiment quickly spread that the discomfiture of the enemy on the frontier ought to bring to an end a state of things which had brought such frightful confusion and havoc. The judges of the Revolutionary Tribunal sickened at their cruel and execrable work; shouting crowds no longer followed the guillotine; and cries of pity often rose for the victims even in the least wealthy parts of the capital. In this condition of opinion the ultimate fall of the supremacy of Robespierre was assured; but it was accelerated by a movement in the governing powers which had bowed under his sway for a time. In a fit, apparently of moody discontent, he absented himself for several weeks from the ruling Committee of Public Safety; and whether he did or did not contemplate the decimation of the down-trodden Convention, the execution of most of his nearest associates, and an absolute dictatorship for himself, most of his colleagues began to combine against him. When he re-

<small>Fall of Robespierre, July 27, 1794.</small> appeared in the Convention, the dark threats he uttered seemed to indicate only more measures of blood; and, under the influence of one or two courageous leaders, even the

prostrate Assembly broke out in murmurs. Next day, after a scene of violent excitement, his arrest and that of St. Just and Couthon was decreed ; and the Revolutionary Mountain at last rose with the Plain and Right against the dreaded tyrant. Robespierre, however, had in the interval invoked the aid of the Jacobin Club and of his satellites in the Commune of Paris ; and he was rescued, with the two other prisoners, while a formidable insurrection was set on foot to overawe the national representation. The sections were, however, divided; a small part only obeyed the Commune; and the majority sided with the Convention, especially after a decree had been made declaring "the triumvirs" traitors to the State. Robespierre and his associates were quickly haled before the tribunal which, so to speak, had become the type of their fearful government; and most of the leaders of the Commune, now again struck down, perished with the abhorred and guilty tyrant. This apostle of blood and his followers were the last of the band, with a few exceptions, which was most stained in the Revolution with crime; and the dagger of Charlotte Corday* had some months before relieved France of the presence of Marat. Execution of Robespierre, St. Just, Couthon, and others, July 28, 1794.

Such was the Revolution of July 1794, or of Thermidor, by the new French calendar. It will always be a subject of reproach to Frenchmen that they bowed their necks to Reflections on this event.

---

* Charlotte Corday, born in 1768, was a young lady of a good family in Normandy, and was a grand-daughter of Corneille. Her imagination, deeply impressed by the atrocities of the Reign of Terror, fired her to assassinate Marat, and she stabbed him in a bath in July 1793. Her execution is touchingly described by Mr. Carlyle.

the yoke of Robespierre; and in this acquiescence we, no doubt, see the national tendency to yield to despotism. It must be recollected, however, that the success of the Jacobins was largely due, in the first instance, to its association with the cause of the independence of France, and to the hold they had on patriotic minds, and that it is impossible at a terrible crisis to check even the worst tyranny at once; and when the danger of foreign war had ceased, the Reign of Terror soon came to a close. As for the horrors of that time, they show how fierce were the hatreds of class which had long existed, and how brutalized a part of the people was; but though France accepted the Jacobin rule, and even welcomed it for some reasons, these atrocities ought, in justice, to be charged against a minority of Frenchmen only—the worst populace of a few great cities, and a band of reckless and audacious demagogues. The Terrorists have been described as men of great powers, and the measures they adopted for the defence of France have been held up as a proof of ability; but this misconception of the worshippers of success ought to be contradicted by impartial history. The Jacobin leaders, certainly, showed energy; but their system led to a civil war which was destructive, and might have been fatal; their policy of force, especially in its social aspects, was cruel, ruinous, and unwise alike; and whatever seems to have been achieved by them was really achieved by French genius and valor. Besides, any credit to be given to them ought to be confined to Danton alone—the Marats, the Robespierres, and their crew, were simply incapable as political chiefs; and not one of the distinguished soldiers who appeared at this crisis was a Terrorist. The efforts of France to resist her foes were heroic, and have hardly,

The Terrorists were not able men.

perhaps, been ever surpassed, but should not blind us by false illusions. The Allies might, without the least difficulty, have entered Paris in the summer of 1793; and, memorable as its struggles were, the Revolution triumphed only through the divisions and negligence of its antagonists. {Notwithstanding the efforts of the French, the Allies could have put down the Revolution.} Nor does the eventful contest of this period detract from the truth that armies of recruits are weak and dangerous instruments of war, and that in the military, as in other arts, experience and training are of the greatest value. The young French levies were for months useless unless supported by seasoned troops. Napoleon, indeed, has said that what was really done was done by the Army of the old Monarchy; and the forces of the Coalition were, in every respect, of better quality than their opponents. But mere organization is not everything in war; and unanimity, numbers, patriotic devotion, and above all, superior strategic skill—mistaken as Carnot was more than once—prevailed as they have prevailed before. These considerations ought not to lessen the admiration which is justly due to the energy and constancy of the French people; they simply explain, on rational grounds, the great success of the imperilled Republic, which national enthusiasm has not unnaturally invested with a character of marvel.

CHAPTER VII.

THERMIDOR. FRENCH CONQUESTS.

Reaction of Thermidor.
THE authors of the Revolution of Thermidor had no conception that what they were about to do would bring the Reign of Terror to a close. Some had been almost as bad as their victims; others were Jacobins of a decided type; and their principal object was to escape death, though the majority of the Convention felt nobler motives. But the fate of Robespierre was a signal for France to throw off a terrible incubus; and a reaction against the Reign of Terror began to set in with that passionate quickness which is a distinctive feature of the national character.

The prisons opened.
Within a few days the astonished multitudes of "suspects" were let out from their prisons; and even the populace of Paris joined in the ecstacy of the hour of deliverance. Before long the atrocities in the South and other places caused general indignation, and several of the monsters who had encouraged these crimes met the fate which they righteously deserved.

Punishment of several of the Terrorists.
Abolition of the Revolutionary Tribunal.
After a time, too, the Revolutionary Tribunal, with its detestable procedure, disappeared; and some of the judges justly perished by the violent means which they had recklessly abused. Meanwhile the Convention, at last set free, endeavored to confirm its restored supremacy, to check tyranny and anarchy alike, and to inaugurate a policy of conciliation. The powers of the Committee of Public Safety

were reduced, and its members changed by a speedy rotation, though this obviously weakened the Executive. The decrees which placed all France "in requisition" to the State were either modified or repealed; and the maximum was abandoned, with the sanguinary laws which sought to force the value of assignats, although the results were not unforeseen. At the same time energetic efforts were made to curb and guard against mob license; the National Guards were again remodelled and recomposed from the middle classes; the band of pikemen were broken up; the authority of the Commune of Paris, already shattered, was still further lessened by dividing its council and limiting its powers; the more violent sections were jealously watched; and, last and most important of all, the revolutionary committees were everywhere suppressed, and the Jacobin Club and its kindred societies, the centre and feeders of agitation, were shut up. The remains, too, of the proscribed Gironde, with the seventy-three imperilled deputies, were invited to return to their seats; compensation was voted, to a certain extent, for some of the worst outrages of the Reign of Terror; and at last Billaud Varennes, Collot d'Herbois, and Barère, the three surviving chiefs of the terrible committee, were prosecuted and sent beyond the seas, though they had taken part with the men of Thermidor. Finally, religion was solemnly declared free, and the churches were given to their congregations, though the sentiment of the Convention remained hostile for the most part to priests of all kinds.

and of the maximum. The forcing of the value of assignats discontinued.

The populace of Paris kept down.

The Jacobin Club suppressed.

In this way the State tried to atone in some measure for the horrors of the past, and the machinery of Jacobin disorder and cruelty was, to a considerable extent, destroyed. The reaction, however, in the ruling powers of France, and the enactments sanctioned by the Convention, expressed but feebly the intense hostility which broke out generally against the whole scheme of Terror. Jacobin functionaries were expelled from their places everywhere ; the National Guards of Paris, filled with the bourgeoisie, showed no mercy to the " tools of Robespierre;" and the young men of the Middle classes formed companies to keep down the mob, and hunted out, as if they had been unsexed, the female furies of the galleries and the guillotine. The example of the capital was followed elsewhere, especially in the large trading cities, which had been treated with such ruthless barbarism ; and the recoil of opinion was so quick and violent that the royalists, who, a few months before, lived in daily dread of a summons to the scaffold, showed themselves, and sometimes oppressed their oppressors. The "Committee of Mercy" into which, it was said, "France had suddenly resolved herself,'" was, in a word, not merciful to the late dominant party ; and, in the rapid oscillation of the public sentiment, not only was clemency lavishly displayed, but the tyrants of the other day received their own measure, and were widely subjected to no little tyranny. At the same time, in Paris and elsewhere, a singular revolution in manners took place, not unknown in other national crises, but strangely rapid and very characteristic. In the extraordinary confusion of the last two or three years property had changed hands to an immense extent ; and a new and large moneyed class had sprung up, formed by the sale of the lands of *émigrés*, by army and other government contracts, and, above all, by jobbing in assignats, and speculating in their continual fall, which no policy of terror could long prevent. This class, persecuted by the Jacobin leaders, now emerged brilliantly to the surface; and the Court and the Nobles having disappeared, it formed the high social life of the capital, and stamped its character on the fashion of the hour. The uncouth savagery which had been supreme was replaced by a costly display of wealth; and the ruling orders banished the memory of the past in a giddy round of excitement and pleasure. The mansions of the Soubises and the Noailles were crowded with a new kind of *noblesse*, and echoed to the sound of *bals à la victime*, confined to the relations of recent sufferers. What was significantly called the *jeunesse dorée* of the changed error, appeared in the salons of the Voltaires, the Condorcets, the Du Deffands; and the wives and daughters of the men of the time, in Ionic garb, and with snooded tresses, aped the graces, the luxuries, and the dissoluteness of Versailles. The raggedness and austerity of 1793 was, in short, cried down; and French nature, volatile and gay, indemnified itself for what it had endured by rushing wildly into joyous amusement. The change was not surprising, though it leaves behind a painful impression of national levity; yet we shall hardly compare it, as it has been compared, to the reawakening of nature in spring, to the letting loose of the ice-bound waters.

<small>The Jeunesse Dorée.</small>

It was impossible but that this vehement reaction should lead before long to renewed troubles. The party of Terror, lately all powerful, had still a considerable hold on the masses, though its chief strength had departed from it; and the harshness with which it was everywhere coerced, and the triumph of the Moderates, now again in the ascendant, filled it with

<small>Renewed troubles.</small>

K

resentment and indignation. Had France, "patriot" orators exclaimed, shaken off an arrogant though abhorred despotism to fall into the hands of moneychangers and scribes? Had Europe been driven from her frontiers, and thousands of her bravest children perished, to substitute for an aristocracy of birth and titles a new aristocracy of the bank and the counter? Was the end of the Revolution to be the complete destruction of its most trusty instruments? Were the measures by which it had saved the Nation, checked dangerous factions, and maintained the poor, to be flouted in the interest of the selfish and rich? Was a dictatorship, stern, perhaps, but glorious, to be converted into a mode of government in which a class maltreated and scorned the people? The extraordinary condition of France gave plausibility and force to these arguments, and supplied discontent with its keenest stimulants. The requisitions and spoliations of the Reign of Terror had inevitably lessened and checked production; and the abolition of the maximum and of the ferocious laws which forced up the value of assignats had concurred to raise the price of commodities, though these expedients had, of course, been less efficacious than their authors supposed. The result was that great scarcity prevailed, and that a sudden and extreme increase in the cost of the necessaries of life took place; and the pressure in Paris became so alarming that the government was obliged to put the poor on rations, and to have recourse to all kinds of expedients to secure for them a scanty subsistence. This distress, general and widespreading, caused a demand for the Jacobin measures to revive; and it is probable, indeed, that the financial system of the Terrorists, execrable as it was, was abrogated with incautious celerity.

Scarcity and distress.

However this may have been, the lower classes in the capital and other parts of France lent themselves before long to the appeals of agitators to rise and regain their lost power; and the irritation they felt was, no doubt, exasperated by the selfish luxury of the new-made rich, by revolutionary hopes not yet extinguished, by ignorance, jealousy, and blind passion. *The Jacobin party tries to rally.*

Such, briefly, was the internal state of France within a few months after the Revolution of Thermidor. The forces of anarchy before long broke out in the chief centre of their power, though they made themselves felt in other places, especially where they had been most repressed. On April 1, 1795, 12th Germinal by the new style, the mob of Paris burst into the hall of the Convention, shouting for "Bread and the Constitution of 1793," which had become the rallying cry of the "patriots;" but it was driven out without much difficulty; and the dispersion of it was chiefly remarkable in that Pichegru, then for the moment on the spot, was called in to put down the rioters—an ominous but significant symptom. *Outbreaks of 12th Germinal April 1,* Some weeks afterwards, on May 20, or 1st Prairial, a more determined, and better organized demonstration took place; the populace, aided by one or two of the sections, invaded the seat of the Legislature again, and savagely massacred one of the deputies, amidst a scene worthy of the worst days of 1793; and a few Mountain deputies, who, it is supposed, were privy to the rising to some extent, went through the form of voting decrees which conceded all the anarchists' demands. *and of 1st Prairial, May, 1795,* This outbreak, however, threatening as it became, was no longer sustained by the potent means ready in the hands of a Danton or a

Robespierre, and was suppressed in a short time; and the National Guards and anti-Jacobin sections were again aided by a force of soldiery, now on the side of authority and the State, not as had been witnessed a few years before. The extinction of this insurrectionary effort enabled the leaders of the Convention to strike down the remaining Jacobin chiefs, and to take severe measures against future disorders. The deputies of the Mountain who had voted for the decrees were executed, or put an end to themselves; and the relics of the Terrorists were proscribed and banished. At the same time the rebellious sections were disarmed; the National Guard was carefully thinned of men suspected of the Jacobin taint, and, for the first time, was, to some extent, placed under regular military control; and provision was made for the immediate removal of the Convention to Châlons in the event of danger, and for summoning to its aid the nearest army. Meanwhile, stern and sanguinary laws were passed against popular and anarchic meetings; the "patriots" complained that they suffered more than they had ever inflicted in the Reign of Terror; and, in the words of a sober historian, "the party of humanity and moderation did not itself abstain from the profuse shedding of blood."

put down and suppressed.

By these means the once terrible power of Jacobinism was altogether broken, though its elements retained indestructible life. The government, however, had no sooner put down one party than it found it necessary to restrain another, for the reaction of Thermidor was becoming dangerous; and though the Moderates in the Convention prevailed, they had no sympathy with the avowed royalists, or even with the reformers of 1789, foremost in the fierce anti-Jacobin

The power of Jacobinism finally broken.

crusade. Coercive measures were also employed against these enemies of the Republic; and thus the ruling powers were on either side beset by exasperated and reckless factions, and with difficulty kept a middle course between them. The government accordingly became weakened; its authority, diffused and no longer concentrated, through the change made in the Supreme Committee, grew vacillating, and, in a great degree, uncertain; and as it rejected the expedients of the Reign of Terror, it was gradually more and more compelled to look to military force for support—the end to which things were beginning to tend. Meanwhile, on all points in the theatre of war, the success of the French arms had multiplied, and the hosts of the Republic were borne forwards on a rapid and overwhelming tide of victory. The fortresses captured in 1793 were quickly evacuated by the Allies; and, after the occupation of Brussels, the conquerors spread over Belgium in triumph, and annexed its fertile provinces to France. Before long Pichegru advanced northwards, while Jourdan turned towards the Lower Rhine; and though this dislocation of the French armies—a characteristic error of Carnot's strategy, which consisted in ambitious movements on the wings of the adversary with a too feeble centre, and was only better than the impotent system of a general advance on an immense divided front—gave the Allied commanders a great opportunity, they separated from each other in eccentric retreat, full of mutual discontent and suspicion. By the close of 1794 Pichegru had overrun a large part of Holland, while Jourdan had gained two important victories on the principal affluents of the Lower Meuse; and within a few

Measures of the Government against the Royalists.

Weakness of the State. Tendency to the rule of the sword.

Great successes of the French against the Allies.

months the United Provinces had been transformed into the Batavian Republic, the House of Orange had been deposed, and the whole Low Countries, from the Scheldt to the Ems, had become merely a French dependency. The war, too, had been carried far into Spain; and events, which for a time had worn a menacing aspect in La Vendée, turned in favor of the Republic once more. In this unhappy region the atrocious cruelties of the Terrorists had caused the insurrection to revive, and to extend over a large part of Brittany; and the prospects of the rising appeared so bright that an English expedition was despatched, with a band of *émigrés*, to aid the royalists. A descent, however, attempted from Quiberon Bay, proved a miserable and inglorious failure; and Hoche, who, like all real Generals, had many of the highest gifts of a statesman, reduced the whole West before long to submission by a policy of conciliation and sagacious firmness, winning the purest fame of the military chiefs of the time.

Conquest of Belgium and Holland, September, 1794, · January, 1795.

Failure of English descent from Quiberon Bay, July 15–20, 1795.

These extraordinary successes of the French dissolved the already yielding Coalition. Prussia, the Power which had chiefly provoked the contest, was the first to abandon the allied cause, and made peace in the spring of 1795. Spain followed her example within a few months; and England, Austria, and Piedmont, with some States of the German Empire, already wearied of a calamitous and unprofitable struggle, alone remained to continue the war. The Republic had thus in two campaigns broken up an alliance which seemed more powerful than that which had humbled Louis XIV.; and it had extended its conquests beyond the limits of the

The Coalition dissolved. Prussia and Spain make peace, April, June, 1795.

most ambitious hopes of the Bourbon Monarchy. The result was in the highest degree brilliant; yet its real causes may be easily noted. Before the Campaign of 1794 had closed, the French armies, already immensely superior in numbers to their antagonists, had become gradually inured to war, and the young levies, after enormous losses, had hardened into truly formidable soldiers. The enterprise of the Republican troops, stirred by the impulse which first gave them strength, by the national passion for military glory, and by reiterated and splendid success, became astonishingly great and daring, and they ultimately gained that moral ascendency over their ill-led and beaten opponents which is one of the chief conditions of success. The conduct, too, of the Allied Commanders was even more pitiable than before; and indignation was justly felt in England against the incompetent Duke of York, and in Austria against the dull Prince of Cobourg, who had contrived in two years to fail in everything. The circumstance, however, has yet to be mentioned which so quickly enlarged the conquests of France, and we shall see it again in operation. The Republican soldiers were not, indeed, always kindly masters in the Low Countries or elsewhere; they were obliged to live on the tracts they occupied, being almost destitute of supplies from home; and their rapid advance was usually marked by excesses of license and by organized plunder. But in these, and in other parts of the Continent, the abuses of Feudalism and of the eighteenth century had undermined the whole frame of society; and the old order of things collapsed when it came in contact with revolutionary passions. Wherever the arms of France made their way, the privileges of the Church and the Nobles disappeared; the Reign of

Causes of this astonishing success of the Republic.

Liberty and Equality was proclaimed, and much that was unjust was swept away; and the result was that the people welcomed the foreign invader in many places, though their liberation cost a heavy price, and that the moral influence of the new French ideas was even more decisive than what were called the fourteen armies of the French Republic.

<small>Continuing weakness of the Republic at home.</small> While France, however, was triumphant abroad, her government* at home remained feeble, and her social condition was in many respects lamentable. Her armies, indeed, with the exception of that which held the mountainous line of the Alps from Dauphiny and Provence to the Genoese seaboard, were, on the whole, in a prosperous state, especially in the rich Low Countries; and the attraction to them became so great that towards the close of 1795 she had probably four hundred thousand men in the field. The peasantry, too, were for the most part thriving, notwithstanding the late maximum and requisitions, for the emancipation of the soil in 1789 had continued to make agriculture improve, and rents and taxes had sunk to almost nothing, under a currency ever diminishing in value. Trade, too, had revived to some extent, the Reign of Terror having ceased to destroy it;

---

* M. Thiers' *Histoire de la Revolution Française* seems to me, on the whole, the best guide for the period between the Revolution of Thermidor and the 18th Brumaire. His account of the internal and financial state of France during these years of disenchantment and exhaustion is lucid and able. The papers by Napoleon, in his *Commentaries*, on Vendémiaire and La Politique du Directoire, should also be read, but they are not just to the Government. The correspondence of the late Mr. Wickham throws much light on the relations between Foreign Powers and the discontented factions in France.

and the assignats, from their enormous fall, becoming almost useless as instruments of exchange, a return to a natural system had begun, and the precious metals slowly reappeared. But, as if to show the irony of fate, the populace of the great cities, which had figured so largely in the Revolution, remained generally in extreme want; and though, as we have seen, a moneyed class had sprung up, this had been at the cost of other classes; and the government, which still went on receiving the imposts of the state in worthless paper, was on the verge of financial ruin. Harassed, too, as it was by contending parties, and itself a mere revolutionary growth, its weakness could only rapidly increase; and, with the Convention, it was completely eclipsed by the splendor of the military power, which had begun to fascinate the masses. A strong Republican spirit, indeed, was still prevalent in the legislature; but though freedom and the Rights of Man were potent spells of victory abroad, they were gradually losing their magic in France. The period of exhaustion and of disenchantment which follows revolutions was soon to open, and the political aspirations of many turned chiefly to repose and a strong government. What that government would probably be in the collapse of settled authority and rule, Burke in England had already distinctly foreseen.

Extreme distress of the great cities.

Exhaustion of the revolutionary spirit.

As the summer of 1795 progressed, the reactionary parties increased in strength. The Republic, though victorious abroad, became associated in the minds of thousands with Jacobinism and the horrors of the past; and a sentiment began to be widely diffused in favor of Monarchy and of the system which had perished only

Desire for repose and a settled government. Reaction towards Monarchy.

in a moment of passion. This feeling allied itself with the desire for quiet which largely prevailed; and though the *émigrés* were generally hated, and the exiled Bourbons had not many supporters, royalist agents made their presence felt, and the air grew thick with rumors of royalist plots. The government and the Convention, too, became more than ever disliked; they were accused of prolonging a usurped power; and as they had lost their hold on the Jacobin "patriots," they were decried in the centres of public opinion, though still upheld by the great mass of the Nation. In this state of things the ruling powers resolved not unwisely to appeal to the people; and the appeal was prefaced by a Constitution which expressed the latest effort of their legislative wisdom. This scheme, called the Constitution of the year III.—the Hegira of "liberty" ran from 1792— plainly showed what were the ideas dominant among the chief French politicians of the hour and in the majority of the Convention. The organic changes of 1789 were ratified by a solemn oath; the Jacobin Constitution of 1793 was pronounced impossible and thrust aside; and the government was declared a Republic, though not without one or two protests. It was sought, however, to provide against the troubles and disasters of the past by a variety of ingenious expedients; and the proposed form of government was, in many respects, decidedly hostile to democratic influences. The Legislature, composed of seven hundred and fifty deputies, was to be elected by a not popular vote, although the election was to be annual; and it was divided into two distinct parts, a Council of Ancients, and one of Five-Hundred, experience having already taught the lesson of the perils attending a single Chamber. An Executive was formed

Constitution of the year III.

of Five Directors chosen by the Councils, and with dependent ministers; and precautions were taken against a recurrence of the tyranny of 1793 by a provision that one Director should retire each year. At the same time, the extravagant local powers which had been created in 1789, and had been so terribly abused, were still further limited; and recent enactments against mob violence were declared essential to the security of the State. In addition, and most important of all, two-thirds of the existing Convention was to be re-elected, and a third part only of the succeeding assemblies was to be at present formed of new members, the mischief of the self-denying ordinance of 1791 being fully understood, and great apprehension being felt of the royalist and anti-republican parties.

This Constitution, which, in the abstract, was not without considerable merit, and might have struck root in different times, was generally well received in France, though it was observed that assent was for the most part passive, and the enthusiasm of past years had died away. The conditions, however, which maintained the existing Legislature in the main unchanged, were violently denounced in several places; and this was eagerly seized as a grievance by the adversaries of the existing order of things. The leaders of the reactionary parties declaimed again the tyrannous Convention; and they were supported by an undefined following of those whom vanity, ambition, and want, led to hope for advantage in new disorders. These sentiments were especially strong in Paris, ever agitated and eager for change; and a formidable opposition to the Constitution, supported largely by the middle classes, gathered in the fickle and excitable capital. An insurrection was planned in the sections in which the malcontents were most powerful; and on October 4 the National Guards of one of the principal sections rose, the expedients of anarchy being thus employed in the turbulence of revolutionary time, by the class which had lately most suffered from them. The incapacity of the military commandant in Paris led quickly to a more general rising; and on the morning of the 4th dense columns rolled through streets and squares towards the Tuileries palace, vociferating against "Conventional traitors." The insurrection appeared as terrible as that of August 10; but a man of action was on the spot to quell it, and the conditions of the struggle were wholly different. The frightened Convention had some hours previously given Bonaparte the command of all the troops in the city; and that officer awaited the attack with composure, though he had only then a few thousand men. The tumultuary assailants were cut down by vollies of grape shot as they appeared; their masses, after a few discharges, broke, and in a very short time hardly a trace remained of what had seemed a most alarming outbreak. The result was, perhaps, in some degree due to the energy and skill of Bonaparte; but probably the greater part of the force of the sections had no real heart in the cause; and as revolutionary passions were dying out, and regular soldiers were now on the scene, the revolt was put down with comparative ease.

Rising of the reactionary sections of Paris, 13th Vendémiaire, Oct. 4, 1795, put down by Bonaparte.

The quick suppression of this outbreak, known as that of the 13th Vendémiaire, was a severe blow to the revolutionary parties, and, for the moment, put them to silence. The authority of the Convention and of the Republican

The authority of the Convention restored.

chiefs, who guided the majority, increased in proportion; and severe measures were adopted against the still formidable National Guard of the capital. This citizen force was in part disbanded, and placed entirely in the hands of the General in command of the regular troops in Paris; and it thus finally lost the character of a power self-elected and independent of the State. The chief result of Vendémiaire, however, was, of course, to strengthen the military power; and Bonaparte learned on that day a lesson he was not likely to forget. On October 26 the Convention declared its mission ended, and closed its sittings; and immediately afterwards the new powers which were to govern France were installed in their functions. *The military power becomes stronger.*

The last part of the rule of the Convention is not less instructive than that which preceded, though of less tragic and striking interest. In less than a year and a half after the Revolution of Thermidor, the national sentiment seemed transformed; the forces of Jacobinism had been put down; and the Republic was threatened by a combination of royalists and anti-republican parties, increasing in strength though not dominant. In this we certainly see clear proof of the mobility of the French character; yet, if we recollect that the excesses of the Reign of Terror were justly abhorred, that the ascendency of Jacobinism was largely due to passions engendered by national peril, and ceased when the crisis passed away, and that old habits, traditions, and beliefs retain always extraordinary power, the change becomes intelligible to thoughtful minds. Concurrently we observe how the hopes and passions of the Revolution begin to fade and wane in the disappoint- *Reflections on the course of the Revolution after Thermidor.*

ment of its most eager supporters; how the State weakens amidst the strife of factions, not morally strong, but selfish and fierce; how a feeling of lassitude creeps over human nature lately so violently stirred, and a desire grows up for rest and order; and how, above all, the power of the sword, sustained by brilliant success abroad, and throwing its weight into the balance at home, casts its shadow on the coming time.

CHAPTER VIII.

THE DIRECTORY. BONAPARTE.

Character of this period. DURING the period we are next to survey, the French Revolution, losing its strength at home, and having triumphed over its foreign enemies, turns definitively into the path of conquest abroad; until, suddenly arrested by unexpected reverses, it collapses under the military rule to which it had been for some time tending. In the internal condition of France in these years we see the causes increasing in force which had been lessening revolutionary passions, and introducing the arbitrament of the sword. Under a system of government, not, indeed, as worthless as it has been described by the flatterers of success, but composed of men not of marked eminence, divided against itself, and sinking in repute, the strife of the dregs of factions becomes more vexatious, and the desire for tranquillity grows more general; and at last, after a long exhibition of weakness, violence, and uncertain counsels, the State falls into the hands of a great soldier, and national peril

1795.   *The Directory.   Bonaparte.*   143

hastens the issue. This consummation—the usual end of epochs of wild and destructive change—is furthered by the advance of prosperity, and by the eagerness of the new interests formed by the Revolution to consolidate themselves; and it is precipitated by the national tendency to bow to power and military fame, and, above all, by the splendid achievements and gifts of the extraordinary man to whom France not unnaturally looked as her champion. But though the decline of the failing Republic is of the deepest interest to the political thinker, History, at this juncture, turns her chief attention to the march of the Revolution abroad, and to its contest with the old Powers of Europe. There we see how the ideas of 1789, though not so decisively perhaps as before, concurred to speed the progress of the arms of France; and how their influence was not unfelt even in the hour of defeat and disaster. There, too, we see how war assumes more ample and magnificent proportions, under the impulse of a new and eventful time, and the inspiration of commanding genius; and we mark, as Bonaparte appears on the scene, how he alike extends the conquests of France and modifies her Revolutionary foreign policy.

For some time after Vendémiaire, the internal state of the Republic presented but few incidents of striking interest. The suppression of the revolt of the sections had, we have seen, quieted the reactionary parties; and though their foes, in consequence, grew more daring, the efforts of these were of little avail, and a Jacobin conspiracy, headed by an enthusiast called Babœuf, came to nothing. Another attempt was also made to descend on the coasts of La Vendée; but the policy of Hoche had borne its fruits, and the West remained in submissive repose, though elements of trouble lurked beneath the surface. The

State of the Republic after Vendémiaire.

majority too, of the former Convention predominated in the new Legislature, though a certain number of the freshly elected deputies were little inclined to republican views; and, for the present, the prevailing sentiment was to maintain the settlement of 1795. The Directory, who composed the government, though less moderate than many in the Councils, and indeed wholly formed of men who had voted for the death of Louis XVI., agreed, nevertheless, with each other for a time, and with the national representation; and though, with the single exception of Carnot, they were not men of peculiar mark, their policy was rather mastered by events than of a decidedly bad character. They had, indeed, *Policy of the Directory.* recourse to one or two expedients of a Jacobin kind, in the exhausted financial condition of the State; and they levied a temporary forced tax on the rich, and were compelled for a few months to return to the arbitrary system of requisitions for the troops. These measures, however, were soon abandoned, and were, perhaps, inevitable in existing circumstances; nor can the Directory be fairly charged with what ought to be ascribed to the tyranny of the past. The same kind of excuse may be urged for another startling and grave act, though not so iniquitous as it appeared. After many attempts to avoid the catastrophe, the Directory, with the assent of the Councils, deprived the assignats of their nominal value, and declared that in all public and private transactions they should be estimated only at their real worth; and before long, therefore, this degraded currency disappeared wholly from circulation. This was National *National Bankruptcy virtually declared.* Bankruptcy in another name; but as the Republic had not the means of redeeming the thousands of millions of notes afloat, and the State could not exist on worthless paper, no other course was, perhaps, possible; and, in any case, the men of this era were not responsible for the original evil. Nor did the abandonment of one of the last devices of a revolutionary age create general discontent; nor was the shock as severe and ruinous as Mr. Pitt and others supposed it would prove. The assignats, we have seen, had for some time been ceasing to be a medium of exchange; their depreciation had been taken into account in all the ordinary dealings of commerce; and the ultimate loss by them was comparatively small, as their real value had sunk to almost nothing. What the paper system had done was to transfer property to an enormous extent by its diminution of fixed debts and payments, and by the scope it gave to jobbing speculations. But these mischiefs were now of old date; and the consequences, cruel and unjust as they were, affected classes rather than national interests.

Preparations were made to renew the war with increased energy in 1796. The military operations of the French, in the last months of the preceding year, had been unsuccessful to a considerable extent, for Jourdan had been driven from Mayence, and Pichegru had dealt treasonably with the enemy in his front; and though a victory had been won by the French at Loano, upon the Italian seaboard, the tide of fortune ran less favorably for the Republic than it had ran before. Two large armies under Jourdan and Moreau were massed apart from each other on the Middle Rhine for a formidable invasion of Western Germany; and a third, composed of about forty thousand men, good soldiers, but in extreme want, was entrusted to the youthful Bonaparte, and confronted— along the coast from Genoa to Nice, which it had occupied for a considerable time—a much greater Austrian

Preparations for the campaign of 1796.

L

and Piedmontese force. The vicinity of the Rhine, therefore, was to be the principal scene of events; but the force of genius transformed the situation. Bonaparte assumed his command in the first days of April, and the presence of a superior mind was at once seen in the operations of the French. Deceiving his adversaries by rapid demonstrations, he quickly broke through their extended centre; and, in a series of brilliant engagements, he divided the Piedmontese from the Austrians, drove both, routed, in separate retreat, and having, as he said, "turned the Genoese Alps," reached Turin in a few days in triumph. He now made an armistice with the King of Sardinia, which placed the fortresses of Piedmont in his hands, and secured his communications with France; and having declined to revolutionize a State which might become favorable to French policy, he at once directed his whole efforts against the Austrians, who, he clearly perceived, were the only foes of real importance in Italy. Advancing with a celerity before unknown, he anticipated his antagonist, Beaulieu, on the Po; and after a murderous struggle at Lodi, he entered Milan, and overran Lombardy, the Austrian commander being unable to contend against such activity and daring, and being outnumbered in every encounter. At Milan Bonaparte was welcomed with delight, the citizens detesting the Austrian yoke, and being inclined to the new principles; but he halted only to strengthen his position; and having terrified into submission the hostile princes of Parma and Modena, he made straight for the line of the Adige, which he had marked out, with true military insight, as the real theatre on which to contend with Austria for the prize of Italy. Having forced Beaulieu across the Mincio, and compelled him to fall back on the Tyrol, he laid siege to Mantua in the first days of June; having previously refused, with equal prudence and firmness, to obey an order of Carnot to march against Rome, which certainly would have led to disaster, by needlessly dislocating the French army.

Great as this success of Bonaparte was, the cabinet of Vienna was not disconcerted, and made vigorous efforts to repair its defeats. The French army in Italy was known to be weak in numbers; the strength of its position in the hands of a great commander was not understood; and it was widely believed that it was doomed to disaster, thrown forward dangerously, as it seemed, round Mantua. The beaten divisions of Beaulieu received large reinforcements from the Austrians on the Rhine; and Wurmser, a veteran of high reputation, advanced, in the last days of July, with an army that seemed more than powerful enough to liberate Mantua, and overwhelm his antagonist. Bonaparte, however, with that rapid decision which is one of the distinctive marks of a great leader in war, forestalled admirably the Austrian movements; and, raising the siege of Mantua at a moment's notice, encountered his enemies as they descended along either shore of the Lago di Garda; and, interposing between their divided masses, defeated them at Lonato and Castiglione. He then turned to pursue his baffled assailants, advanced boldly to the verge of the Tyrol, and routed Wurmser again in the defiles of the Brenta, after a march of extraordinary daring and quick- *[The Austrians send an army to raise the siege of Mantua, and to crush Bonaparte.]*

[He defeats Wurmser in a series of engagements.]

Aug. 3—6.

ness; and though the tenacious Austrian chief got into Mantua by a circuitous movement, he had lost the greater part of a gallant army. The Austrian government, however, still persisted, and a fresh force, under the command of Alvinzi, was once more directed against the adversary, who, it was thought, must succumb to such repeated efforts. The attack proved dangerous in the extreme; the Austrians, though disseminated in separate masses, forced one of the chief positions of their foes; and Bonaparte, with the main body of the French, was almost driven from the barrier of the Adige. Alvinzi, however, paused at the decisive moment; his dexterous adversary fell on his rear, displaying the greatest fertility of resource; and victory at last declared for the French, after a protracted struggle along the dykes of Arcola. The campaign, nevertheless, was not yet ended; and after recruiting his worn-out host, Alvinzi again approached the Adige. The decisive encounter took place on January 14, 1797; and the Austrians, divided and baffled once more, were routed with terrible effect at Rivoli, on the eastern shore of the Lago di Garda. This brought hostilities to an end for a time; Mantua opened its gates in a few days; and Bonaparte stood in triumph on the line which he had made the centre of his operations, having annihilated three armies, each stronger than his own.

This splendid campaign, still perhaps unrivalled, raised Bonaparte at once to the summit of fame. Its astonishing results were in some degree due to the revolutionary influence of France, but far more to the capacity for war of the young leader who had appeared on the scene. Bonaparte, in this admirable passage of arms, had displayed all the qualities of a great captain; sagacity, resolution, boldness, vigor, a perfect knowledge of the theatre of operations, and a skill in arranging his forces on' it, which completely bewildered his inferior opponents. There was, too, another general cause for his success which gave a character to his strategy, and has wrought a marked change in the art of war. In consequence of the multiplication of roads it had become possible to make more rapid marches than Generals of a former age could attempt; and, owing to the progress which had taken place in husbandry, an army could now often rely for supplies on the districts which it happened to go through. The old system of slow advances, depending mainly on magazines, and retarded by fortresses and such obstacles, had thus become, in a great degree, obsolete; quick and daring attacks and brilliant manœuvres, the troops living on resources found on the spot, had been made more practicable than they had' ever been; and Bonaparte had thoroughly grasped this truth, though it had been partially recognized before, and it was obviously suggested by examples already set by the revolutionary armies. In this campaign we see plainly that he conducted war upon these new principles; and, though other causes no doubt aided, the circumstance partly explains his success in so often routing his adversaries in detail. Nor had he shown the qualities of a soldier only in this memorable and arduous contest; he had given proof of no common statecraft, and especially of a secret contempt for the propaganda of revolutionary ideas, of which the French armies were

Character of his strategy.

the principal centres.* He had refused, we have seen, for political reasons, to overthrow the Sardinian throne; and, to the astonishment of his lieutenants, he had soon afterwards negotiated with the Pope and the Grand Duke of Tuscany, avowed enemies of the Revolution, in an antirevolutionary and diplomatic fashion. It had become already evident that a leader had appeared who, for good or evil, had little sympathy with the fanaticism of liberty and the Rights of Man, powerful levers, as yet, of French influence abroad.

State craft of Bonaparte.

Meanwhile a very different contest had been waging beyond the Rhenish frontier. Following the essentially vicious plans of Carnot, Jourdan and Moreau had made their way into Germany, divided by a wide space of country, the first moving along the Thuringian range, the second skirting the Black Forest. The young Archduke Charles retreated before them, though with an army nearly equal in strength; and he fought an indecisive battle with Moreau at Neresheim, near the Upper Danube. As the French generals, however, moved slowly, and made no signs of effecting their junction, though now only a few marches apart, the Archduke assumed the offensive; and leaving a detachment to hold Moreau in check, he marched against that leader's isolated colleague, thus imitating the manœuvres of which Bonaparte was giving such splendid examples in Italy. The

Campaign of 1796 in Germany. Defeats of the French.

The Archduke Charles.

Ability displayed by him.

---

* Napoleon's policy in 1796-7 is set forth by himself in his *Commentaries*. M. Lanfrey, in his *Histoire de Napoleon I.*, describes it with great ability, but in too harsh colors. See chapters 6, 7, and 8 of the work.

operations, however, of the Austrian commander were wanting in the perfect skill and energy conspicuously displayed by his far greater rival. Jourdan, indeed, was beaten in detail, and fell back discomfited to the Rhine; but he was not pursued with daring and vigor, and he reached his winter quarters comparatively unhurt. Moreau, too, after the defeat of Jourdan, got safely out of a most difficult position, and made good his retreat through the intricate defiles and rocky crags of the Swabian Alps; and he even drove his antagonist back, though probably had he been boldly attacked by the Archduke after he had been left without support, his army would have been almost destroyed. Germany was thus cleared of its French invaders, and the Republic met a decided reverse; but nothing really great was accomplished; and the campaign is a striking example how military conceptions, however excellent, must be as well executed to have marked results. The Archduke, however, justly acquired renown; the errors of Carnot were perceived, and the events of the year proved that in war, as in other arts, the same original thoughts, under similar conditions, occur sometimes to different minds.

The state of the Republic had not improved while Bonaparte had been conquering on the Adige. The prosperity of France, indeed, had gradually augmented, as time weakened the effects of the Reign of Terror; the distress of the great cities lessened; and the revenue had begun to show signs of progress. But, in the transition from the paper system, the finances were inevitably strained to the utmost; the part of the Debt remained unpaid which had escaped the Jacobin sponge; and the treasury was extremely ill-managed, as even the administration of it had been withdrawn by the Constitution from the Executive government. Complaints, therefore, abounded everywhere; and the animosities had only increased in bitterness, which threatened the State, and made it insecure. As Vendémiaire receded into the past, the royalists and anti-republicans grew in strength; and they drew to their party a great many of the disappointed and discontented men who always abound in a revolutionary time, and a still increasing number of the new aristocracy of wealth, who had no genuine republican tastes, and whose real aspiration was for rest and enjoyment. Dissensions, too, broke out within the Directory itself; and two of the Five, of whom Carnot was one, inclined at least to sentiments opposed to those which prevailed in the old Convention; ever true, in the main, to some ideal of a Republic, whether moderate or not. The strife of factions was quickened by the elections held in 1797, which displaced many of the "Conventionals," as they were called—the restriction was by this time removed which had been imposed in 1795—and filled the Legislature to a large extent with deputies of reactionary views. The royalists and anti-republicans of all kinds began now to assert their power; and the opposition to the government was seconded by reckless and widespread intrigues and conspiracies. Pichegru, whose royalist leanings had been avowed, though his treason had not been yet divulged, became a chief director of these dishonorable plots, the inevitable growth of a revolutionary era; and though the reactionaries were, in the mass, opposed to violent changes in the State, they lent themselves to designing leaders. Non-juring priests and long-exiled *émigrés* began soon to return freely; the Powers at war with France had numerous agents in correspondence with the malcontents; and plans were set on foot for a Bourbon

[marginal notes:]
Internal state of the Republic; revival of factions.

Royalist and reactionary schemes.

restoration, to be sustained by a rising in La Vendée. In this emergency the three Directors who adhered to the existing order of things, sought for aid from the power alone capable of throwing a decisive weight into the scale, and not disloyal to their authority if not particularly attached to it. Hoche moved an armed force to the capital, and Augereau, despatched from his camp by Bonaparte, was placed at the head of seventy thousand men to carry out the intended design. On September 4 the Tuileries palace, where the Councils held their ordinary meetings, was once more surrounded by bands of soldiers; and within a few hours most of the reactionary deputies were imprisoned and their seats declared vacant; and the principal conspirators, with Pichegru at their head, were on their way to a place of foreign banishment. The remains of the thinned and purged Legislature voted readily the proscription of many suspected persons, and one of the hostile Directors was included in the list, Carnot having fortunately effected his escape. The triumph of the Republicans, in what was named the *coup d'état* of the 18th Fructidor, was for the moment general and complete; but the success of this and similar acts of violence—for which happily no word exists in our language—could only hasten the military domination which was already beginning to be felt everywhere. It was also a significant mark of the time that the populace of Paris, growing weary of political changes which had proved abortive, and of the struggles of warring factions, had looked on with passive indifference at the peril of the Republic and its temporary success. Coup d'état of the 18th Fructidor, September 4, 1797.

Meanwhile Bonaparte had been extending the power of France in the Italian Peninsula, and, after a brief and brilliant cam- Conclusion of the campaign of Italy.

paign, had brought the war with Austria to a close. The first success of the French on the Po had agitated the States between the Appenines and the Alps; and national and revolutionary passions had made the invaders welcome in many places, though sentiments were a good deal divided, and the excesses of the so-called liberators—especially the robbery of works of art, which were sent as spoils to the museums of Paris—had caused more than one angry rising. After the complete triumph of 1796 the opinion of the masses became more evident; and though the old aristocracy of Venice remained bitterly hostile to the French ideas, the Modenese, the subjects of the Pope, and the great body of the people of Lombardy, had risen against foreign or hated rulers, and attached themselves to the victorious Republic. Bonaparte, wielding already enormous power, ably turned the movement to his own advantage, and to that of the Directory in a secondary degree; he obtained considerable territories from the Pope, as the price of sparing Rome and the adjoining Provinces; and while he levied ample contributions from them, he gave or promised the Italians "liberty" within the districts he had annexed or occupied. He steadily carried out, however, this policy of compromise, and of moderating Revolution; and, while he treated the Italian States and their Sovereigns with a view rather to his own objects, or to immediate political interests, than with the least regard to Republican notions, it was observed that he had no sympathy with what he contemptuously called the multitude, and that he thoroughly despised its hopes and passions. Meanwhile, his army, largely recruited from all parts of France, had grown truly formida-

Conciliatory policy of Bonaparte; his anti-revolutionary views.

He marches on Vienna from Italy.

1796.   *The Directory.   Bonaparte.*   155

ble; and he took the field again in the spring of 1797. Austria had no forces sufficient to oppose his march; and though the Archduke Charles made a gallant resistance, Bonaparte swept over the Italian Alps and hastened down their German slopes towards Vienna. An armistice was signed on April 7, within sight of the domes of the Austrian capital; and Bonaparte, having with a force comparatively small conquered from the Var almost to the Danube, and broken the strength of the Austrian Monarchy, dictated in a few months the terms of peace. By this treaty, known as that of Campo Formio, Austria ceded Belgium to the French Republic, and, as head of the Empire, agreed to the cession of the German Provinces on the French bank of the Rhine; and she consented that Lombardy and several adjoining States should be formed into a Cisalpine Republic, of course a mere dependency of its French original. In return for these immense losses, Bonaparte flung her Venice as a spoil, notwithstanding a protest from the Directory; and his conduct in this was very characteristic. The Venetian oligarchy had certainly been a thorn in his side while he was on the Adige; and after he had disappeared beyond the German Alps it had stirred up an insurrection in his rear. But, long before the peace of Campo Formio was made, the Republic had become a democracy apparently subservient to French authority; and, nevertheless, Bonaparte deliberately sacrificed a people and a State, once an ally of France, in order, as he avowed, to sow dissensions among the late Coalition, which, with the exception of the Power aggrandized, resented the transfer of Venice to Austria. The act was not so ineffably base as it has

Treaty of Campo Formio, October 17, 1797.

Gains of France.

Sacrifice of Venice.

been described by historical censors; but it was very significant of a policy of craft, of expediency, and of hard self-interest, opposed to all the revolutionary professions.

<small>Reflections on the conduct of Bonaparte.</small> In this manner a youth of twenty-seven had struck down the only remaining enemy feared by the Republic on the Continent, had consolidated and widely increased its conquests, and had shed a glory on the arms of France more splendid than she had ever known. The right of France to what the national sentiment had recognized as her natural limits had been admitted by her great German rival: her influence extended, beyond, from the Adige to the Texel; and a dream which Richelieu would have dismissed as idle had been realized in perfect completeness.

<small>Enthusiasm in France at his successes.</small> A burst of enthusiasm went up from the popular heart to hail the warrior who had done these great deeds; and the name of Bonaparte, scarcely known before, was in every mouth in France as a word of marvel. Hardly less astonishment was felt in Europe, too, at the extraordinary achievements of the young conqueror; and the feeling <small>Admiration felt for him in Europe.</small> was largely mingled with genuine admiration. The diplomatists of Piedmont, Austria, and Rome, had recognized in Bonaparte a kind of sympathy with the established Powers and old order of Europe, surprising in a negotiator of a Revolutionary State; and several of them had said that no other General of the devouring Republic would have been so moderate. Bonaparte had also treated his defeated opponents with delicate and becoming courtesy; and he had displayed to soldiers and statesmen whom he wished to please the charm of a manner which possessed an inscrutable and mysterious fascination. He

was thus an object of the respect and flattery of even the most resolute enemies of France ; and he was regarded by the enfranchised Italians as a deliverer all the more to be loved because one of their own race and blood.

Surrounded thus by a halo of glory, Bonaparte left Italy to return to France, and after passing hastily through Rastadt, where the States of the Empire were negotiating a peace that seemed inevitable after Campo Formio, he quietly returned to the modest house in Paris which he had quitted a comparatively unknown soldier. He was greeted with an enthusiasm such as never had been seen since the days of Louis XIV., though, either from inclination or a studied policy, he avoided the public gaze, and seemed to court solitude. The capital shone in an array of splendor which contrasted strangely with the horrors of a few years before; and the conqueror of Arcola and Rivoli was the only object in the eyes of the multitudes who crowded to celebrate his great exploits in festivals in which the antique pomp of the Roman Commonwealth curiously blended with the glitter and luxury of a modern age. How long would the obscure Heads of a divided, feeble, and revolutionary government withstand the influence of the young hero, who seemed to carry fortune at the point of his sword; how long could the Republic co-exist with this glorious personification of the military power, which already encompassed it on every side?

He returns to France, and is received with acclamation.

December, 1797.

CHAPTER IX.

EGYPT AND THE 18TH BRUMAIRE.

The Directory jealous of Bonaparte.

THE homage rendered to Bonaparte, and the great influence he already enjoyed, gave umbrage to the Republican government. The causes of dissension were already numerous, for the haughty independence of the young General, his contempt of all military schemes but his own, his sacrifice of Venice, and the sovereign attitude he had assumed in the negotiations with foreign Powers, and, above all, his supremacy over his troops, had been viewed with alarm and suspicion; and when, after his return to France, he was welcomed as the image of her glories, his ascendency irritated the eclipsed Directory. Nor did the subsequent conduct of Bonaparte tend to reassure the weak chiefs of the State, who dreaded an authority they did not themselves possess. Though he continued to live in extreme simplicity, and seemed to prefer the society of men of letters and science to political affairs, he had let fall expressions which revealed a dislike of a feeble and disunited government, and the junta in office instinctively felt that his presence was a rebuke and menace to them, though jealousy was masked under a show of deference. Either from a desire to get rid of a foe, or possibly from a higher motive, the Directory soon tried to engage Bonaparte in an enterprise which, if of tempting promise, was one of extraordinary difficulty and peril. England, after Campo Formio, was the only great Power that remained at war with the victorious Republic; and the Directory, exasperated at a recent failure to negotiate with a British envoy, invited Bonaparte to make a descent on our coasts, a project for which Hoche—that remarkable man had just died, amidst general regret—had always had a strong predilection. An expedition of this kind, however, had been unsuccessful in 1796, and the battles of Camperdown and of St. Vincent had annihilated the fleets of the Batavian Republic and of Spain, now an ally of France; and Bonaparte declared the scheme premature, and suggested another which he thought more hopeful. His mind, imaginative and calculating alike to a degree of force which has been seldom witnessed, had even in Italy turned to the East and the ancient centres of historic power; and he proposed to invade and occupy Egypt—that stage on the way from Europe to Asia which has always attracted the thoughts of ambition. The Directory joyfully sanctioned a plan which would certainly remove a dreaded rival, and, if successful, would make France predominant in the Mediterranean Sea; and Bonaparte was given ample means to carry out the intended design. His preparations were made with a secrecy and skill which showed a high faculty for organization; convoys were collected in the Italian ports, and troops directed upon the sea-coast, so as to conceal the project as long as possible, and in May, 1798, the expedition set sail from Toulon. It consisted of a powerful fleet and army; and its leader perhaps entertained hopes of imitating the career of Alexander, and, after subduing and colonizing Egypt, of marching from the Nile to the Indus.

They engage him to attempt a descent on England.

He proposes to invade Egypt.

Expedition to Egypt.

While this enterprise was being set on foot, the Congress of Rastadt had been sitting, and negotiations were going on for peace on the Continent. Prussia, which since the treaty of 1795 had almost become an ally of France, had secretly rejoiced at the defeats of Austria, and saw in the present confusion of Europe the means of extending her power in Germany, fell in with the policy of the Republic; and, in consideration of benefits to herself, assented to French annexations on the Rhine, to the humiliation of lesser German States, and to the annihilation of Imperial Bishoprics, a favorite object of the Directory. This selfish and unpatriotic state-craft—a main cause of that habit of aggression and of intervention in the affairs of Germany which Prussian writers have laid to the charge of France for their own ends—was opposed by many of the German princes; but, as Austria had retired from the contest, and the divided Empire was left without a head, a renewal of the war appeared impossible. This would have been the case in ordinary times; but ancient privilege and democratic ideas were in a state of angry collision in the countries approached by the French revolution; and though hostilities had not broken out, the prospects of peace did not brighten. Causes of fresh troubles quickly arose when Europe was in this disturbed condition, and they were aggravated by the republican ardor and arrogant pretensions of the Directory, though the real impulse lay much deeper. Before Bonaparte had left Italy, Genoa had formed herself into a Ligurian Republic; and not long afterwards a democratic rising occurred in several of the Swiss cantons, and after a sanguinary civil war an Helvetian

Republic had been established by French influence and French bayonets. This was followed by a violent outbreak in Holland, which for a time completely overwhelmed the party of the House of Orange, and of the old order of things; and before long the French invaded the territories of the Pope, set up a Roman Republic in his States, and filled Piedmont with revolutionary agents, against the conditions of recent treaties. The march of the Revolution hastened, accordingly, in a state of nominal peace as well as in war; and the French government encouraged its progress by their fanatical zeal and reckless want of scruple. It is not surprising, therefore, when France had lost for a time her most dreaded commander, that several of the European Powers should have begun to watch events, and prepare for war; that the negotiations should have proceeded slowly; and that even Austria should have thought of arming once more, more especially as the genius and the gold of Mr. Pitt had been engaged in endeavoring to cement again the Coalition which had been recently dissolved.

The Continent was in this unquiet state when an unexpected event decided the issue to which affairs had been slowly tending. Bonaparte had reached in safety the shores of Egypt, the French fleet, though with immense convoys, having eluded the watch of the English cruisers, and having even had time to seize and occupy the great Mediterranean fortress of Malta. His army had landed, and, crossing the verge of the Desert, had routed the Mameluke horsemen in a battle fought within sight of the Pyramids; and he had triumphantly made his way to Cairo, where he had endeavored to establish a French colony. But in the meantime his fleet had been com-

Bonaparte lands in Egypt, July 1, 1798.

Battle of the Nile, Aug. 1, 1798, and destruction of the French fleet.

M

pletely destroyed by the great English sailor whose manœuvres at sea bore a certain resemblance to his own on land; and he seemed cut off with his army from France, and imprisoned within his precarious conquest. The victory of Nelson determined the Powers which hitherto had been afraid to strike, and new names were added to the list of the enemies of the hated Republic. Hostilities were proclaimed in the winter of 1798, and it soon became evident that the contest would rage from the Zuyder Zee to the Straits of Messina, and would spread over part of the Turkish Empire. The Porte undertook to attack Bonaparte; the Court of Naples set an army on foot to invade the newly-created Roman Republic; Austria prepared for a fresh struggle on the Rhine and the Adige, aided by a large reinforcement from Russia, which had only threatened in 1793. Except Prussia, Germany generally concurred; and England gladly threw her sword into the balance. The Directory, elated by late successes, met the challenge of its foes with defiance, and looked forward confidently to a new series of triumphs. An unhappy incident which had lately occurred, and which threw a dark stain on the House of Austria—the murder of the plenipotentiaries of France at Rastadt—had given the Heads of the Republic the strength arising from widespread national indignation; and, as they had, so to speak, organized the *levée en masse* of a few years before, by the celebrated measure called the "Conscription," which at this moment is the foundation of the enormous armies that cover Europe, they prepared for hostilities on the greatest scale.

Renewal of the war in Europe.

Murder of the French plenipotentiaries at Rastadt, April 28, 1799.

The Conscription.

The campaign which followed is of little interest as

an illustration of the art of war. On both sides the antiquated system of timid operations along an immense front, and of pausing at obstacles, was, in the main, adopted; and Switzerland became the chief scene of the strife, in deference to the wholly unsound theory that the possession of a mountain range ensures a decisive advantage to a belligerent, apart from any other consideration. Though generally ill-led, the allied armies had for months a great superiority over the French; and they certainly might have invaded France, and not improbably have occupied Paris, had they been directed with real energy and skill. In the South, indeed, the Neapolitan levies were routed with ease upon the Tiber; and under the impulse of the success of their foes, Naples was changed into the Parthenopæan Republic, and the King of Sardinia was expelled from Piedmont. But on the points where the contest was most important, fortune was long adverse to the French armies; and they lost the fruits of the glorious struggle of 1796, though ultimately saved from the extreme of peril. Jourdan was defeated with heavy loss at Stochach, between the Swabian Alps and the Lake of Constance; and had not the Archduke Charles been compelled, by the military or Aulic Council at Vienna, to waste his strength among the hills of Uri, he might have crossed the Rhine, invaded Alsace, and turned the whole line of the French in Switzerland. Meanwhile the Austrians, feebly resisted, had forced the great barrier of the Adige, and before long the warriors of Mantua and Rivoli were driven from the Mincio across the Adda, pursued by the enemies they had so often beaten, and by a Russian army under Suwarrow, a celebrated veteran of the reign of Catherine. Moreau, who had been for some time in disgrace, for supposed complicity with the crime of Pichegru, which had come to light after the 18th Fructidor, was now raised to command in Italy, and endeavored to effect his junction with Macdonald, coming up from the South across the Apennines; but though Suwarrow showed no skill, the two French generals were completely beaten along the historic banks of the Trebbia. This was followed by another defeat at Novi; and though the populations of the new Republics remained true to the French cause, the allied armies overran the Peninsula, and Italy was lost more quickly than it had been won, with the exception of Genoa and a few other fortresses. The war might have been easily carried into France had the allies now acted with real vigor; but a fatal error caused a sudden change of fortune. A combined English and Russian force, under the too celebrated Duke of York, had made a descent on the coasts of Holland; and the Archduke Charles was directed, on the Lower Rhine, to co-operate with this remote detachment. This movement, made against the will of the Austrian chief, weakened the force opposed to the French in Switzerland; and Massena, the ablest lieutenant of Bonaparte, and trained in the lessons of 1796, seized the favorable opportunity presented to him. He fell on the Russian Korsakoff in his front, and crushed him in a great battle at Zurich; and Suwarrow lost three-fourths of his army in a fruitless attempt to support his colleague. This reverse as usual, caused dissensions to break out in the camp of the allies, and these were only increased

Battles of the Trebbia and Novi, June 17, 18, and 19, and August 15, 1799.

The French driven from Italy.

Failure of English descent on Holland.

Battle of Zurich, September 25–28, 1799.

by the inglorious failure of the Duke of York in his advance into Holland, which the Archduke's diversion could not really aid. Offensive operations were given up, and the territory of France remained intact; though the armies of the coalition, with Italy in their grasp, had their outposts on the borders of Provence. It saves France from invasion.

Meanwhile, torn by intestine factions, the government of France had been declining rapidly; and the state of the Republic had become lamentable. The *coup d'état* of the 18th Fructidor had given a triumph to the extreme republicans; and the expiring remains of the Jacobins lifted their heads again in a threatening manner. The Directory and the Councils, becoming alarmed, turned violently against the enemies they feared; and several "patriots" of a Jacobin type having been returned at the election of 1798, the reckless course was again taken of declaring the seats of these deputies vacant, as had been done in the case of the opposite party. The Constitution was thus set at naught twice; and though the conduct of the ruling powers was less to blame than at first sight appears, the Republic became more feeble than ever, and degenerated into a divided oligarchy, discredited, unpopular, and merely upheld by the military force on which it rested. The renewal of the war in 1798 gave extreme offence to the wealthy classes, and roused once more anti-republican hopes, though the fate of the envoys at Rastadt had, we have seen, provoked a storm of indignation; and measures on which the Directory unwisely ventured—a renewal of the forced tax on the rich, and a declaration which practically swept away the greater part of the remaining Debt—caused widespread irritation and alarm. At Lamentable internal state of the Republic. Strife of factions.

The reverses of 1799 cause all parties to combine against the Directory.

this crisis the reverses of 1799 came to exasperate passion and discontent, led to fresh exhibitions of weak oppression, and precipitated the decline of the imperilled State. All parties combined against the Directory, with characteristic national vehemence, in the panic caused by defeat and fear; and two of the Directors were thrown out as a sacrifice, though the change could produce no good consequence. Meanwhile, the beaten chiefs of the armies, who for some time had chafed a good deal against a despised civilian rule, exhaled their grievances in angry complaints; and popular leaders, appearing once more, clamored for the energy of 1793, and compelled the government to have recourse to laws of an extreme kind against priests and *émigrés*, and to arbitrary military and financial experiments.

Weakness and ruin of the State.

At the same time, at the news of the success of the allies, La Vendée showed symptoms of rising; the sources of revenue quickly dried up; the armies, driven upon the frontier, from the fertile tracts on which they had lived, were reduced to a state of extreme want; and between dread of a counter-revolution, and of a revival of the Reign of Terror, the thoughts of all the moderate part of the nation turned eagerly to what had long been their wish—a strong government that would defend France, and save the interests produced by the Revolution. In the shipwreck which menaced the sinking Republic, the ominous words "we must have a chief" dropped from Siéyès,* the most far-sighted of the gov-

Desire for a strong Government.

Siéyès.

---

* The Abbé Siéyès was born in 1748, and in 1784 was made Vicar-General of the diocese of Chartres. He devoted himself to political speculation, and having written a pamphlet on the state

erning Five; and in the Legislature, the armies and the great body of the people, a sentiment which had been growing up that a complete change of system was needed acquired at once irresistible force.

While this was the state of France and Europe, Bonaparte, undismayed by dangers around, had been carrying on his daring enterprise in the corner of Africa where he seemed imprisoned. *Fortunes of Bonaparte in Egypt.* Having, in some measure, pacified Egypt by a policy of mingled craft and rigor, he advanced into Syria across the isthmus, not impossibly—such was the wide sweep of that dazzling yet capacious intellect— with an ulterior design of reaching Persia and descending on India by the Euphrates. He was, however, baffled by English energy in an attempt to secure a hold on the coast; and having, to his bitter disappointment, raised the siege of Acre, he was forced to retrace his steps to Egypt. He was before long assailed by the Turkish hordes sent by *He fails at Acre, March to May, 1799.* the Porte to assure his overthrow; but he defeated them with terrific carnage; and having reached the seaboard, not far from the spot where he had disembarked more than twelve months before, he received intelligence for the first time of the great reverses of 1799. His resolution was taken at once; and if ambition was his ruling motive, it is puerile to charge him with fear and per-

of the Commons in France, which became famous, was returned to the States-General in 1789. His courage, however, was not equal to his intellect, and he sank into nothingness during the most stormy times of the Revolution. Having joined the party which overthrew Robespierre, he afterwards became one of the Directory, and promoted the Revolution of the 18th Brumaire. He sank into inglorious wealth and repose during the Empire, and lived to see Louis XVIII. restored to the throne.

On hearing the news of the state of France, he leaves Egypt.

fidy. He gave his command to Kleber, his well-tried lieutenant, his army being at the moment safe, and even without an enemy at hand; and he set off without delay for France, where, he rightly conjectured, his presence was sought, and where, too, such a man was wanting. He landed in October, 1799, on the shores of Provence, having fortunately slipped through the English fleets; and his landing, when known, became the signal for a burst of national and heartfelt welcome which revealed the instincts of the great mass of Frenchmen. At every stage on his way to Paris he was greeted by enthusiastic crowds, as the last hope of France in her hour of misfortune; and the feelings of the soldiery rose to the height of fanaticism at the sight of their well-known leader. In the capital the excitement was intense; the populace and the garrison openly hailed the conqueror of Italy as the Chief of the State; and even the Councils and the Directory, swept along by the vehement tide of opinion, felt or feigned reverence and exultation.

Enthusiasm with which he is received on his way to and in Paris.

He at once becomes the real centre of power.

In this state of affairs the existing government could not continue for any length of time. Within a few days Bonaparte had become the real centre of political power; all parties, except the extreme Republicans, who instinctively felt he was a deadly enemy, and especially the new aristocracy of riches, gathered around him with anxiety and hope; and the chiefs of the Army readily concurred, although divided by mutual jealousies. Two of the Directors, Siéyès being one, belonging to the enlightened Moderates, assented to the Revolution visibly impending; and a majority of the Ancients agreed to second another *coup d'état* in the interest of Bonaparte. That leader, who with his wonted insight had seemed to keep aloof, and had bided his time, now made his preparations for the crisis at hand; and if his acts were marked by stratagem and guile, they were not stained by the cruelty and blood which had hitherto been the disgrace of similar changes. On the allegation of a Jacobin plot in Paris, the Ancients voted, on the 18th Brumaire (November 9, 1799), that both the Councils should repair to St. Cloud, the object being to deprive the Legislature of the means of resistance, and to dissolve it quietly. Meanwhile, the garrison of the capital had been gained; watches had been placed on the National Guards, and the Heads of the long powerless Commune, in order to prevent a further outbreak; the habitation of Barras, Gohier, and Moulins, the three Directors, not in the secret, was surrounded by troops; and Siéyès and his colleague Ducos broke up the government by a formal resignation of the offices they held. Bonaparte was thus made suddenly master of Paris, with the soldiery and its leaders devoted to him; and as all that he had done was welcomed by the immense majority of the citizens, his easy triumph appeared assured. Of all Powers, however, a popular assembly most keenly resents an act of indignity; and the Council of Five Hundred, when it found itself deceived and decoyed away on a mere pretext, broke out in fierce and threatening complaints, though largely composed of the very party which secretly desired a change in the State. On the following day, Bonaparte appeared at St. Cloud, "to explain," as he said, "his conduct;" but he was met with exclamations of hatred and terror; and for a moment his position was critical, for the

He prepares a coup d'état to change the government.

The 18th Brumaire, Nov. 9, 1799.

Scenes in Assembly at St. Cloud.

guard around the Assembly wavered. The die, however, had been cast; the president of the Five Hundred, Lucien, a brother of Bonaparte, declared the Council lawfully dissolved; the hall was cleared by armed men of hostile deputies, and a sufficient number remained to sanction the already accomplished transfer of power. A provisional government was next appointed; but though it was composed of three consuls, two being Siéyès and his facile colleague, Bonaparte, as First Consul, was really supreme.

Formation of a provisional government. Bonaparte First Consul.

Such was the *coup d'état* of the 18th Brumaire, one of the principal events in the French Revolution, and, indeed, in the annals of modern Europe. The Republic was to exist for a time in name, as the Roman Senate survived Pharsalia; but though the truth was veiled under decent forms, the new Cæsar was everything from the first; and history before long was to repeat itself, and to see the rise of a Cæsarian empire. In overthrowing the existing government of France, Bonaparte, doubtless, acted without scruple, and was not superior to ambitious selfishness; and in the snare he laid for the Five Hundred—an unwise deception, which provoked to anger an assembly really not hostile—we see that contempt of popular sentiment, and of everything associated with popular forces, which was a distinctive mark of his character, and one of the most striking defects in it. But the Catos who denounce Brumaire as a crime and an "assassination of French liberty" simply misunderstand or distort facts; and views such as these entirely miss the true nature of the French Revolution. Bonaparte had really France on his side

Character of the Revolution of the 18th Brumaire

Reflections on the conduct of Bonaparte and on the march of events.

in thrusting the Directors from their seats, and merely accelerated the course of events which had long pointed to military rule; and History can fairly say for him that the Dictatorship he seized was perhaps needed, was certainly the choice of the French People, and, as he truly boasted, "cost not a drop of blood." As for the "liberty" which he has been charged with destroying, it was a mere figment without real existence; and he could not have struck the Republic down had it had a root in the national heart. In fact, the Revolution, in its whole course, had been unfavorable to the growth of true popular rights and of republican institutions in any real sense; and the nature of events and the disposition of Frenchmen had concurred to produce that despotism of the sword of which Bonaparte was only the most splendid image. It would have been a task of extraordinary difficulty to have founded anything like freedom upon the corruption of the old Monarchy; and the Legislation of the National Assembly, and the passions generated in the war that followed, only led to anarchy and tyranny combined. As for the Republic, it was the mere offspring of passion; and, after the experience of the Reign of Terror, a reaction against it quickly set in, which, notwithstanding all the Directory could have done, would have proved irresistible in the course of time. Besides, in the actual state of France and Europe, a Republic which required the nurture of peace could hardly have acquired in any case stability; the short-lived Republic which was set up soon yielded to the influence of the sword; and, tried among a people ill suited to it by temperament and historical tradition, it could, perhaps, only end in failure. The proneness of Frenchmen to bow to power and to admire military grandeur and suc-

The coup d'état was not a crime.

cess hastened the Revolution already at hand, when a crisis of national danger appeared; and the Hour, when it came, found a Man who satisfied the wants, the hopes, and the fancy of the Nation. In these circumstances the 18th Brumaire can be hardly matter of surprise or censure, though in the suddenness of the Revolution itself we see another proof of the passionate mobility and changeableness of the French character.

CHAPTER X.

MARENGO. LUNEVILLE. AMIENS.

Wise and healing policy of the First Consul. THE first care of the new ruler of France—the ascendency of Bonaparte was at once complete—was in some measure to restore the finances, the condition of which had become deplorable. The First Consul had brought to this task a resolute will, a commanding intellect, and a faculty of organization perhaps never surpassed; and enjoyed advantages, to carry out his object, beyond the reach of the fallen government. The moneyed classes, who had given him support in the Revolution which had placed him in power, advanced readily considerable funds to supply the needs of the exhausted treasury; and, as the resources of France were really immense, trade revived and the revenue increased at the first sign of order and *Financial reforms.* confidence. The government, however, had recourse to other means to place the finances on a better footing, and to some extent to improve public credit. Bonaparte obtained the services of a very able man, who had refused to hold office from the Directory; and under the skilful care of Gaudin—a minister of real capacity and worth—a series of admirable reforms were begun in the whole financial system of the State. The iniquitous forced tax on the rich was abolished; and while the direct taxes which since 1789 had formed the only ordinary sources of supply were distributed and raised with a regard to justice, an attempt—feeble indeed, and tentative at first, but ultimately leading to marked results—was made to return to some of the indirect taxes, which had been recklessly and unfairly removed in the transports of revolutionary passion. At the same time a thorough change was made in the mode of collecting the public imposts, which had been wasteful and offensive alike ; and, by arrangements in some degree borrowed from the practice of the old Monarchy, but modified and improved by modern experience, receipts were rendered more quick and certain, while considerable sums were immediately obtained from the new officials who had become collectors. Provision was also made for the payment of the debt, or rather what remained of it, which had been unpaid for a considerable time, and before long national insolvency had ceased. The surviving Jacobins and extreme Republicans complained truly that more than one of these measures had too much in common with the old order of things; but with the First Consul this was an idle objection, and these reforms were alike judicious and able. Sufficient means were in this way obtained to satisfy the most pressing wants of the State, and especially to relieve the armies, the distress of which had become lamentable; and the foundations were laid of financial order. The

First Consul, however, went much further; and, as soon as he had secured power, he endeavored to bind up the wounds of the Nation, and to mitigate the animosities which distracted France. His position and the accidents of his life contributed largely to serve his purpose; for, as authority really centered in his hands, and he had taken no part in the Revolution, it had become possible, especially in the comparative quiescence of the passions of the past, to carry out a policy at once more equable, more firm, and of a more conciliatory nature than the Directory or Convention could have attempted. The benefits he conferred in this respect on France from the first moment do not admit of question. His attention was directed to the clergy first, who, as we have seen, had been an object of jealousy and proscription for many years, and had been persecuted with fresh rigor after a brief instant of illusory clemency. The First Consul, until the time should arrive for a permanent settlement of ecclesiastical affairs, procured the repeal of the most severe laws of the Revolution against the Catholic priesthood; and he weakened a source of sacerdotal hate by substituting for the irritating test imposed by the National Assembly a simple oath of allegiance to the State, to be taken by clergymen of all descriptions. This wise policy made good subjects of thousands of men who had hitherto used their influence against the whole course of the Revolution since 1789; and as ministers of religion of all kinds were not only tolerated but even encouraged, while perfect freedom of conscience remained, the fierce dissensions lessened to some extent which had been so grievous in this particular. The next soothing measure of the First Consul was to abolish many of the sanguinary decrees indiscriminately passed against the *émigrés* in a mass, and to extend an amnesty to certain classes of them; and in this manner a number of exiles who hitherto had fought in the ranks of her foes began to return to France, to support the new government, and to detach themselves from the Bourbon cause. Finally, the troubles which had arisen in La Vendée were appeased, to a considerable extent, by recurring to the judicious policy of Hoche, carried out with a firm yet clement hand; and though one or two severe examples were made, the system of moderation was the general rule. *Pacification of La Vendée.*

By these prudent and just measures the State, which seemed in hopeless decline, regained speedily new life and vigor; and France was restored in a few months to an extent which might have been thought impossible. Meanwhile the task of framing a new constitution for the still nominal Republic had been given to Siéyès, the ablest of the makers of systems who had been so numerous in the Revolution. It would be hardly necessary to notice the results of this work, which left the greatest changes of 1789, now beyond recall, entirely intact, and merely substituted a new State machinery for that which had been swept away, if it were not that the "Constitution of the year VIII."—this was the name of the new political growth—illustrated curiously the cast of thought now prevalent among men of experience in France, and supplied some of the illusory forms which concealed the power of the new Chief of the State. *Rapid recovery of France.*

The real objects of Siéyès were to maintain popular rule in appearance, and yet to curb the excesses of popular license, and at once to create a strong government, and to guard against *Constitution of the year VIII.*

the irregular tyranny of which he had seen such frightful examples. For this purpose, in strange contrast with the ideas of not many years before, his scheme preserved an image of popular rights, and declared that Sovereignty belonged to the people; but it confined the whole administration of the State, even in its lowest departments, to certain lists of citizens, and it distributed the Legislative and Executive powers between a council of State and a Tribunate, charged respectively to propose and discuss all measures, a Legislative Assembly the duty of which was to enact laws without the agitation of debates, a Senate to nominate to all great offices, and a Grand Elector and two Consuls to govern under all kinds of restrictions. By these means the ingenious designer imagined that he would reconcile democracy with stability, order, and political freedom; but it is unnecessary to say that his pretty system found little favor in the sight of the ruler of France. Bonaparte allowed the limitations on popular rights in the choice of functionaries to continue for a time; and he approved of the silent Legislature and the divided duties of the Tribunate and the Council of State; for such an arrangement, he clearly saw, weakened any influence these bodies could possess. But he insisted on curtailing the privileges of the Senate, and in removing checks on the Executive power; and he placed himself, with the title of First Consul, and with absolute control over the whole scheme of government, in the stead of the Grand Elector and his two dependents. The dictatorship of the First Consul was to last for ten years, and a second and third consul, mere shadowy names, were to veil the reality of a single ruler.

In this way the despotism of one man, surrounded by merely nominal restraints, became definitely established in France, and the supremacy of Bonaparte was consecrated by law. The Constitution received the sanction of an enthusiastic popular vote, significant of the national instincts and character; and before long Siéyès and his late brother Director gave way to two new consuls, who, though able men, were merely the willing agents of power. The government of France, however, at this juncture was only a small part of the First Consul's task; he had, if possible, to repair the disasters of war, and to roll back the Coalition from the frontiers. These cares had, of course, engaged his thoughts as soon as the reins of power had come into his hands; and, supported by a strong national sentiment, and by able and skilful lieutenants, and employing the growing resources of the State with absolute authority and consummate art, he soon reorganized the shattered armies and revived the military strength of France. One circumstance was of happy omen to him, for the Czar, after the defeat at Zurich, had ordered Suwarrow to return home; and thus the forces of the Allies were reduced by a large contingent of hardy warriors. The German Empire and England, however, remained in the field; and while an army of considerable but inferior strength threatened Alsace from Western Bavaria, Austria had assembled a very powerful force to secure the conquests she had made in Italy, and having reduced the Italian fortresses still garrisoned by weak French detachments, to invade the borders of Dauphiny and Provence. In this state of affairs the First Consul formed a plan of operations which has been always

His despotism is established, surrounded by merely nominal restraints.

Reorganization of the French armies.

Plans of the First Consul.

N

thought one of the most dazzling of his military conceptions. The force of the enemy in Bavaria was not so great as it ought to have been, regard being had to the whole theatre of war; and the great Austrian host on the western verge of Italy was dangerously exposed on this secondary frontier, to an attack from Switzerland, which projected, like a huge natural bastion, along its flanks and rear. Bonaparte, accordingly, arrayed a force superior to that in its front in Bavaria, which was to descend rapidly from the heads of the Rhine, and, under Moreau, to take the foe in reverse; while he prepared secretly a second army, with which, concealing his design to the last moment, he resolved to cross the great Swiss Alps, and to fall on the Austrians and cut off their retreat.

The campaign of 1800. Operations began on both sides in the spring of 1800 on the theatre of war. Leaving Ott to undertake the siege of Genoa, and covering his line of retreat with a large scattered force, Melas, the Austrian commander-in-chief in Italy, advanced to the Var and had soon taken Nice. Meanwhile, Moreau had set his army in motion; and though too timid to carry out the project of striking his enemy in the rear by crossing the Rhine at its heads at Schaffhausen, he had nevertheless invaded Bavaria, forced back his weaker antagonist Kray, and, as had been agreed on, was able to send a considerable detachment across the St. Gothard, to cooperate with the First Consul. That great commander had in the interval drawn together gradually from all parts of France the troops intended for the decisive stroke; and he screened the movement with such skill that the Austrians believed it was nothing more than the preparation of a levy of conscripts. By the middle of May 50,000 men, ready for the field, were on the Swiss frontier, and everything had been arranged with clear forethought for overcoming the great barrier before them. Sending a column by the ordinary pass by Mont Cenis to deceive the enemy as long as possible, the First Consul directed the mass of his army over the Great St. Bernard; and from May 16 to May 19, the solitudes of the vast mountain tract echoed to the din and tumult of war as the French soldiery swept over its heights to reach the valley of the Po and the plains of Lombardy. A hill fort, for a time, stopped the daring invaders, but the obstacle was passed by an ingenious stratagem; and before long Bonaparte, exulting in hope, was marching from the verge of Piedmont on Milan, having made a demonstration against Turin, in order to hide his real purpose. By June 2 the whole French army, joined by the reinforcement sent by Moreau, was in possession of the Lombard capital, and threatened the line of its enemy's retreat, having successfully accomplished the first part of the brilliant design of its great leader. *The First Consul crosses the Alps May 16—19, 1800.* *The French army enters Milan, June 2.*

While Bonaparte was thus descending from the Alps, the Austrian commander had been pressing forward the siege of Genoa and his operations on the Var. Masséna, however, stubbornly held out in Genoa; and Suchet had defended the defiles of Provence with a weak force with such marked skill that his adversary had made little progress. When first informed of the terrible apparition of a hostile army gathering upon his rear, Melas disbelieved what he thought impossible; and when he could no longer discredit what he heard, the movements by Mont Cenis and against Turin, intended to perplex him, had made him hesitate. As soon, however, as the real design of the First Consul was fully revealed, the brave Austrian chief resolved to force his way to the Adige at any cost; and, directing Ott to raise the siege of Genoa, and leaving a subordinate to hold Suchet in check, he began to draw his divided army together, in order to make a desperate attack on the audacious foe upon his line of retreat. Ott, however, delayed some days to receive the keys of Genoa, which fell after a defence memorable in the annals of war; and, as the Austrian forces had been widely scattered, it was June 12 before fifty thousand men were assembled for an offensive movement round the well-known fortresses of Alessandria. Meanwhile, the First Consul had broken up from Milan; and whether ill-informed of his enemy's operations, or apprehensive that, after the fall of Genoa, Melas would escape by a march southwards, he had advanced from a strong position he had taken between the Ticino, the Adda, and the Po, and had crossed the Scrivia into the plains of Marengo, with forces disseminated far too widely. Melas boldly seized the opportunity to escape from the weakened meshes of the net thrown round him; and attacked Bonaparte on the morning of June 14 with a vigor and energy which did him honor. The battle raged confusedly for several hours; but the French had begun to give way and fly, when the arrival of an isolated division on the field, and the unexpected charge of a small body of horsemen, suddenly changed defeat into a brilliant victory. The importance was then seen of the commanding position of Bonaparte on the rear of his foe; the Austrian army, its retreat cut off, was obliged to come to terms after a single reverse; and within a few days an armistice was signed by which Italy to the Mincio was restored to the French, and the disasters of 1799 were effaced.

The French recover Italy.

This splendid success has been always considered one of the most wonderful of its author's achievements. Yet, though the daring passage of the Alps was a military combination of the highest order, carried out generally with the greatest skill, the movements of Bonaparte in this campaign hardly equalled those of 1796, and the march on Marengo gives proof of that over-confidence and sanguine ardor which were the chief defects in his genius for war. While Italy had been regained at one stroke, the campaign in Germany had progressed slowly; and though Moreau was largely superior in force, he had met more than one check near Ulm, on the Danube. The stand, however, made ably by Kray, could not lessen the effects of Marengo; and Austria, after that terrible reverse, endeavored to negotiate with the dreaded conqueror. Bonaparte, however, following out a purpose which he had already made a maxim of policy, and resolved if possible to divide the Coalition, refused to treat with Austria jointly with England, except on conditions known to be futile; and after a pause of a few weeks hostilities were resumed with increased energy. By this time, however, the French armies had acquired largely preponderating strength; and while Brune advanced victoriously to the Adige—the First Consul had returned to the seat of government—Moreau in Bavaria marched on the rivers which, descending from the Alps to the Danube, form one of the bulwarks of the Austrian Monarchy. He was attacked incautiously by the Archduke John—the Archduke Charles, who ought to have been in command, was in temporary disgrace at the Court—and soon afterwards he won a great battle at Hohenlinden, between the Iser and the Inn, the success of the French being complete and decisive, though the conduct of their chief has not escaped criticism. This last disaster proved overwhelming, and Austria and the States of the Empire were forced to submit to the terms of Bonaparte. After a brief delay peace was made at Luneville in February 1801 ; and the glorious provisions of Campo Formio were ratified and extended in the interests of France. The principle of the French " natural boundaries " was confirmed again by a second cession of Belgium and the western bank of the Rhine; and the young Republics created in Italy—they had remained true to their allegiance to France—were, save at Rome and Naples, set up again, and recognized by Austria, although the objects of the bitter aversion she naturally felt for what represented revolution and defeat. The Grand Duke of Tuscany, an Austrian prince, was in addition deprived of his duchy, to be conferred on an Infant of Spain, a Power now wholly dependent on France ; and the First Consul pursued the system of secularizing, as it is called, the great German Bishoprics, in order to satisfy the greed of Prussia, to bind her more closely to the French alliance, and effectually to divide Germany. The Pope, however, was recalled to Rome, as the First Consul had need of his support in a great measure already impending ; and, at the intercession of Russia, Naples was spared, and hopes were held out to the dethroned King of Sardinia. In negotiating this treaty, which not only assured to France the coveted boundary of the Rhine, but made her dominant over half the Continent, Bonaparte had shown the art of the young General of 1796, and the same contempt of revolutionary principles. But he had assumed a more dictatorial tone, and hardly a trace of the moderation remained of which he had given proof when his power was uncertain. The change was felt, and it was generally perceived by the representatives of the old Powers of Europe that the ambition and craft of the military genius who ruled France might be at least as dangerous as the propaganda of Republican liberty. England was now again left alone to contend against the State which had twice defeated Europe; and many circumstances concurred to make her wish to give up the struggle, at least for a time. Her ascendency on the sea had become as evident as that of her antagonist on land. She had swept the fleets of France from the ocean, and conquered most of the French and Dutch colonies ; and, in the existing state of the world, the rival nations could not find a theatre for a decisive encounter. Mr. Pitt, too, had retired from power; the continuance of the war had become unpopular, and even the Tory majority in the two Houses felt that an interval of repose would be welcome. Events hastened the consummation to which things had been of late tending. An English force had landed in Egypt, and, retrieving years of military discredit, had compelled the veteran army of Bonaparte to capitulate after a gallant struggle, and Egypt had been definitely lost to France. On the other hand, the First Consul had combined a formidable league against England, headed by the maritime Powers of the North ; and though this alliance was quickly dissolved, it caused apprehension not lessened by the failure of Nelson to destroy a French flotilla off the coast of Boulogne. After long negotiations peace was signed at Amiens, in March 1802, France retaining all her continental conquests and recovering some of her colonies, England keeping Ceylon and Trinidad; and though statesmen felt that it was only a truce, the two nations rejoiced that the sword had been sheathed. One article in the treaty, bitterly discussed, was soon to become of unhappy importance. Malta had been wrested by our fleets from the French; and it was stipulated that the great fortress should be restored to its original possessors, on the condition, however, perfectly understood, that France was not to make fresh annexations in Europe.

March-April 1801.

Treaty of Amiens, March 27, 1802.

Great results obtained by the First Consul.

In this way the most dreaded enemy of France retired from a contest of nine years, and the supremacy of her rival on the Continent was confirmed. The Peace of Amiens was immediately followed by a general pacification of Europe; and the ruler of France stood before the world encompassed by a fresh halo of glory and renown. Within the space of a year and a half that wonderful man had raised France from what seemed hopeless prostration and anarchy, had given her order, allayed her troubles, revived her strength, and struck down her foes; and he had consolidated her triumphs by a series of treaties which made her arbiter of the finest part of Europe. The prospect was magnificent, and appeared serene; but would the warrior who had gathered in his hands the stormy forces of the Revolution, pause in the intoxicating career of victory? Would not the confusion and change of Europe offer to his ambition a perilous field; would not the animosities of defeated Powers come into fierce collision with his imperious rule and the order of things which he wished to establish ; would not the despotism he was inaugurating in France, though, perhaps, inevitable in her present state, accelerate the tendency to foreign conquest which she had displayed for several years?

CHAPTER XI.

THE CONSULATE. RENEWAL OF WAR.

DURING the period which followed the Peace of Amiens,* the First Consul had leisure to make great changes in the internal government of France, to carry out the policy of

Internal Government of the First Consul.

* M. Thiers, in the *Histoire du Consulat et de l'Empire*, has described in the minutest detail, and with a masterly hand, the internal Government and the foreign and domestic policy of Napoleon. This work should be studied for its copious information; but in peace as in war the brilliant author surrounds his ideal with deceptive splendor. M. Lanfrey, in his *Histoire de Napoleon I.*, has said all that could be said on the other side, and has painted the vices and mischiefs of Napoleon's despotism, and the faults of the Emperor's character, with much skill and power. The *Commentaries*, and especially the *Correspondence* of Napoleon, show what he was as a ruler and administrator as well as a warrior, and the works of MM. Bignon and Fain may also be consulted. The correspondence of Lords Grenville, Wellesley, Sidmouth, and Castlereagh, of Mr. Pitt and Mr. Fox, and the *Memoirs* of Prince Hardenberg, show what Napoleon's régime appeared to English and German statesmen ; and Alison's *History*, though disfigured by party views, contains a full account of the Consular and Imperial system of Government.

reconstruction, and of moderating and reconciling the remains of factions begun after the 18th Brumaire, and at the same time to increase his own domination, and to weaken whatever seemed hostile to it. His measures of reform and pacification had already been followed by good results, but many of the institutions of the country he ruled, and its social frame in some of its parts, were shattered, distorted, and out of joint, after the frightful shock of the Revolution; and an opportunity was afforded him to reconstitute the polity of France in several respects, to leave a permanent mark on it, and to influence powerfully the national life, in what he conceived the interests of the State, and in furtherance certainly of his own objects. Bonaparte, as we have already said, in consequence of the antecedents of his career, and of the firm hold he preserved of power, was in many particulars fitted for this work; his great ability gave him some qualifications for it, and what was more important, the circumstances of the time concurred largely to serve his purpose. The Revolution had now permanently set free the soil, had removed mischievous restrictions on trade, had relieved Frenchmen of feudal shackles, had secured a general equality of rights more real than the fanciful Rights of Man, and had laid the foundations of a material prosperity which was to become equally brilliant and solid; and terrible as its devastations had been, these blessings were great and were to prove lasting. But while in the highest places of government it had ended only in a long succession of weakness and oppression, for the present closed by a splendid but weighty despotism of the sword, it had also left considerable parts of the national organization a mere chaos; and order, tranquillity, and reform were

The time favorable for reconstructing society in France.

1802-3. *The Consulate. Renewal of War.* 187

needed in the administrative system, and the ecclesiastical and even social arrangements of the long disturbed and agitated country. At the same time the gradual subsidence of past animosities had grown more evident; the desire for repose had become supreme in the extinction of political hopes and passions; the one thought of the numerous classes which had gained advantage from the Revolution was to disregard its ideals and to reap its benefits under a regimen of settled authority and law; except a few royalists and extreme anarchists, all parties accepted facts as they were; and the Nation, entranced by the spell of glory, and grateful also for splendid services, looked up to Bonaparte with unthinking confidence. A great field lay open to the First Consul, and the soil was ready for his strong hands to turn.

The attention of Bonaparte was first directed to the whole internal administration of the State. The reforms effected in the finances had restored credit and assured the revenue; and the causes were not in operation yet which in this respect were to lead alike to illusory prosperity and real exhaustion. But almost everywhere else, disorder prevailed; and if much that the First Consul did has been censured by able thinkers, many of his creations have obtained the sanction of national approval and have become permanent. One of his chief cares was to accomplish a change in the general judicial system of France, which the National Assembly had, with strange unwisdom, exposed to the evils of popular election, and which now required a thorough amendment. The appointment of judges was properly secured, as in England, to the Executive government; justice was brought nearer home to all Frenchmen by increasing the number of in- *Reforms in the State.*

The Judicial system.

ferior judges; and uniformity in the distribution of rights was obtained by establishing a series of appellate tribunals, in some degree resembling the old Parliaments, but with a better and modern procedure. This important reform, in which we again see the ancient Monarchy imitated and improved, was certainly marred by the institution of special courts for political offences; but it must be recollected that a system of this kind had at all times existed in France, and never was so fearfully abused as during the period of the Revolution.

The Code. The next great work of the First Consul was to give the Nation the one general Code which the National Assembly had projected, and the Convention had endeavored to begin; and in a few months, under his energetic impulse, the medley of usages and written observances, confused, uncertain, and huge in bulk, which had formed the canon of rights in France, were fused into a harmonious body of laws, the real merit of which is seen by their extension over a great part of Europe, though their genius is in many respects despotic. This noble achievement was of course, in the main, the task of professional lawyers; but Bonaparte may claim to have been its chief author, and in some places even the text of the Code bears the mark of his keen and powerful intellect. Perhaps, however, the most notable of the internal changes Centralization of local powers. made at this time was the Revolution which the First Consul wrought in the arrangement of local powers in the State, and the relations of these with the supreme government. The Convention had, as we have seen, limited the extravagant authority given by the National Assembly to local bodies which had proved so mischievous in the Revolution, and Bonaparte carried to the furthest extent the principle of

1802-3. *The Consulate. Renewal of War.*

restriction and compression. The powers of the provincial and municipal Assemblies were almost everywhere wholly suppressed; the influence of the Communes, including that of Paris, already curtailed, was reduced to nothingness; the National Guards were made simply a submissive appendage of the Army; and France in local affairs was practically ruled by a bureaucracy of sub-prefects and prefects, in close dependence on the central government, and in many respects with a strong resemblance to the royal intendants of the Bourbon Monarchy. Prefects and sub-prefects.

The next great measure of the First Consul was the renewal, under altered conditions, of that alliance between the State and the Church, which had existed in France since the dark ages. He had, as we have said, on his advent to power, put an end to the persecution of the clergy; but after the events of past years, confusion prevailed in all parts of the Church, and its relations with the people and the government alike were jarring, irregular, and ill-defined. A bitter feud divided the nonjuring priesthood from those who had taken the oath of 1790-91, and communicated itself to their flocks everywhere; and as the great majority of the bishops were *émigrés*, and many of their Sees had become vacant, whole districts were without the episcopal rule which is an essential part of Roman Catholic discipline. Besides, France had been under a kind of interdict since the property of the Church had been swept away, and the position of its ministers changed by the Legislation of the National Assembly; and the open disfavor of the Holy See had added to ecclesiastical disorders, been a source of real weakness to the State, and shocked the consciences of millions of Frenchmen. In
The Concordat.

this state of things the First Consul, after long negotiations with the Papal Court, at present really well-inclined to him, obtained what was called a Concordat with Rome, the first of many arrangements of the kind, which in some measure at least reconciled the ecclesiastical and civil powers in France, allayed many of the troubles of the Church, and at once bound it up with the new order of affairs and placed it under the control of the government. By this famous compromise, complete freedom to all sects was permanently assured; the confiscations of the Church lands were confirmed; the number of Sees in France was greatly reduced, and their occupants, with the whole body of clergy, were made simply pensioners of the State; and the supreme authority of the civil ruler in ecclesiastical matters was solemnly asserted. But on the other hand the Catholic religion was declared that of the Nation as a whole, its organization was upheld by law, and its teachers given a recognized rank; and if the Church lost finally its ancient pretensions, and was associated with a Revolutionary State, its internal condition was rendered secure by the support and favor accorded to it, and the strife within it was greatly lessened by the complete equality with which its Ministers, whatever their antecedents, were always treated. The re-establishment of the Church in France, and its restoration to a place in the State, were celebrated by religious ceremonies at which Bonaparte assisted in person; and—strange spectacle in that age of wonders—the aisles of Notre Dame, where a few years before the Goddess of Reason, in the midst of Revolutionary worshippers, held her orgies, echoed once more to the sacred services of the most mystic form of the Christian faith at the bidding of a revolutionary soldier.

It may be doubted whether the Concordat <small>Its effects.</small> has ultimately advanced religion in France, while it has placed the Church and all spiritual affairs in complete subjection to the secular arm. It tended, however, to restore order, to allay discord, and to promote peace; and if it enlarged the influence of the new ruler, it is too much to say that he had no other motive. The Concordat was followed by a scheme of public instruction which also extended the power of <small>Public Instruction.</small> the government over the Nation by putting intellect under the control of the State; but here also it is unfair to assert that this was the sole object of the First Consul. The general effect of the various measures of which we have faintly <small>General results of these reforms.</small> traced the outline was to improve extremely the administration of affairs, to diffuse tranquillity, and upon the whole to contribute to the national welfare; and if some of these reforms, especially the return to centralization in local government, have had evil results of their own, and if they certainly made despotism more wide-spread and universally felt, they have almost all survived to this day, and have satisfied the wants of the great body of Frenchmen. The First Consul, however, took other means to consolidate his sway which we must briefly notice. His <small>Changes in the army.</small> authority rested ultimately of course on the instrument by which he had attained power, and he not only improved the discipline and organization of the French Army, but in a great measure transformed its spirit, overcame the jealousies of its chiefs which had made themselves more than ever apparent, and converted into enthusiastic devotion to himself its National and Revolutionary instincts. But like all soldiers who have displayed capacity as rulers for political affairs, he concealed the omnipotence of the sword in the State, and he endeavored to obtain support for his government from the elements of civil life in the Nation by associa-ting it with a great mass of interests created by, and dependent on, himself. For this purpose, while he generally maintained the equality of Frenchmen before the law, he gradually formed out of the official classes, which he multiplied in every conceivable way, an aristocracy of a new type; and he tried by every means in his power to amalgamate it with whatever remained of the aristocracy which the Revolution had spared. To accomplish this object he introduced again all kinds of distinctions in social life—the Legion of Honor was the most remarkable—and at last ventured on restoring titles; and by these means he no doubt strengthened the attachment to himself of the upper orders of Frenchmen who had risen to influence through the Revolution, and even allied them to some extent with the thinned relics of the old Noblesse; though this new patriciate, as has always happened in similar cases, was a poor creation, unstable, untrustworthy, and little respected. Before long he effected another great change, which indicated whither events were tending. The Consulate for ten years became one for life; the authority of the Senate, composed of the creatures of the new ruler, was at once augmented and made more to depend on his will; and while the restrictions on the popular voice invented by Siéyès were nominally lessened, the Tribunate which had offered a show of opposition on several occasions to the autocrat in power, was reduced in numbers, carefully weeded, and practically merged in the mute Legislative Body. This "reform of the constitution" of the year VIII., which made Cæsarian despotism perfect, was, as before, sanctioned by a general vote of an overwhelming majority of Frenchmen.

Modification in a despotic sense of the Constitution of the year VIII.

By these means the government of Bonaparte became essentially the domination of one man, well ordered, spreading itself everywhere, gathering to itself all the forces in the State, shaping and controlling the national life, and surrounded by a gradation of powers and a set of influences which gave it a support. A considerable part of the new mechanism of the State had much in common with the ancient system which the National Assembly had tried to destroy for ever; but though a certain resemblance existed, the rule of Bonaparte, in most essential points, differed widely from that of the Bourbon Monarchy; for if it was more despotic and sometimes oppressive, it was more national, and on the whole just. Its great and fatal evils of course were that it left everything to the will of one man, that it was wholly inconsistent with anything like liberty, that it more or less weakened the national energies, even when apparently most beneficent; that it was, at best, attended with precarious good, and might issue in grievous mischiefs; that, in a word, even in its most brilliant form, it was despotism with all the resulting perils. The Dictatorship, however, of the First Consul, vicious though it was as a scheme of government and destined to end in terrible misfortune, had nevertheless the real excellences that it secured internal quiet to the State and gave France a variety of institutions which have stood the infallible test of time, and that it alike protected the order of things which had grown up under the Revolution, and recon-

Partial Resemblance of the new Government to that of the Monarchy.

Its evils.

Its merits.

O

ciled it in some degree with the past; and it is for this, among other reasons, that it remains dear to the memory of Frenchmen. As the administration of Bonaparte at home was generally at this period moderate, the benefits that followed were almost unmixed. He, indeed, showed himself implacably severe to the remaining dregs of the Jacobin faction; and more than once treated with unsparing tyranny those whom he called the "men of the September massacres." But he went on steadily with the auspicious work of reconciling and moderating parties; and he finally closed the list of the *émigrés*, and admitted numbers of the exiles into the service of the State. At the same time the noble system of public works which have illustrated his era was set on foot; the canals and roads which had been the pride of the ancient Monarchy, and for many years had been in a state of decay, were restored; and new towns springing up in La Vendée, the capital adorned with magnificent buildings, and the Alps spanned by vast military lines, attested the energy of the chief to whom France had committed her fate.

Wise Administration of the First Consul.

Meanwhile Bonaparte already wearing, as it was said, "the shadow of a kingly crown," promoted carefully, by indirect means, the domination he had directly established, and hastened the movement towards monarchy which had been visible even before his time. He abolished the ceremonies in which the Republic commemorated the execution of Louis XVI., and caused the remains of Turenne—the great hero warrior of the most glorious days of Louis XIV., which even Jacobin frenzy had spared, though during the excesses of the Reign of Terror it had desecrated the rest of the Bourbon kings—to be transported solemnly to the Invalides, and buried with

He encourages the movement towards Monarchy.

1802-3. *The Consulate. Renewal of War.* 195

extraordinary pomp. He had already taken up his abode at the Tuileries, and effaced the marks which revolutionary passion or republican frenzy had left on the spot; and he held what really was a Court, with its accessories of etiquette and splendor, in that seat of fallen yet not forgotten royalty. At the same time he adopted a regal style in his correspondence with foreign Powers; and though in his relations with the Bodies of the State he preserved forms of simple equality, and spoke and bore himself as a private citizen, he always appeared in Paris with a magnificent retinue, and flattered the populace with the display of grandeur. He also encouraged in every way the luxury and taste of the Bourbon days, and spoke with contempt to those in his confidence of the savageness of revolutionary manners and of the absurdity of republican ways; and in his serious moments he would often dwell on the instability of the institutions of France, on the necessity of settled power in an old State, on the evil effects of the philosophic theories—the ideology he scornfully called them—which had swayed the minds of men a few years previously. Nor were the tendencies of which he set an example less clearly apparent in the tone of general opinion, practice, and sentiment. France teemed with addresses shedding incense on "the new Saviour of social order;" and the Press, lately so anarchic and wild, but now controlled by a watchful police, poured forth homage in floods to greet the ruler who had "closed the terrible age of Revolution." In the same way the mimicry of Republican tastes which had been the mode of a short time before disappeared in the salons of the capital; the cant of classical liberty was heard no more; ladies put off the Ionic costume of the Aspasias and Phrynes, of Greek times; and military brilliancy, costly liveries, and

Change of manners in France.

the graces, the finery, and the frivolity of Versailles, showed themselves again in the new masquerade in which the high life of Paris and France figured. The First Consul had literally become the "mould of form" for nine-tenths of Frenchmen, and all France yielded to the spell of his influence.

<small>Foreign Policy of the First Consul.</small> While Bonaparte had been thus extending his sway, and reorganizing and transforming France, he had not been less active and stirring abroad. In his foreign relations at this period he pursued the policy of craft and interest inconsistent with the ideas of 1789, which had distinguished his earliest efforts, and he displayed an imperious will and grasping ambition; but if he gave proof of that lust for power and domination which was to end in ruin, it should be recollected that the circumstances of the time, and even the conduct of some foreign Powers, contributed to place him in the position he assumed. As if to show his contempt of Republican dreams, he made the Infant of Spain, whom he had chosen for the purpose, King of the ceded Grand Duchy of Tuscany; and in this manner he riveted a yoke already becoming difficult to bear, on the abject necks of the Spanish Bourbons. At the same time he annexed Piedmont to France, on the plea that the King had given up the throne; and though he checked revolutionary ideas in Italy, he made the Pope and King of Naples feel that they held their possessions at his will and pleasure. Meanwhile he increased the hold of France on her new conquests and dependent Republics; and, as might have been expected, he fashioned the offspring to the submission to himself which the parent displayed. As President he ruled the Cisalpine Republic, considerably enlarged by the treaty of Luneville,

<small>Its craft and ambition.</small>

1802-3. *The Consulate. Renewal of War.* 197

and given the general name of the Italian nation ; he managed Holland through a Constitution on the model of that existing in France, and though he left Switzerland nominally free, he practically controlled it as a French Province. The most remarkable advance in his power, however, arose from his intervention in Germany, due mainly to the quarrels of German potentates. The secularization of the Bishoprics, which had been a principle of the Peace of Luneville, led to angry contentions between the German Courts, each eager for a greater share of the spoil ; and Austria and Prussia made such exorbitant demands that the Sovereigns of the lesser States applied to the powerful ruler of France for aid. The First Consul gladly became a mediator, and secured a considerable increase of territory to Bavaria, Baden, and Würtemberg, while, to the extreme satisfaction of Prussian statesmen, he still further enlarged the bounds of Prussia with the view of strengthening her against Austria, thus following traditional French policy which he had made in a special way his own. In this manner the influence of France, great in Germany since the day of Richelieu, was increased in an extraordinary degree ; but if the policy of Bonaparte was hard and calculating, and Germans learned to lament the results, they might bear in mind who called in a protector when they indulge in homilies on French aggression.

French intervention in Germany.

In this way, in the midst of apparent peace, the domination of France was extended, and her ruler became the undisputed arbiter of Europe from the Baltic to the Mediterranean. It was impossible but that the growth of this power should vex and alarm the only State which had as yet contended successfully with

Great extension of French power and influence.

France; and English statesmen, who had perceived from the first that the peace of Amiens could not last long, began to apprehend that war was near. This was not the case, it was universally felt, of a Republic weak and distracted at home, though strong in its arms and ideas abroad, the existence of which was always precarious; it was that of a gigantic Despotism, directed and swayed by commanding genius, and all-powerful in France as well as in Europe; and Whigs and Tories equally agreed that the present state of the Continent was a danger to England. In this condition of feeling causes of dissension arose quickly between the two Powers: English politicians not unjustly complained of the enormous extension of French power and influence, and Bonaparte retaliated by denouncing the asylum given to conspirators against his rule in England, and the hostility of the English Press, of which the freedom shocked his despotic instincts. Meanwhile, on the ground of the virtual infraction of the treaty of Amiens by French ambition, Malta was not ceded at the time arranged; and recriminations on this subject ended in a scene of violence in which the First Consul, breaking out into a real or feigned passion, spoke menacingly to our envoy in Paris. The publication of a French State paper, revealing a design of regaining Egypt, increased the quickening elements of discord, and a kind of challenge which Bonaparte, with his usual scorn of popular forces, threw out generally to the English Nation, aroused an indignation impossible to allay. After fruitless negotiations touching Malta, which, though a principal occasion of the strife, had become merely an incident in it, war was renewed between the two countries; and in

Disputes with England. March to May, 1863.

Renewal of war with England May 18, 1803,

May, 1803, the great Powers of the West had again closed in mortal encounter. It is vain to measure the provocation on either side, though in view of the recent aggrandizement of France, the retention of Malta was not contrary to the real spirit of the treaty of Amiens, and though in defying the free opinion of England, the First Consul made a signal mistake which illustrates one of his chief defects as a politician. But if the war was, perhaps, inevitable—for the preponderance of France was perilous in the extreme to England, and this justifies the acts of our statesmen—the renewal of the contest was to be deplored. It was to end in frightful misfortune to France, after raising her to the summit of glory; it was to give England imperishable renown, indeed, and yet to expose her to terrible dangers, to retard her social progress for years, and to involve her in a system of politics with which her people could have no sympathy.

CHAPTER XII.

THE EMPIRE TO TILSIT.

THE new war between England and France was embittered by passion, and a death-struggle from the first. The First Consul now took up with ardor the idea of invading our shores, which he had considered premature a few years before; and he applied for months his commanding intellect to preparing the means of a formidable descent. Times had changed since he had advised the Directory to pause, and not to run the risk of the enterprise; he had

The First Consul plans a descent on England.

absolute control of the naval resources of France, Holland, and Italy, largely increased, with those of Spain soon to be added to them; his military forces overawed Europe, and nothing seemed too difficult for the daring warrior who had hardly met a check in his career of triumphs. Within a short time an immense flotilla, comprising more than two thousand boats, and light vessels with powerful guns, had been constructed along the seaboard extending from La Rochelle to Antwerp; and by degrees this menacing array was drawn together to the coast of Picardy, and, under the protection of miles of batteries, was collected in the narrowest part of the Channel, within sight of the white cliffs of Dover. Meanwhile troops had been marched in thousands from all parts of the dominions of France; and before long the country from Dunkirk to Etaples bristled with the camps of the warlike masses which had been marshalled for the great expedition. Boulogne, and the small adjoining ports, were chosen as the places of embarkation; and the arrangements of Bonaparte were so well laid that his whole army, with its vast material, could be moved on board in a few hours, and the flotilla could be made ready for sea within the space of a single tide. It was not the purpose, however, of this great commander to expose this armament, formidable as it appeared, without ample protection, to the English fleets; and to accomplish this object he matured designs which have always ranked among his ablest projects. He calculated that the English Admiralty, imagining that the descent would be tried with the powerfully armed flotilla alone, would guard the Channel chiefly with small vessels; and if so, it might become feasible, notwithstanding the naval

The flotilla and camp of Boulogne.

Project of covering the descent by a large fleet in the Channel.

strength of England, to bring a great fleet into the narrow seas, and under its cover, at the decisive point, to effect in safety the dangerous passage. For this purpose he planned a variety of schemes to draw away our squadrons from the waters of Europe, and to concentrate an armada of fifty sail of the line in the straits that divide the two countries; and though his combinations ultimately failed, they were more nearly successful than is commonly supposed.

While Bonaparte was thus straining every nerve to master what he called "the wet ditch" of the Channel, a lamentable incident occurred which has left a deep stain on his public life, and was ultimately attended with eventful results. The First Consul had, we have seen, shown generous clemency to the *émigrés*, and most of them had returned to France, and even largely entered his service. A certain number, however, had remained in exile; and a part of these men, associated with one or two chiefs of the late western insurgents, had joined in conspiring against the ruler whose power it was hopeless to shake openly. As far back as 1801 an attempt had been made against the life of Bonaparte, by firing what was called an infernal machine, as he was proceeding to the opera; and this was undoubtedly a royalist plot, though attributed at first by its intended victim to the survivors of the anarchist faction. These machinations, which had never ceased, became more active when the war again broke out, and a project to assassinate the First Consul and to destroy his government was formed in England, though it is unnecessary to notice the monstrous charge that English statesmen connived at it. The Count of Artois, to his lasting discredit, was cognizant of this criminal purpose, and it is

Conspiracy of the émigrés against the First Consul.

said, even took part in it; and though the leaders were men who had fought in the ranks of the Breton royalists, Pichegru, who had been exiled since Fructidor 18, was an accomplice to a certain extent; and Moreau, who had become hostile to Bonaparte, unwisely listened to the tempter's voice, though innocent of any murderous intent. The heads of the conspiracy, with Pichegru and Moreau, were arrested in Paris before they could effect their purpose; and one of the prisoners having deposed that a Bourbon prince was to join in the enterprise, the attention of Bonaparte was unhappily turned to the Duke of Enghien, a scion of the race, whose presence on the borders of the Black Forest had, with other circumstances, aroused suspicion. The unfortunate prince was suddenly arrested, though on German territory, and hurried to Paris; and though guiltless of all real crime, was shot by the sentence of a military commission, after a trial which does not deserve the name. Some of the conspirators were afterwards justly executed; and the tragedy was closed by the banishment of Moreau, and by the suicide of Pichegru* in his place of confinement.

<small>Execution of the Duke of Enghien, March 21, 1804.</small>

The death of the Duke of Enghien was a crime which shows what despotism could effect in France, though largely entitled to national gratitude, and seldom marked by mere vulgar cruelty. It is, however, unfair to regard this act as an assassination of the worst kind, for there were grounds to suspect the Bourbon princes; allowance must be made for that dread of murder which has unhinged even the most powerful intellects; and Bonaparte had a

* There seem to be no grounds for the charge that Pichegru was strangled in prison by the order of the First Consul.

right to make an example of the *émigrés*, who wickedly sought his life, though he unfortunately selected an innocent victim. The deed, moreover, was less culpable than the slaughter of the French envoys at Rastadt; and if it can be only at best palliated, it is right to bear in mind that the age had acquired a character of violence and angry passion. The immediate effect of this tragic event was to hasten the movement towards Monarchy to which everything had been inclining. The possibility of the sudden death of Bonaparte, which had been brought before the public mind, caused men to hope that the evil results of his disappearance would be at least lessened if he were at once placed on an hereditary throne; and the sentiments of the Nation made it eager to surround its ruler with the pomp of sovereignty. The First Consul naturally flattered these ideas, but whether from a desire to draw a distinction between the position of the Bourbons and his own, or from a wish for new and peculiar greatness, he refused to accept the title of King. At last he selected the ancient dignity which had come down from the time of Charlemagne; and amidst enthusiastic demonstrations of joy he was proclaimed Emperor of the French in May 1804, designing himself Napoleon, by his Christian name, according to the usage of Crowned Heads. The Empire, limited to his descendants, was upheld by dignitaries, in part borrowed from the Germanic model, and in part from that established by the ancient Kings of France; and its military character was fitly expressed by the appointment of sixteen marshals chosen from among the principal chiefs of the Republican armies. At the same time fresh changes

This event hastens the movement in favor of Monarchy.

The First Consul proclaimed Emperor of the French, May 18, 1804.

were made in the shadowy institutions of the work of Sieyès; and the senate was enlarged, while the popular tribunate was still further weakened, and at last suppressed. More important, certainly, than this mere shifting of the apparatus of despotic power, was the inauguration of the imperial Court, in which the aristocracy of the new era vied with survivors of the old *noblesse*, in flattery, vanity, and ostentation.

Coronation of Napoleon Dec. 2, 1804. On December 2, Paris flocked to witness the spectacle of the Coronation. In gratitude to the restorer of the faith in France, the Pope had come from Rome to hallow the pageant, and had departed from the usage which his predecessors had imposed on the haughtiest of the German Emperors. The Pontiff, attended by a procession, in which mitres and crosses were strangely mixed with the sabres and banners of the imperial guard, passed along the Seine to the ancient Cathedral, raised centuries before by the good St. Louis, and still towering in lofty state above the wrecks of the revolutionary tempest. The walls of Notre Dame were hung with tapestry rich with the golden bees of the new Sovereign; the dim light, which showed nave and aisle, fell on the ranks of the Bodies of the State, of the representatives of foreign Powers, of deputations from the chief towns of the Empire, all arrayed in costly and orderly pomp; and, as the sacred procession entered, choir and organ pealed forth a solemn chant, and the prelates of the renovated Church of France knelt reverently to implore the apostolic blessing. Meanwhile Napoleon had left the Tuileries, escorted by the new great officers of State, and with the company of his marshals by his side; and as he moved slowly along the ways which had seen all that was worst in the Reign of Terror, cheers burst exultingly from the thronging crowds, hailing a master as they had hailed liberty. On the arrival of the Emperor the assemblage in the Church stood up to greet him, amidst the swell of sacred music and the blare of trumpets; and it was with sentiments of mingled curiosity and awe that the spectators beheld the conquering soldier, wearing the golden laurel of the Cæsars on his brow, do homage to the successor of the Galilean fisherman. The ceremony now began, and Pius VII. poured the mystic oil on the kneeling Sovereign, and invested him with the lesser emblems of power, the consecrated Sword, and imperial Sceptre; but as he was about to complete the rite, Napoleon took the Crown from the hand of the Pontiff, and, with a significant gesture, placed it on his head himself, in witness of the supremacy of the State, and of his own paramount and chief authority. The Emperor then ascended a throne, encircled by a following in which great names of the Bourbon Monarchy stood by the side of republican soldiers and politicians; and as the hymn arose which had fallen on the ear of Charlemagne when saluted Emperor of the West, the acclamations that echoed from Notre Dame were caught up by the vast crowds outside, and the roar of artillery joined in concert. The satirist may ridicule whatever was incongruous or out of date in the spectacle, but History notes its more suggestive features—how the Revolution, in Napoleon's hands, arrayed itself in the forms of the Past, did external reverence at least to the symbols of majesty, order, and antique tradition, and embodied itself, so to speak, in the type of contented servitude and military despotism.

Before long, however, pageants of this kind gave way to the sterner scenes of war renewed over the greater part of the Con- *New coalition against France.*

tinent. The execution of the Duke of Enghien, and the violation of the territory of a German State, had given natural offence to the Powers of Europe; and fresh causes of irritation arose, when, by a transformation expressive of his power, Napoleon converted the Italian Republic into a vassal Monarchy ruled by himself, and incorporated Genoa into the French Empire. Mr. Pitt, too, had returned to office; and his efforts, in the increasing peril of England, to reunite a confederacy against her foe, soon shaped alarm into definite purpose, and revived the Coalition ever ready to combine. By the summer of 1805 England, Austria, Russia, Sweden, and Naples, had entered into a close alliance; and it was hoped that even Prussia would join the league, as the overwhelming preponderance of France had begun to affect the policy of that Power, and to make it apprehensive for its own safety. Four lines of invasion were marked out by those who directed the Allied councils; the first by the North German seaboard, the second up the valley of the Danube, the third from the Adige into Italy, and the fourth along the Neapolitan coast; but the second attack only was to be made in force; and the Austrians and Russians who were to attempt it were separated from each other by the immense distance between Bavaria and the Galician frontier. These faulty dispositions were not lost on the great soldier who had so often triumphed over disunited and ill-led enemies; and Napoleon prepared to defeat the Allies by operations worthy of his genius for war. Comparatively neglecting the subordinate attacks, he resolved to meet the second in irresistible strength, and to crush the Austrians before the Russians could

Plan of the attack of the Allies.

Campaign of 1805.

Napoleon quits Boulogne, and surrounds and captures an Austrian army at Ulm, Oct. 19, 1805.

1805. *The Empire to Tilsit.* 207

aid them; and as soon as he had ascertained that his lingering fleets could not reach the Channel to cover the descent, he broke up with his whole army from Boulogne, and marched with extraordinary speed to the Rhine, while powerful detachments from Holland and Hanover descended on the Maine to join in the movement. By the second week of October these converging masses, directed with admirable precision and skill, had gathered on the rear of the Austrian army, which had been imprudently advanced on Ulm; and within a few days an iron net was thrown round the doomed and baffled host, and it was forced to surrender with Mack its chief. The whole vanguard of the Allied armies had been thus annihilated by a simple manœuvre resembling that which had destroyed Melas; and Europe never witnessed such a scene again until it was reproduced in our own days by the capitulations of Metz and Sedan.

This wonderful success was soon, however, to be chequered by a tremendous disaster on the element on which all the efforts of France were destined only to end in failure. We have referred to the combinations by which Napoleon endeavored to collect a fleet of overwhelming force in the Channel; and these became in the highest degree formidable, when, in the autumn of 1804, Spain placed her naval forces in his hands. In the spring of the succeeding year a large French squadron set sail from Toulon, and, rallying a Spanish squadron at Cadiz, arrived safely in the West Indian seas, its object being to attract Nelson from European or English waters, and then, joined by a squadron from Brest, to make as quickly as possible its way to Boulogne, and so cover

Battle of Trafalgar and destruction of the French and Spanish fleets, Oct. 21, 1805.

the projected descent. The first part of the scheme completely succeeded; Nelson was led away in a fictitious chase; the French Admiral Villeneuve left the West Indies with a long start over his dreaded rival; and though he was not met by the Brest fleet, he could have hardly been stopped had he made directly for the Channel, which, as Napoleon calculated, was but ill-guarded. But Villeneuve was timid, and inclined southward; a light vessel detached by Nelson, with admirable forethought, gave the alarm; an indecisive action, off the coast of Spain, induced the Frenchman to bear up for Ferrol; and though he had still not a few chances of success, for he had been strengthened by another squadron, he shrunk from his foes, and put into Cadiz. Within a few weeks his whole fleet was destroyed in the greatest naval battle of modern times; and this crushing victory, though dearly bought by the death of the greatest of English seamen, brought all further attempts of invasion to an end. Yet the glory of Trafalgar ought to blind no one to the imminent peril which England escaped; Napoleon's manœuvres were nearly successful; and had Villeneuve had a ray of the genius of Nelson, he would, in all probability, have made the descent possible. What saved England was not the defence of the Channel, which was left too feebly guarded, but the terror of her fleets, and the demoralization of her foes; and though Napoleon ought to have taken these moral elements more fully into account, he was not far from accomplishing his design. We believe, however, that he entirely underrated the resistance which he would have to encounter had he succeeded in making the descent; the English army was of considerable strength; and on this, as on other occasions, he unduly disregarded the enor-

The project of the descent might have succeeded.

mous power of national forces under certain conditions. He might have captured London, but he would, we think, have been ultimately imprisoned within his conquest.

Trafalgar, however, was soon forgotten in the exultation of a career of victories. The disaster of Ulm put an end to the scheme of invasion formed by the Coalition; and, having sent detachments to subdue the Tyrol, Napoleon, with the mass of his forces, marched down the Danube on the Austrian capital. The army he commanded was the finest which France, perhaps, ever sent into the field; it had been trained in its camps at Boulogne to the highest point of endurance and vigor; it had been organized upon the system of *corps d'armée*, and separate reserves, since adopted by all Continental armies; though it numbered several German contingents, it was not filled with unwilling auxiliaries, as became the case in subsequent campaigns; and if it had suffered greatly in its late forced marches, it presented a combination of freedom of movement, of activity, energy and trustworthy force, which justified the name of the Grand Army, thenceforward given it by its mighty leader. *Napoleon marches on Vienna. The Grand Army.*

The conquering host rolled swiftly onwards, a few Austrian divisions and the Russian army, which had reached the Inn, falling back before it; and after passing the undefended lines of the feeders of the great Austrian stream, it was in possession of Vienna at the middle of November. Meanwhile the Russians, led by Kutusoff, a captain destined to future renown, had judiciously retreated into Moravia, opposing, as obviously was the course of prudence, time and distance to the far advancing enemy; and before long they were encamped round Olmutz, supported by several Austrian detachments. *Vienna occupied Nov. 13, 1805.*

P

Napoleon, however, having become master of the bridges of Vienna by a stratagem, crossed boldly to the northern bank of the Danube, carrying out his system of daring movements, and relying on the ascendency of immense success; and towards the close of November the Grand Army was collected, apparently in a disseminated state, but really within the hands of its chief, in Lower Moravia, around Brünn and Austerlitz. His position had now become critical, for Prussia, terrified at recent events, had begun to arm, and was about to descend through Bohemia on the French line of retreat, and the Archduke Charles, with his brother John, was hastening with a considerable force from Hungary; and had the Allies simply awaited events, Napoleon must have retired before them. The Czar, however, Alexander, against the advice of Kutusoff, resolved to attack the French Emperor—that great captain had purposely assumed a timid attitude to deceive his foe—and in the last days of November, the Allied forces broke up from Olmutz, and marched on Austerlitz.

Battle of Austerlitz, Dec. 2, 1805. Ruin of the Allied army.

An ambitious attempt to out-flank Napoleon, and intercept his retreat on Vienna, unduly weakened the line of his enemy; he seized an opportunity which he had foreseen; and, after a fierce and murderous struggle, the Allied army was pierced in the centre, and became a mass of shattered and ruined fragments. The Sun of Austerlitz, to which the conqueror was wont to refer with just pride, saw the warlike strength of the Coalition struck down.

Peace of Presburg, Dec. 15, 1805.

This great victory—the masterpiece of Napoleon's tactics on the field of battle— was followed in a few days by a peace, made at Presburg. The Czar lost nothing but military fame;

but Austria was compelled to surrender Venice, annexed to the new Italian kingdom; and she ceded the Tyrol to Bavaria, and recognized the Elector as an independent Sovereign. Baden and Würtemburg were also enlarged, and the Elector of Würtemburg made, too, a King; and thus Austria, the old rival of France, was reduced to a Power of the second order, and the policy was carried on of extending the influence of France among the minor States of Germany. The King of Naples was soon afterwards dethroned, as a member of the late Coalition; and the Emperor of Austria, with a just sense of dignity, acknowledged his position, and abandoned his claims to the German Empire, long an appanage of his House. Bavaria, Baden, and Würtemburg, with some lesser States, were now formed by Napoleon into what he called the Confederation of the Rhine; and those German Powers which, in the late campaign, had proved useful and willing allies, became mere vassals of the French Empire, with their military forces in the hands of his chief. In this state of things Prussia was left wholly isolated; and she was soon to reap the fruits of a policy which, beginning in aggression, had ended in greed. Partly from alarm, and partly owing to an alleged violation of her territory by the French, Prussia had, we have seen, prepared to attack Napoleon, when dangerously exposed, in the rear; but after Austerlitz, her government recurred to its former course, and had accepted Hanover, for some time occupied by the French armies, as the price of a renewed alliance with France, though this perfidy was justly condemned by her people, and could only provoke the scorn of Na-

Changes effected by it.

Austria ceases to be Head of the German Empire.

The Confederation of the Rhine.

Isolation of Prussia.

Conduct of that power.

poleon. The spoliation of the patrimony of the Crown caused England at once to declare war against Prussia; and that Power, having endeavored secretly to form a new Coalition against France, and a chance of peace with England having arisen on the accession of Mr. Fox to power, Napoleon dealt with Prussia after her own measure, and offered to make over Hanover to Great Britain. This, and one or two other acts of the kind, proved too much for the patience of the Prussian court; and, in September, 1806, it recklessly drew the sword, amidst the exultation of an army proud of the great traditions of Leuthen and Rosbach. A daring offensive movement was begun; and by the first days of October the Prussian forces had crossed the Elbe, and carelessly advanced, extended along an immense line, from the Lower Saale to the Thuringian Forest. The Grand Army which, since Austerlitz, had remained, for the most part, in Germany, and had been gradually directed on the Maine, was now moved through the Franconian defiles; and, issuing from the valley of the Upper Saale, fell on the rear of its incautious foe, and overwhelmed the Prussians in a great battle at Jena, and another fought on the same day at Auerstadt. This success proved decisive, though Napoleon's manœuvres were hardly as skilful as in previous campaigns; in a few days the whole Prussian army, driven across the Elbe, had either disappeared or become a mass of demoralized captives; Berlin had been opened to the conquerors; and the French standards had advanced to the Oder, the military Monarchy of Frederick the Great having been crushed in about three weeks.

This astonishing triumph in its rapid suddenness

surpassing all that he had as yet achieved, impelled Napoleon to fresh efforts. Russia had declared war before the rout of Jena, and had marched an army across her frontier ; a few thousand defeated Prussian troops had escaped to the northern verge of the Monarchy ; and, disdaining the perils of a winter campaign, the victor resolved to press forward, and to bring the war to a speedy conclusion. His legions were soon upon the Vistula; and having crossed that great barrier stream, he endeavored to bring his enemy to bay in the vast region of marsh and forest formed by the Bug, the Narew, the Ukra, and other rivers of Western Poland. But here his method of rapid invasions, his troops living on the territories they entered, received a check from the forces of Nature, significant of its essential dangers ; the Grand Army was arrested in its march, and exposed to cruel privations and want in the midst of barren and pathless swamps ; and after a series of fruitless engagements, it fell back from Pultusk to the Vistula. The French Emperor now put his soldiers into winter quarters along the line which extends from Warsaw to Thorn and the Baltic, and made preparations to besiege Dantzic ; but he was not given the repose he expected. The Russian commander Benningsen, proud of having resisted the conqueror with success, attempted to assail him in his cantonments ; and moving his army behind the screen of the lakes which fill the distance from the Narew to the Passarge, fell on the extreme left of the French divisions along the seaboard of Eastern Prussia. Napoleon, however, had anticipated the stroke ; and his antagonist having begun to retreat, he pursued and attacked the Russians at Eylau on February 8, 1807.

Indecisive battle of Eylau, Feb. 1807. The battle was terribly and sternly contested; and though the Russians retired from the field, the losses of the French were so heavy that they were not equal to prolong the contest. Napoleon was now in real danger, far away *Peril of Napoleon.* from France, and with the great Powers of Germany conquered, but indignant, occupying his retreat; but he stood firm and applied himself with more than even his wonted energy to restore his forces. Troops were raised in thousands from all parts of the Empire, of which its chief wielded the ample resources with extraordinary administrative skill; and in a *Reorganization of the Grand Army.* few months the havoc of war was repaired, and the Grand Army in greater strength than before. Hostilities were resumed in June; and Benningsen imprudently advanced to attack an antagonist greatly his superior in force. The Russians were soon repelled from the Passarge; *Decisive victory of the French at Friedland, June 14, 1807.* and Benningsen, in an attempt to get back to the frontier, having crossed the Alle with extreme incaution, Napoleon fell on him with terrible effect, compelled him to fight with his back to the stream, and routed him on the 14th of June, not far from the little town of Friedland. This stroke was decisive; before a week had passed the Grand Army was on the banks of the Niemen; and, with Dantzic, the whole remaining provinces of the Prussian Monarchy passed into the hands of the conquerors. Within less than two years the imperial eagles, which crowned the standards of the French armies, had flown from the British seas, across prostrate Germany, to the distant verge of the Russian empire; war had never been seen in such grandeur before; though Napoleon's movements had not been free from hazards which had attracted the attention of a few thoughtful minds, though unseen by the crowd in the glare of victory.

In this series of triumphs we see the strategy of 1796 repeated, on a larger scale, and with greater results. To seize the decisive points in the theatre of war, to bring a superior force upon them, and to interpose between divided enemies and beat them in detail by rapid manœuvres, were the main objects of Napoleon's movements; and he generally attained them by daring attacks, and by forced marches which placed his soldiers on the most vulnerable parts of the hostile line. In these campaigns, however, he had been greatly seconded by the mistakes of enemies, who had usually contrived to present themselves to his crushing blows; his system, as we have seen, had shown signs of failing when exposed to the strain of natural obstacles; and as the armies he led were infinitely better than those of the Allies in every respect, his exploits were not perhaps so wonderful as those around Mantua and on the Adige. Such exhibitions of military force had, however, never been made before; and the antiquated methods of slow advances, of timid movements upon an immense front, and of never passing an untaken fortress, were finally abandoned by European generals. Thus in war, as in many other particulars, the French Revolution wrought changes which had made it a new era in the History of the World; and the strategy of Napoleon, in some of its aspects, was an expression of the increased energy and activity generated by that event. The scenes which followed the victory of Friedland rather bore a likeness to a strange romance than to the ordinary arrangements of affairs of State. Unable to

Characteristics of these campaigns.

Changes in the art of war.

Meeting of Alexander and Napoleon on the Niemen, June 25, 1807.

resist, the Czar sued for peace; but Napoleon welcomed Alexander as a friend, for he wished to make him subserve his policy; and after interviews between the two potentates, held chiefly in a floating tent on the Niemen, in the presence of the French and Russian armies, peace was made at Tilsit, on the north Prussian frontier. By this celebrated treaty Prussia was deprived of more than half her former possessions, and became a mere vassal of the French Empire; a kingdom of Westphalia was carved out of her Elbe Provinces and added to the Confederation of the Rhine; and her conquests in Poland were given to Saxony—she had taken part with France in the late campaigns—under the curious name of the Grand Duchy of Warsaw. At the same time France and Russia united in an alliance of the most intimate kind; the Czar recognized the French Empire, and pledged himself to uphold its power, and—what was more important —he undertook to offer his mediation to England, and, if she refused it, to go to war with that Power. In return for a co-operation which appeared to set a seal to his domination in the West, Napoleon promised to second the designs of Russian ambition in the North and East; and he consented to the annexation of Finland, and of the provinces of Turkey north of the Danube, insisting, however, that Constantinople should, in no contingency, become Russian. The conqueror justified the dismemberment of Prussia, and her seeming ruin as a State, by a reference to the proclamation of Brunswick in 1792.

Treaty of Tilsit, July 7 and 9, 1807.

Alliance between France and Russia, and dismemberment of Prussia.

Objects of Napoleon in making the treaty.

The purpose of Napoleon in making this treaty was to obtain a complete and enduring guarantee for the supremacy of France on the European Continent, to divide Germany more thoroughly than before, and to subject her everywhere to French influence, and, finally, to raise a new foe against England, whose efforts might lead to important results; and it appeared an admirable scheme of state-craft, if such disturbing elements as national passions and the jealousies of rulers had no existence. The dangers, however, that lay hid under the new arrangement of the map of Europe, and in the results of French conquests, were as yet withdrawn from almost every eye; and the power of Napoleon was now at its height, though his empire was afterwards somewhat enlarged. At this period that gigantic rule extended undisputed from the pillars of Hercules to the furthest limits of Eastern Germany; if England still stood in arms against it, she was without an avowed ally on the Continent; and, drawing to itself the great Power of the North, it appeared to threaten the civilized world with that universal and settled domination which had not been seen since the fall of Rome. The Sovereign of France from the Scheldt to the Pyrenees, and of Italy from the Alps to the Tiber, Napoleon held under his immediate sway the fairest and most favored part of the Continent; and yet this was only the seat and centre of that far-spreading and immense authority. One of his brothers, Louis, governed the Batavian Republic, converted into the Kingdom of Holland; another, Joseph, wore the old Crown of Naples; and a third, Jerome, sat on the new throne of Westphalia; and he had reduced Spain to a simple dependency, while, with Austria humbled and Prussia crushed, he was supreme in Germany from the Rhine to the Vistula, through his confederate, subject, or allied States. This enor-

His power at its height.

Extent of the French Empire.

Vassal kingdoms.

Allied and subject States. mous Empire, with its vassal appendages, rested on great and victorious armies in possession of every point of vantage from the Niemen to the Adige and the Garonne, and proved as yet to be irresistible; and as Germany, Holland, Poland, and Italy swelled the forces of France with large contingents, the whole fabric of conquest seemed firmly cemented. Nor was the Empire the mere creation of brute force and the spoil of the sword; its author endeavored, in some measure, to consolidate it through better and more lasting influences. Napoleon, indeed, *The Empire promoted civilization in some respects.* suppressed the ideas of 1789 everywhere, but he introduced his Code and large social reforms into most of the vassals or allied States; he completed the work of destroying Feudalism which the Revolution had daringly begun; and he left a permanent mark on the face of Europe, far beyond the limit of Republican France, in innumerable monuments of material splendor. And thus it has happened that much that he founded has survived his fall and his short-lived conquests; the extent of his sway may be still traced by the reach of institutions established by him; and even nations who felt the terrors of his sword and rose justly against his domination, still acknowledge that his rule was not without good, and have a kind of sympathy with the modern Cæsar.

Nor did the Empire at this time appear more firmly established abroad, than within the limits *Prosperity of France.* of the dominant State which had become mistress of Continental Europe. The prosperity of the greater part of France was immense; the finances, fed by the contributions of war, seemed overflowing and on the increase; and if sounds of discontent were occasionally heard, they were lost in the universal acclaim which greeted the author of the national greatness, and the restorer of social order and welfare. The Jacobin faction had long shrunk out of sight; the memory of the Revolution and the Reign of Terror was felt as a foolish or hideous dream; the public tranquillity was undisturbed; and, in the splendor and success of the Imperial era, the animosities and divisions of the past disappeared, and France seemed to form a united People. If, too, the cost of conquest was great, and exacted a tribute of French blood, the military power of the Empire shone with the brightest radiance of martial renown; Marengo, Austerlitz, Jena, and Friedland could in part console even thinned households; a career of glory opened on soldiers which, if brief, was not seldom brilliant; and the chiefs of the armies, enriched with the wealth of vanquished Provinces and subject Kingdoms, and invested with lofty and sounding titles, forgot the rivalries of an earlier time, and joined in docile homage to their great master. The magnificent public works with which Napo- *Public works of Napoleon.* leon adorned this part of his reign, increased this sentiment of national grandeur; it was now that the Madeleine raised its front, and the Column, moulded from captured cannon, which a fresh outburst of Jacobin frenzy overthrew, only a few months ago, in the presence of the mocking enemies of France; and Paris, decked out with triumphal arches, with temples of glory, and with stately streets, put on the aspect of ancient Rome, gathering into her lap the gorgeous spoils of subjugated and dependent races. The government of *Character of* the Empire had by this time become of a *his Government.* purely monarchic type; it had abolished all republican forms, even to the calendar of 1793, and had made dukes, counts and barons by scores, out of the leading men of the new age; but if it showed the defects of an absolute power, it was still essentially the firm, national, and equal despotism of the Consulate, reconciling parties, keeping down anarchy, and as yet acceptable to a people which had forgotten even the thought of liberty. Nor had the great reforms of the Consulate been without ample and beneficent fruit; religious passions had altogether subsided; and the State was administered with an energy, a regularity, and a general equity, which France had never experienced before.

Elements of weakness and decay in the Empire. Yet, notwithstanding its apparent strength, this structure of conquest and domination was essentially weak, and liable to decay. The work of the sword, and of new-made power, it was in opposition to the nature of things; it came in conflict with national traditions, with popular instincts, with moral forces; and it was to illustrate the old fable of the Titans heaping Pelion on Ossa, and being overwhelmed by the bolts of Olympus. The material and

Indignation of conquered nations. even social benefits conferred by the Code, and reform of abuses, could not compensate vanquished but martial races for the misery and disgrace of subjection; and, apart from the commercial oppression of which we shall say a word hereafter, the exasperating pressure of French officials, the exactions of the victorious French armies, and the severities of the conscription introduced among them, provoked discontent in the vassal States on which the yoke of the Empire weighed; and made the people of the Confederation of the Rhine, of Germany, and even by degrees

Tendency of Germany to unite through common suffering. of Italy, more or less hostile to the rule of the stranger. The prostration, too, of Austria and Prussia, which had been the result of late events, had a direct tendency to make these Powers forget their old discords in common suffering, and to bring to an end the internal divisions through which France had become supreme in Germany; the recent formation of a Saxon Poland, an evident protest against the Partition, could not fail ultimately to give umbrage to the Czar; and the triumphant policy of Tilsit contained the germs of a Coalition against France more formidable than she had yet experienced. At the same time, the real strength of the instrument by which Napoleon maintained his power, was being gradually but surely impaired; the imperial armies were more and more filled with raw conscripts and ill-affected allies, as their size increased with the extension of his rule; and the French element in them, on which alone reliance could be placed in possible defeat, was being dissipated, exhausted, and wasted. Add that while it was being thus sapped at the root, the Empire had been continually growing, with a growth too rapid to be sound or lasting, that the ambition of its chief appeared to enlarge as the circle of his conquests expanded, and that the old League of the Continental Powers against the Revolution was being gradually changed into an alliance, unrecognized as yet, but being formed of nations against a military despot; and we shall understand what perils lurked beneath the surface of the imperial sway which overawed Europe.

Jealousy of Russia.

Decline of the Grand Army in strength.

Nor was the Empire, within France itself, free from elements of instability and decline. The finances, well administered as they were, were so burdened by the charges of war, that they were only sustained by conquest; and, flourishing as their condition seemed, they had been often cruelly strained of late, and were unable

The resources of France unduly strained.

to bear the shock of disaster. The seaports were beginning to suffer from the policy adopted to subdue England; and though the Emperor made persistent efforts to prepare for "an Actium in the British Channel," they invariably ended in disgrace and failure. Meanwhile, the continual demands on the youth of the nation for never-ceasing wars, were gradually telling on its military power; Napoleon, after Eylau, had had recourse to the ruinous expedient of taking beforehand the levies which the conscription raised; and though complaints were as yet rare, the anticipation of the resources of France, which filled the armies with feeble boys unequal to the hardships of a rude campaign, had been noticed at home as well as abroad.

Moral evils of the rule of Napoleon. Nor were the moral ills of this splendid despotism less certain than its bad material results. Too much, indeed, has perhaps been made of the political corruption of the imperial system; for though instruments of new power are peculiarly subject to this baneful influence, it does not appear to have been worse than it had been under the fallen Monarchy; and the France of Napoleon did not parade the shameless dissoluteness and social vices which had characterized part of the republican era. It is also unfair to ascribe to the Empire the want of eminence in art and letters which we see in France during the whole period from 1789 to 1815, for this deficiency was mainly due to the concentration on alien subjects of the energies of the French intellect, even if it be true that the attempts made by the Emperor to remove the dearth were rather calculated to prolong and increase it. Still the inevitable tendency of the Empire, even at the time of its highest glory, was to lessen manliness and self-reliance, to fetter and demoralize the human mind, and to weaken whatever public virtue and mental independence France possessed; and its authority had already begun to disclose some of the harsher features of Cæsarian despotism. This was seen not merely in arbitrary acts, but in suspicious jealousy of any forces or influences not controlled by the State, and in an interference, petty and vexatious alike, even with the arrangements of social life; and the effects were slowly provoking ridicule or discontent, though the murmurs as yet were scarcely heard.

The great and paramount cause, however, of the insecurity of Napoleon's Empire was that its existence hung not only on the life, but on the will of its mighty creator. With- *Insecurity of his power which depended mainly on himself.* out solid foundations abroad, and springing from Revolution at home, it was, in the main, the work of a single man; and it might obviously perish as quickly as it arose by the death of its chief, or through the failure of the gigantic projects which he could design and compass, without the least check on his undivided power. And the Sovereign who wielded this immense authority was a soldier who had hardly known defeat, who stood at the head of gigantic armies, and whose soaring imagination, urged by ambition, was one of the most distinctive of many splendid faculties! And the ruler who had reached these heights of grandeur had overthrown the Old Order of Europe, and had placed his foot on the necks of conquered nations; yet was really sustained only by the unstable forces of a State recently torn by Revolution, and by a Nation of which the inconstancy had been stimulated of late by every possible means, which could pass with the rapidity of thought from enthusiastic devotion to scorn and hatred, and which, especially at the touch of misfortune, could suddenly awake from gilded servitude, and with strange levity repudiate what it had seemed to revere! Should that vaulting ambition o'erleap itself, should disaster overtake the spoiled child of fortune, should that despotism weigh with too heavy a burden, in what perils would the Empire be involved, amidst a hostile Europe, and a France linked to Napoleon chiefly by the frail tie of success?

CHAPTER XIII.

THE EMPIRE TO 1813.

BEFORE the war which ended with the Peace of Tilsit, the conduct of Napoleon had, in many respects, been that of a great and sagacious ruler. He had doubtless, even then, given proof of a passion for power, and of grasping ambition, had revealed a purpose to extend still further the domination of France on the Continent, had committed a great political mistake in irritating and defying England, and had justly outraged the opinion of Europe by the execution of the Duke of Enghien; and as the character of man does not really change, though circumstances may largely affect his acts, it is possible to show that, from the beginning of his career, he was one and the same in his essential nature. But History,

Retrospect of the policy of Napoleon.

in judging the leaders of States, can hardly enter into this minute inquiry; and as it contemplates the public life of Napoleon during the first part of his wonderful career, it can excuse much that is more or less blameworthy, and finds more to admire than to condemn. Many of the reforms of the First Consul remain monuments of his great capacity, and his despotism in France, though heavy from the first, was also attended with immense benefits; and if he annexed half-subject Italian provinces, if he increased the influence of France in Germany, if he precipitated an unfinished quarrel with England; nay, if he put to death iniquitously a Bourbon Prince, his policy and conduct in these particulars may be justified, in a greater or less degree, from the peculiarities of the time, the condition of Europe, the traditions of France for long ages, the antecedents of the aggressive Republic, and the violence and confusion of an era of Revolution. But conquest, and all engrossing power on a scale hitherto unknown in Europe, had the influence on this extraordinary man which they have exercised on natures of the same kind; they enlarged the scope of his daring ambition, and made his sanguine intellect believe that nothing was beyond the reach of his efforts; and they led him into a series of acts, the imprudence and inexpediency of which were perceived even by ordinary men, and which hastened, probably by many years, the ruin of that colossal dominion, which, however, could not have been lasting. We have already seen that the Treaty of Tilsit tended to unite Germany, and even Russia at last, in hostility against the French Empire; and from this time forward Napoleon engages in enterprises and in a course of policy, in which, if we still see his genius for war, and his skill in admin-

It changes for the worse after Tilsit.

Q

istering affairs of State, we more often trace the excesses of mere force, the presumptuous over-confidence of success, and the exaggerated notions of arrogance and pride.

One of the first cares of the French Emperor, after sheathing his victorious sword at Friedland, was to mature a scheme for subduing England, and forcing her to accept a humiliating peace, which had occupied his thoughts for a considerable time, and became known as the Continental system. The Directory had, many years before, attempted to injure British commerce by excluding English and colonial produce from the ports and territories of France and her allies; and England had retaliated by severe measures which even the occasion could hardly justify. Such acts, however, were trifling compared to the vast plan for ruining England through her trade, which Napoleon conceived in 1806—7, and which forms one of the most striking instances in which despotism has set itself to contend against nature. The Lord and controller of five-sixths of the Continent, he deliberately resolved to close Europe, along its circumference, to access from England; and for this purpose, by two famous ordinances, known as the Berlin and Milan Decrees, he declared that English and colonial merchandize should be confiscated wherever it was found, in the Empire or its allied States, and that even shipping which touched at British harbors should be included in the general proscription. As France commanded the entire coast from the Baltic to the Mediterranean seas, and Russia fell in with Napoleon's project, the effect of this scheme, if fully realized, would have been to shut out England from all the best markets, to cripple her resources, and to blight her industry; and though it was never even

The Continental system, 1807-8.

nearly carried out, it certainly did her a great deal of injury. The consequences, however, to the French Empire and its dependencies were to be far more disastrous.* The Continental system caused frightful distress in a short time in every maritime town from Riga to Amsterdam and Venice, and blotted, as it were, their prosperity out, by sapping and impeding their trade; and it created general and just discontent in all the allied and vassal States, and even within the limits of France, by depriving millions of the conveniences of life, and by subjecting the mercantile and manufacturing classes to the oppressions and exactions of a host of officials charged to enforce its harsh and unfair restrictions. This system, in fact, was a vexatious tyranny which did palpable and wide-spread mischief, and brought the sense of wrong home to innumerable hearths; and it quickened the exasperation and animosity of the subjugated but reluctant Continent. This, however, was hardly its principal result; the iniquitous provisions of his commercial policy being largely eluded outside of France, Napoleon was urged still further to stretch the boundaries of his overgrown Empire, and to proceed to fresh annexations and conquests; and this supposed necessity, in conjunction with the promptings of his ever-growing ambition, contributed greatly to his final overthrow.

<small>Its mischievous effects upon the Empire.</small>

<small>It urges Napoleon to make conquests.</small>

The establishment of the Continental system caused Napoleon at once to turn his eyes to Spain and the neighboring kingdom, Portugal, which, though still in-

* The ruinous effects of the Continental system in weakening the Empire and impelling Napoleon to fresh conquests are well pointed out in M. Lanfrey's *Histoire de Napoleon I.* vol. iii. chap. 10.

dependent States in name, had, and Spain especially, become subject more or less completely to the ruler of France. An event which occurred in the autumn of 1807 accelerated a design already formed, and he resolved to drive the Sovereigns of the Peninsula from their thrones, and to convert it into a vassal Province. Russia, after Tilsit, as had been agreed, had offered her mediation to England, and had declared war when it had been refused; and as Napoleon, with the consent of the Czar, had proposed to force Denmark to place her resources at the disposition of the two potentates, the English ministry had anticipated the stroke, and, as the Danes would not give up their fleet, had caused Copenhagen to be bombarded. On the plea that this act, the harshness of which was infinitely more apparent than real, permitted him to do what he liked in Europe, Napoleon pushed forward an army on Lisbon, and proclaimed that the House of Braganza had ceased to reign; and soon afterwards he gradually introduced considerable forces into Spain, which took possession of the frontier fortresses and ultimately advanced beyond Madrid. The dissensions of the imbecile Spanish Bourbons facilitated the Emperor's unscrupulous policy; and Charles IV., the nominal King, having refused to sanction an abdication in favor of his son extorted from him, Napoleon induced the whole royal family to accept him as the arbiter of their rights, and having brought them together at Bayonne, obtained from the old King a cession of the Crown, and immediately conferred it on his brother Joseph. This treacherous deed of violence and wrong, though accompanied by a new Constitution for Spain, which put an end to many inveterate abuses, led to unexpected and momentous consequences. The pride of the Spaniards was stirred to its depths; the Nation sprang as a man to arms, to resist the detested yoke of the stranger; juntas, as they were called, promoted and organized an insurrection in every province; and in an incredibly short time great bands of levies, far from worthless foes in a land of mountains, had, with what existed of the regular army, fallen on the invaders wherever they could be found, and encircled them, as it were, with a consuming fire. The rising was vigorously supported from England, and before long its effects were remarkable. Napoleon had been completely surprised, in his usual scorn of popular feelings; his forces in Spain were widely scattered, and unable to keep the country down; and though his soldiers were easily victorious in one or two engagements in the open field, one of his lieutenants, Dupont, was obliged to surrender with a large detachment in the Sierra Morena, and another was ignominiously driven out of Castile. Meanwhile, a British force under Sir Arthur Wellesley—a name destined to illustrious fame—had defeated the French divisions in Portugal, and had also compelled them to capitulate; and a French squadron in the harbor of Cadiz had been destroyed or forced to strike its colors. Before the autumn of 1808 the imperial eagles had been made to fly in disastrous retreat towards the seat of their power, and not a Frenchman south of the Ebro was seen.

General rising in Spain, May, June, 1808.

Capitulation of Baylen, July 19, 20, 1808.

First appearance of Sir A. Wellesley on the scene. Convention of Cintra, Aug. 30, 1808.

Great reverses of the French.

These disasters amazed and excited Europe, and filled Napoleon with indignation. His renown, he knew well, was the mainstay of his power; and he poured troops into Spain in thousands to subdue what he called "a rising of the mob." His disciplined armies soon scattered in flight the levies that ventured to cross their path; and, having swept through the Somo Sierra pass, he installed his brother in pomp in Madrid. But the national resistance lived on; it broke out in a savage guerilla warfare, in a country made for a movement of the kind; and Saragossa gave a glorious example of a defence imitated by other cities. Napoleon, however, went on persistently with the work of subjugation; and before long he had crossed the Guadarramas again, in pursuit of a small British army, which from Leon had threatened his line of retreat, but was retiring before his overwhelming forces. His march was interrupted by the news that the attitude of Austria was becoming dangerous; so quitting the Peninsula, he returned to France; and the enemy whom he had hoped to crush not only effected his escape to the sea but inflicted a check on one of his best lieutenants. By this time, however, a fresh contest had begun on another theatre of war. Encouraged by recent events in Spain, and supported by the British exchequer, Austria rose suddenly and declared war; and the Archduke Charles, in April 1809, advanced with a large army from the Inn to the Iser, his object being to surprise the French and their allies, dispersed widely on either bank of the Danube. Napoleon, however, who had arrived from Paris, had just time to anticipate the stroke; and drawing together his scattered divisions with admirable precision, quickness, and art, he turned the Austrian left wing, broke through its centre, and compelled the Archduke to take refuge, completely defeated in a game of manœuvres, not the least wonderful in the Emperor's career, behind the neighboring hills of Bohemia. The imperial legions once more poured victoriously down the valley of the Danube ; and within a month from the opening of the campaign, Vienna was, for the second time, in their power. Napoleon, however, was not able in 1809, as in 1805, to master the bridges near the capital ; and in an attempt to cross to the northern bank of the Danube, and to bring his antagonist there to bay, he met a serious reverse at Aspern, his army being divided on the stream, and a sudden flood having carried away the artificial passages he had made. *Reverse of Napoleon on the Danube at Aspern, May 21, 22, 1809.* This disaster, however, was repaired by prodigies of perseverance and skill; and by July 5, the whole Grand Army, with reserves summoned from Italy and the Rhine, had made its way over the firmly-held river, and debouched into the great plain of the Marchfield, from an island in which it had been camped and fortified. The battle which ensued was bloody and terrible ; a vigorous effort made by the Archduke against the French left proved nearly successful ; but the Austrian centre and right were pierced ; and *Battle of Wagram and victory of the French, July 6, 1809.* Napoleon, after a desperate struggle, in which nearly 300,000 men fought, stood at last triumphant on the low hills of Wagram. The blow, though not nearly so overwhelming as those of Austerlitz, Jena, and Friedland, was too much for the strength of Austria, and peace, purchased by fresh cessions of territory, was made at Vienna in autumn. *Treaty of Vienna, Oct. 14, 1809.*

This campaign restored the power of the conqueror; and a subsequent event appeared to increase it. Napoleon had married several members of his family into royal Houses—vassal Sovereigns could not refuse him anything—and after Wagram he found means to repeat the experiment in his own person. His wife Josephine had borne him no child, and in order to strengthen and prolong his dynasty he obtained a divorce, and soon afterwards married a youthful daughter of the Emperor of Austria, the Archduchess Maria Louisa. This marriage was celebrated with extraordinary pomp, and seemed to set a seal on his greatness; nor was the advantage for a time illusory, as Austria, wearied with repeated defeats, for the present inclined to a French alliance. England, backed by the insurrection of Spain, now became once more the only open foe of the master of more than thirty legions; and had Napoleon, at this juncture, made the Peninsula feel the whole power of his arms, he could, humanly speaking, have subdued the country, and kept it free from English intervention. But the Emperor comparatively neglected Spain, for his armies had routed the Spanish levies in several engagements in 1809, and, if they had been foiled by a British force at Oporto, and in a struggle at Talavera, they had lately compelled it to retreat into Portugal; and as the conquest appeared nearly complete they were scattered over a variety of points, and nowhere collected for a decisive movement, although in numbers extremely formidable. This state of things was thoroughly understood by a commander whose wisdom was to throw a momentous weight into the scale of fortune, and who had perceived with profound insight the weak point in Napoleon's system of war, and the best method to cope with it. Sir Arthur Wellesley—become Lord Wellington for his success at Oporto and Talavera—had seen clearly that the rapid invasions of the French armies without regular supplies might be encountered by obstacles and want; and as the forces of Napoleon in the Peninsula appeared unlikely to draw together, he had satisfied himself that he could find the means of maintaining himself against any probable foe, and, in any event, of re-embarking his troops. For this purpose he caused a position on the verge of Portugal, between the Tagus and the sea, to be fortified with extreme care and secresy; and he gave orders that, should the French advance, his army should retreat to this place of vantage, destroying, as it fell back, the adjacent regions. The consequences of these masterly arrangements were memorable in the highest degree. Napoleon, ignorant of what his antagonist had done, directed Masséna, in the summer of 1810, "to drive the English into the sea;" but the French army was far too weak for the purpose; and when, having been checked at Busaco, it arrived before the impenetrable Lines—ever since famous as those of Torres Vedras— after a march of suffering through a wasted country, it recoiled amazed from an impassable barrier. After a series of attempts to bring Wellington to bay, Masséna was ultimately compelled to retreat; and he reached the frontier with the mere wreck of an army ruined by disease and privations. *Memorable campaign of Torres Vedras, and complete defeat of the French, June, 1810. May, 1811.*

The issue of this remarkable campaign caused wonder and hope to thrill through Europe. The forces of Napoleon in Spain were immense; and yet the conqueror had been worsted, at the decisive point, by a small army; *Great results of this campaign, and its influence on Europe.*

and a way to encounter him seemed discovered. Soldiers began to study the strategy of Wellington as they had studied that of the French Emperor; and the name of Torres Vedras was in every mouth as that of Rivoli and Arcola had been. Meanwhile, Germany shook fiercely in her bonds; secret societies spread the flame of patriotism, and invoked vengeance on the detested foreigners; and though the courts of Austria and Prussia stood timidly aloof, and the princes of the Confederation of the Rhine continued to lick the hand of their master, the divided members of the great Teutonic family drew towards each other with the feelings of a common nationality and hate of oppression. Disturbances, too, broke out in Holland, half ruined by the Continental system; symptoms of discontent were apparent in Italy; and the tale of Continental troubles was increased by a violent quarrel between Napoleon and the Pope. Nor was France free from anxious symptoms; Bordeaux, Marseilles, and the seaport towns were full of sounds of anger and distress; the steady consumption of war in Spain had made the conscription extremely unpopular; taxation and bankruptcies had enormously increased; and notwithstanding a watched Press, and mute or obsequious Bodies of State, unquiet murmurs began to be heard and even to threaten a distant tempest. The real strength of the imperial armies had also become more and more weakened; the soldiers of Wagram were very inferior to those who had marched from the camp at Boulogne; and the addition of feeble boys to the ranks, and of auxiliaries listless if not false, had gone on with accelerated speed. Every sign, in a word, of coming danger, which could have been noted in 1807, had grown more visible in 1811; and the birth

Agitation in Germany and Holland.

Murmurs in France.

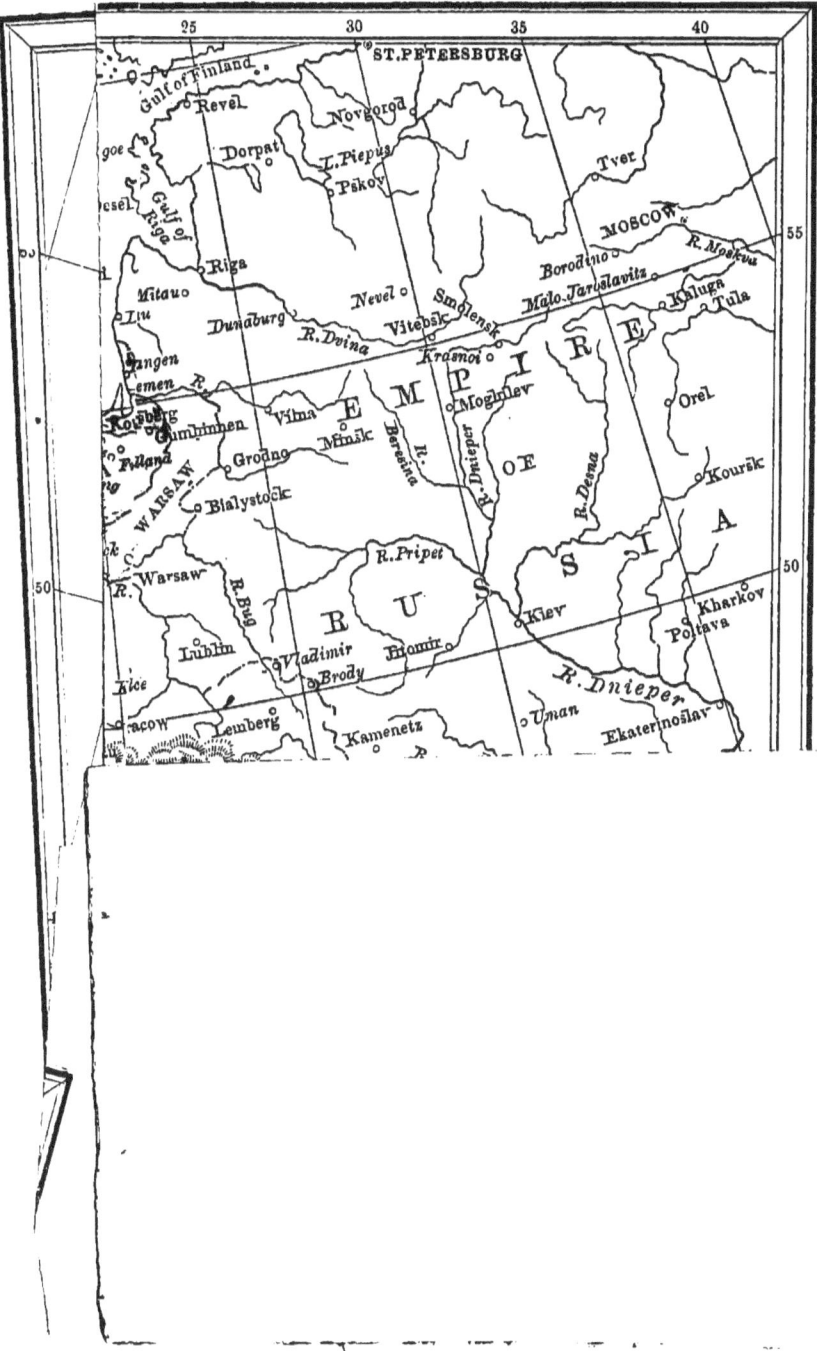

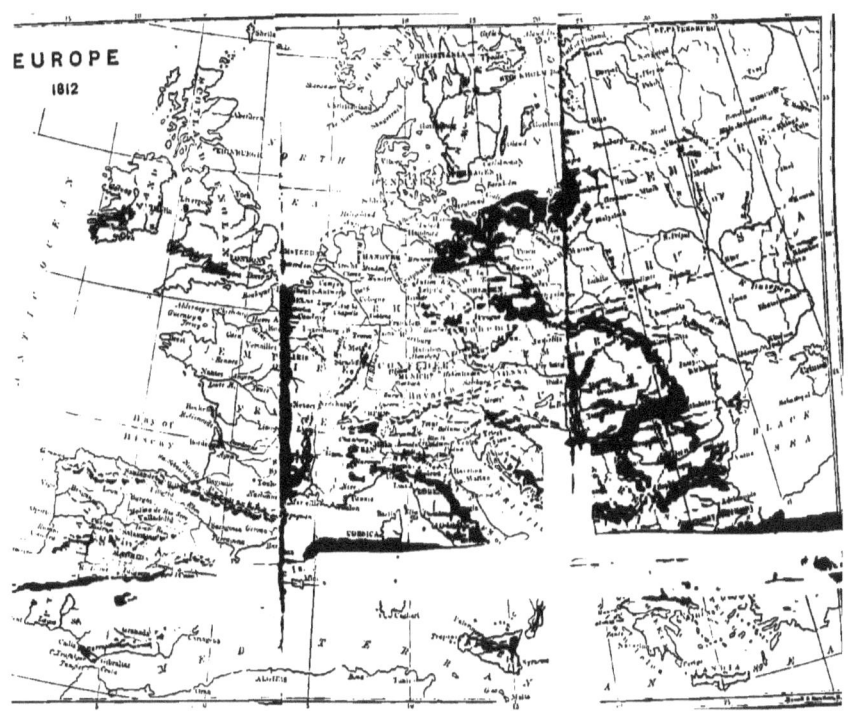

of a son at this time to Napoleon, was not felt to be, in general opinion, as it would have been a few years before, an assurance of the stability of his throne. The conqueror, however, from the height of his splendor could not see the shadows that were creeping on; and in the face of the Continent, awed but indignant, he incorporated Rome, Holland and the Hanse Towns in the territories of the French Empire, in order to complete his rule in Italy, and to carry out more thoroughly the Continental system. *Birth of a son to Napoleon, March 20, 1811.*

These aggrandizements could not fail to arouse the jealousy of the only State on the Continent which still preserved a shadow of independence. The Czar had soon abandoned the alliance of Tilsit; he had resented a refusal of the French Emperor to pledge himself not to restore Poland or to make additions to the Grand Duchy of Warsaw; and he protested against the annexation of the Hanse Towns, and the occupation of Prussia by French troops which had been continued ever since Friedland. Napoleon had retorted by insisting on the necessities of the Continental system; and increasing coolness became open dissension, Alexander having, in self-defence, relaxed some of its worst restrictions. Napoleon resolved in 1811 to invade Russia the following year; and the preparations he made for the enterprise surpassed all that he had yet attempted. Austria and Prussia were compelled to promise him support; the princes of the Confederation of the Rhine were ordered to have their contingents ready; material of war in immense quantities was accumulated in the North German fortresses; enormous magazines were formed to afford subsist- *Jealousy of the Czar, and disputes with Russia.* *Napoleon prepares to invade Russia, Nov. 1811, May 1812.*

ence to half a million of men, for the difficulty of following the usual system of war in Russia had been foreseen; and the whole forces of Western Europe were banded together for an expedition unequalled in its gigantic conception. Slowly and by degrees the prodigious host, an assemblage of many races and tongues—Italians, Germans, Dutch, Poles, and even Spaniards and Portuguese, commingled with the dominant French—was moved from distant points on the Continent; and by the early spring of 1812 it was aggregated on the plains of Northern Germany. The Emperor, leaving Paris in May, was soon at Dresden, where old Europe, in the persons of humbled and vanquished Kings, bowed in homage before the revolutionary Cæsar; and on June 24, 450,000 men, with 60,000 cavalry, and 1,200 guns, crossed the Niemen from the verge of Prussia, and entered the borders of the Russian Empire. Wilna was attained in a few days; but the difficulties of the vast enterprise had already made themselves seriously felt; desertion and disease had set in; the march of the columns had been delayed by the mass of impediments on their track; and Napoleon was obliged to make a long halt while the Russian armies, which had advanced to the frontier, escaped from his well-designed manœuvres, and though separated and feebly led retired slowly into the distant interior.

Campaign of 1812.

The Grand Army crosses the Niemen, June 24, 1812.

Retreat of the Russians.

The French Emperor had now the means, without incurring any serious risk, of dealing Russia a decisive stroke; he might have avenged a great public crime, and proclaimed the freedom of the Polish Nation. But he characteristically preferred a merely hollow alliance with the Austrian

Political mistake of Napoleon in not restoring Poland.

and Prussian Courts to the Polish People; and though his armies were crowded with Polish soldiers, he intimated to a deputation at Wilna that he could not undo the work of the shameful Partition. He broke up from Wilna in the middle of July, leaving the greater part of his impedimenta behind, in order to pursue his retreating enemies, who, divided into two great masses under Barclay de Tolly and Bagration, held an extended line on the verge of Lithuania, from Drissa on the Dwina, to the heads of the Dnieper. *He pursues the Russians.* Napoleon's movements were made slow by bad roads and the want of supplies, already causing havoc among his troops; and Barclay, carefully eluding his foe, succeeded in joining his colleague at Witepsk, and concentrating the united Russian forces, about 250,000 strong. The Grand Army had, by this time, lost considerably more than a third of its numbers, the young soldiers who filled its ranks, and the auxiliaries, disappearing in thousands; but Napoleon, hoping to out-manœuvre his opponent, marched upon Smolensko, in order to turn the positions of the Russians, or to compel them to fight. *Difficulties of the Grand Army.* Barclay, however, now in supreme command, and imitating the defensive method of Wellington, merely checked the Emperor and fell back, destroying the country upon his way, and Napoleon at Smolensko only found ruins, and a battle continually eluding his grasp. He resolved still to continue the pursuit; but it is a mistake to suppose that he took no precautions; on the contrary he sent large detachments to cover and secure his flanks and rear; he ordered large reserves to come up from Germany; and he directed immense magazines to be formed at Smolensko, Wilna, and other places. Having thus, as he thought, made his *Precautions taken by Napoleon.*

advance safe, he set off from Smolensko with about 160,000 men, drawn on through the vast expanses of Russia by the hope of ever-receding victory; but still Barclay stubbornly retired, and the invaders became more and more weakened. At last the indignation of the Russian army at its prolonged retreat led to the removal of its chief, and Kutusoff—the able veteran of 1805—having been appointed to the command by the Czar, was reluctantly forced to offer battle. The encounter took place at Borodino, on the way to Moscow, on September 7. It was murderous beyond all past experience; and though the Russians lost the position, their antagonists could hardly claim a triumph. Kutusoff, however, judiciously fell back, and on September 15, 1812, the Grand Army was master of Moscow, the extreme limit of the march of the Tricolor.

He marches into the interior of Russia.

Battle of Borodino, Sept. 7, 1812.

The Grand Army enters Moscow, Sept. 15, 1812.

The daring advance into the heart of Russia, enormous as the losses of the French had been, now seemed justified by the event; and Napoleon expected to dictate peace. A tremendous catastrophe was, however, to show what patriotism and hatred could plan and accomplish. The governor of Moscow set fire to the city in order to cut off its resources from the French, and as it was chiefly constructed of wood, it was soon a desert of devouring flame. Napoleon, however, still lingered on the spot, convinced that the Czar would yet treat; though Kutusoff, meanwhile, with prudence and skill, had drawn together his shattered forces, and was already menacing the Emperor's retreat. The hope of negotiation having proved fruitless, the Grand Army at last left the ruins of Moscow on Octo-

The Russian Governor of Moscow sets fire to the city.

Napoleon delays in the hope of peace.

ber 19, the intention of Napoleon being to march southward, and to attain Lithuania through a country in which his soldiers could find the means of subsistence. The movements, however, of the French were sluggish, for they had loaded themselves with the spoils of Moscow; and after an indecisive action at Malo Jaroslavetz, the Emperor abandoned his previous design, and retreated by the way he had before advanced. The sufferings of the French in this wasted region became gradually more and more intense; famine, aided by cold, destroyed thousands; Kutusoff hung on the flanks of the perishing host, annoying it with bristling swarms of Cossacks; and the Grand Army which, before leaving Moscow, was still more than 100,000 strong, dwindled into a mass of 40,000 fugitives before it reached the remains of Smolensko. News of fresh misfortunes were here received; the magazines had been hardly formed; two Russian armies, bearing before them the detachments he had left to protect his flanks, were gathering to bar the Emperor's retreat, and the only chance of safety was to press onward, and endeavor to open a way to Wilna. The wreck of the Grand Army, before long joined by the divisions which had tried to cover its wings, toiled feebly along the Lithuanian wastes, pursued, as hitherto, by its relentless foes; and, after increasing losses and horrors, it found itself on the Beresina, assailed and almost surrounded by hostile forces. It ought to have been destroyed to the last man; but its remains were saved by the skill of its chief, and the terror his name still spread around; and, strewing its path with the dying and the dead, it gradually approached the still distant frontier.

Beginning of the retreat from Moscow, Oct. 19, 1812.

Horrors of the retreat.

Imminent peril of Napoleon and the remains of the army.

Passage of the Beresina, Nov. 25-28, 1812.

Napoleon leaves the army for France, Dec. 5, 1812.

At Smorgoni Napoleon gave the command to his brother-in-law, Murat, the new King of Naples, and hastened off to France to raise fresh levies—a step which has been very differently judged—and after he had gone, the dissolution of the ruined array went on more rapidly. Con-

Destruction of the Grand Army.

siderable reserves, which had come up, were involved in the fate of the survivors of Moscow; and after plundering the magazines at Wilna, the thinned remnants of the once mighty host repassed the Niemen in little knots and bands, of which some were rallied behind the Vistula. More than 550,000 men, including reserves, had entered Russia, and it is doubtful if 50,000 of these were ever seen again with the eagles.

Reflections on this catastrophe.

The causes of this tremendous ruin, the prelude to Napoleon's fall, may be indicated in a few words. Something may be ascribed to the bad composition in every respect of the Grand Army, and something to the effects of the cold; and the conduct of Barclay, after Smolensko, and of Kutusoff, during the retreat, was able. The constancy, too, of the Russians was great; and the burning of Moscow certainly had immense, and possibly decisive, results in depriving the invaders of winter quarters. Napoleon may also have shown a want of his usual energy at Maroslavetz, and perhaps on one or two other occasions; he probably ought not to have left his army;

Causes of the ruin of the French.

and his manœuvres to overwhelm his enemies failed, though marked by his accustomed skill. The paramount cause, of the disaster, however, was that Napoleon's system of daring invasion was adopted on an extravagant scale, and was encountered, after some faulty operations, by the Russian commanders in the fitting way; the Grand Army perished from want, led on hundreds of miles in a barren country; and, curiously enough, the very means which Napoleon employed, at the outset of the campaign, to secure its support only led to mischief, for its impedimenta paralyzed brilliant manœuvres, which otherwise might have brought the war to an end. The example of Wellington at Torres Vedras contributed thus to this mighty overthrow; but Napoleon was anything but the madman which he has been called by superficial critics; and it is at least doubtful whether he would not have triumphed, had not Moscow been suddenly destroyed—a contingency on which no leader could reckon. He was a great commander in 1812, as he was throughout his military career, though his over-confidence was more apparent then than it had been on previous occasions; and, apart from the enterprise itself, undertaken in the pride of ambitious power, the chief mistake he probably made in the campaign was that of a politician, not of a chief of armies—the not disarming the Czar on the frontier by liberating the Polish race from its chains.

CHAPTER XIV.

FALL OF NAPOLEON.

AFTER leaving the remains of the Grand Army—he had hoped that it would rally at Wilna—Napoleon returned to Paris in disguise through the frozen plains of Poland and Germany. The reception he met was very different from that which

Return of Napoleon to Paris.

had greeted the warrior of 1799; and though the official *noblésse* of the Empire concealed their alarm by increased servility, France maintained that silence which is often ominous. An incident during his absence had revealed how really precarious was his Revolutionary throne; an obscure republican of the name of Malet had deceived persons in high places by the news of the Emperor's death; and Napoleon heard with amazement and anger that even the Bodies of the State had never thought of his infant son as his possible successor. To strengthen his dynasty, on paper at least, he declared the Empress Regent in the event of his death; but graver matters soon engrossed his thoughts. The Prussian Contingent in the Grand Army, having advanced only a short way into Courland, had made good its retreat comparatively intact; and, on being apprized of the issue of the Campaign, its commander, York, openly revolted from the French, and went over with his men to the Russian camp. This defection proved the shock that lets the avalanche loose, and sets it in motion to change the landscape. Northern Germany rose as a man to arms; the Prussian army —it had been organized after Jena on that peculiar system of which we have seen the astonishing results; and it was even now capable of large expansion, though, in deference to Napoleon's jealous will, reduced to a small standing force—compelled its ruler to declare war against France; insurrections broke out in the Hanse towns; and the heave of a great national stirring was seen in Saxony and the States of the Confederation of the Rhine, and even in Austria under absolute rule. The Czar, who had followed the march of Kutusoff, encouraged this

Conspiracy of Malet.

Defection of York, Dec. 30, 1812.

Rising of Germany, January—March, 1813.

universal movement; and in the first months of 1813 the Russian and Prussian armies, seconded by a great wave of popular war, were sweeping over the North German plains, and effacing the signs of French domination. Murat fled with the ranks of the Grand Army, giving up the command to Eugène Beauharnais, the viceroy of the Italian Kingdom; and that chief, conducting the retreat with skill, and undismayed by the flood of enemies, made good with difficulty his way to the Elbe, though obliged to abandon the French garrisons in the fortresses on the Oder and Vistula.

<small>Retreat of the French, February—March, 1813. Energy of Napoleon.</small>

Napoleon heard this intelligence with scorn and wrath, and addressed himself to pluck safety from danger. He treated the rising of Germany with contempt, as he had treated the rising of Spain, warned his crowned vassals to be on their guard against what he called a "Jacobin movement," and to have their contingents ready by the spring; and wrote to his father-in-law, the Emperor of Austria, already hesitating in the French alliance, that he reckoned with confidence on Austrian aid. His real power, however, was of course in France; and he strained his great faculties to the utmost to repair the disasters of 1812, and to make preparations for a fresh struggle. The resources of France were still great; she still lavished them to maintain her power, though cruelly stricken and discontented; and by summoning old soldiers to the eagles, by making regular troops of the National Guards, and by anticipating the conscription of the succeeding year, Napoleon set on foot, in a few weeks, the enormous mass of half a million of men, and even gave it military organization and form. These levies, however,

<small>His immense preparations to repair his fortunes.</small>

<small>Bad condition of the French levies.</small>

though still bearing the honored name of the Grand Army, had little in common with the band of Austerlitz; every arm, especially cavalry, was weak; and though under a great commander they were to show that they could gain battles, they formed a very imperfect instrument of war. The Emperor took the field in the last days of April, and in a short time the survivors of the awful retreat, drawing from the Elbe to the Elster and the Saale, had joined in Saxony the new legions which had, as it were, sprung from the earth at the bidding of their renowned master. By this time the Russian and Prussian armies had crossed the Upper Elbe and exposed themselves to the Emperor's blows, in the hope of gaining the support of the vassal South German States; and they fell on the French as they were advancing on Leipsic, through the broad plains of Lützen. The encounter was stern, but skill prevailed; and though the success of the French was really trifling, the trained soldiers of the Allies were forced to retire before troops composed largely of young conscripts. The star of Napoleon seemed now to emerge in splendor again from passing clouds; the subject Kings of Bavaria and Saxony made haste to put their contingents in his hand; he entered Dresden in a few days in triumph; and, as the Russians and Prussians continued to fall back, he pursued them to the verge of Silesia, and defeated them in a great battle at Baützen, one of the most remarkable of his wonderful exploits. He had now approached the Oder and Vistula, and had he prolonged this victorious march he would certainly have set his garrisons free, and perhaps have crushed for a time the rising of Germany. He thought, however, that a delay of a few

Campaign of 1813.

Battle of Lützen, May 2, 1813.

Battle of Baützen, May 20—21, 1813.

Success of Napoleon.

weeks would greatly improve his unformed armies ; and confident that a decisive triumph would lay his enemies prostrate at his feet, he consented, Austria having intervened, to an armistice which, as events turned out, was a capital and striking political mistake.

Armistice of Pleiswitz, June 4, 1813.

The negotiations that followed form a signal proof how ambition and pride may blind genius. Austria evidently at this moment held the balance between the belligerent Powers in Germany; and though the Austrian Germans wished for war with France, the Cabinet of Vienna, after Lützen and Baützen, thought peace with Napoleon an essential object, and proposed terms which would have left him master of France, Italy, Holland and Belgium, providing only for the independence of Germany, and the suppression of the Confederation of the Rhine.

Austria proposes terms to Napoleon which he unwisely rejects.

Napoleon, however, had no desire for peace; he had established his armies along the Elbe in positions where he hoped to renew the glories of 1796 on a grander scale, and to defy even all Europe in arms, when his military strength should have been more developed; and he refused to listen to the proposals of Austria, apparently indifferent to what her forces might be, to the disaffection of the Germans in his ranks, which had become manifest for some time, and to the national and angry rising already threatening on every side. In this state of things the Austrian Government, forgetting the old dislike of Prussia, and the recent ties that bound it to France, and yielding to imperious public opinion, inclined gradually towards the Allies; but no engagements were definitively formed, until events on a distant theatre of war determined a hitherto halting purpose. After Torres Vedras, Wellington had fought with varying success in 1811; but in the following year —his own forces having been increased by Portuguese levies made good soldiers by his skilful hand, and drafts from Russia having weakened the French—he invaded Spain, winning a great battle at Salamanca upon the Tormes; and though ultimately obliged to retreat, he liberated a considerable part of the Peninsula. In 1813 he dealt the decisive stroke; advancing from Portugal with an army superior in numbers for the first time to its foes; and aided by masses of Spanish levies, he routed the French with great loss at Vittoria; and in a short time he had reached the Pyrenees, and stood on the verge of that mighty Empire which had seemed invulnerable a few months before. This splendid success decided Austria: she threw in her lot with the Allies: and the most formidable Coalition she had ever yet encountered, encircled France, already worn-out and exhausted.

Napoleon, it is unnecessary to say, made a fatal mistake in rejecting these terms; if he believed that Austria was false, his conduct was arrogant and over-confident. Hostilities began on August 10, on an immense circle from the Oder to the Elbe, and from the Bohemian range to the Baltic, the centre of operations being the plains that form Saxony and the south of Prussia. Napoleon, as we have seen, had occupied the Elbe, and held its passages in great strength, throwing out secondary forces as far as the Elbe and Oder on either side; and from this position he hoped to defeat his enemies, and repeat the dazzling strokes by which he had ruined Würmser and Alvinzi in detail. The conditions, however, of the contest had changed ; it was more difficult to reach divided enemies in the broad space between the Oder and the Elbe, than in the narrow area between the Tyrol and the Adige ; the allied commanders had learned the Emperor's game ; and, above all, the levies of the French were very inferior to the allied armies, composed largely of seasoned troops fired by a sentiment of national hatred. The general plan of the Allies was to avoid Napoleon when he attacked in person, but to fall on his most distant lieutenants, and gradually to converge on their dreaded adversary when his strength had been thoroughly impaired; and as even in numbers they were greatly superior, about 550,000 to 360,000 men, they justly calculated on success at last. Their first movements, however, were ill-designed, and gave Napoleon a brilliant victory which in previous campaigns might have proved decisive. In the absence of the Emperor, who had set off against the Prussians in Upper Silesia, the Austrians and Russians under Schwartzenberg moved through the Bohemian hills on Dresden ; but their operations were uncertain and slow ; their great antagonist had time to return ; and they were completely defeated in a pitched battle, in which Moreau, who had joined their ranks, from animosity to the ruler of France, met a death unworthy of a French commander. *[margin: Plan of the Allies.]* *[margin: Battle of Dresden, Aug. 27, 1813.]*

Napoleon thought that he had now the Coalition in his power, but he was to be taught by a striking example how firm was the constancy of his present enemies. He despatched a force through the Bohemian passes to intercept the retreat of the Allies ; and, in the days of

Marengo and Rivoli, the manœuvre would probably have been successful. Either through his own overconfidence, however, or from errors in which his lieutenants fell, the detachment was too weak to make victory certain; and it was crushed at Culm by an attack of the Allies, who, instead of surrendering, as had been expected, assailed the French with determined energy. This victory redressed the balance of fortune, and events followed which turned the scale. Adhering to their scheme, the Allies fell on the distant lieutenants of the Emperor; one was defeated on the Katzbach in Silesia, another at Grossbeeren in Prussia, and a third with crushing effect at Dennewitz; and, instead of being rent asunder by his blows, the firm arrays of the allied armies drew in gradually their immense circle, and gathered upon their hemmed-in foes. Meanwhile the Grand Army was fearfully diminished by losses in the field, disease, and want; the Confederate Princes of the Rhine grew doubtful, and gradually assumed a menacing attitude; the auxiliaries deserted from the French in thousands, and vast masses of insurrectionary levies hung on the skirts of the dwindling host, keeping up a ruinous and unceasing warfare. The time had come at last for more daring movements; and Blucher, the vigorous chief of the Prussians, with Bernadotte—once a Marshal of France, but now transformed into a Swedish Prince—crossed the Elbe in the last days of September while Schwartzenberg issued again from Bohemia, the object of the Allies being to meet at Leipsic and overwhelm their adversary. Napoleon, had his movéments been free, might perhaps even yet have baffled his foes; but he could not trust

1813.   *Fall of Napoleon.*   249

his vassals in his rear; and he was slowly but surely forced upon Leipsic, and compelled to fight at great disadvantage. The first encounter took place on October 16; and though the Allies were at least 230,000 strong and the French not more than 150,000, the terror inspired by the Emperor was such that the battle had no decisive result. By the 18th, however, great reinforcements had poured in to support the Allies; the Saxon contingent abandoned the French on the field of battle, and fiercely attacked them; and, after a desperate conflict, the Grand Army, which fought magnificently when brought to bay, was gradually compelled to leave Leipsic. The destruction of the single bridge on the Elster, on the line of retreat, caused frightful confusion; a large part of the French army was cut off; and the victor of many fields was driven to the Rhine, leaving his garrisons on the Oder and Vistula to their fate. A gleam of success shone feebly on the retiring host; Bavaria had joined the Coalition, and Napoleon crushed a Bavarian force that had placed itself recklessly on his path; but in the first days of November the allied standards, borne by the power of embattled Europe, lowered on the imperilled Empire from across the Rhine. *Great battles of Leipsic, Oct. 16 and 18, 1813. The French driven to the Rhine.*

Such had been the results of the campaign in Saxony; and though the defections of the German troops, which contributed largely to the final issue, might silence those who have been lately holding up French military honor to the scorn of Europe, Germany had been set free from foreign invasion, and her people had shown heroic patriotism. In other parts of the theatre of war, fortune had also turned against the French Emperor. Austria had invaded *Defeats of the French in Italy. Wellington invades France.*

Italy from the north; Eugène Beauharnais had been beaten on the Adige; and Wellington, after a vigorous conflict with Soult, one of the ablest of the Imperial lieutenants, had descended on France from the Pyrenean frontier. Thus war gathered from all sides on the Empire, and the internal condition of that huge structure showed ominous signs of collapse and ruin. The Princes of the Confederation of the Rhine had before this abandoned their master; the Kingdom of Westphalia had already fallen; and Holland, and even Belgium, wasted by the conscription of the Continental system, had either risen or threatened revolt; while far to the South, Murat—"a paladin in the field, and a fool in the closet," in Napoleon's phrase—was trafficking with Austria, to save Naples. In France, too, the late mistress of Europe, the state of affairs was extremely alarming, and everything portended approaching disaster. 1813, following 1812, and the devouring years of the Spanish war, had consumed the military strength of the Nation; and only the shadows remained of the proud legions which had once trampled on prostrate Europe. Even the material of war was wanting in old France; it had been dissipated on a hundred fields, or transported to the Adige and the Elbe; and the finances, once upheld by the spoils of conquest, had suddenly failed, and were wholly exhausted. Nor was the temper of the Nation such as could endure invasion or continued defeat; its ardor of 1793 had died out; long wars and despotism had impaired its energy; and it was rather overwhelmed by the sense of misfortune, than resolved bravely to meet and subdue it. Though, too, the numerous classes and interests enriched by the Empire still clung to it, they

Revolt of the allied and subject states.

Desperate condition of the Empire.

secretly felt the general discontent; and the very servility of the instruments of power adding to the dangers arising from the instability of a Revolutionary State, and the mobility of the national character.

Napoleon did not yield to despair, though ruin seemed on all sides imminent. He might at this juncture have obtained peace by ceding part of the frontier of the Rhine; but he thought of little but a death-struggle. He gave orders to summon to the field all Frenchmen who had served in the army, though he characteristically refused to appeal to the nation; and, calculating that the Allies would not move till spring, he prepared to contend for the greater part of the Empire. The remains of his forces were distributed along the immense front, from the Scheldt to the Adige, as he believed that he would have time to reinforce them; and though he finally abandoned Spain, he resolved to strike for the whole Rhine and Italy. Had he been permitted to mature his plans, it is difficult to say what the result might have been; but the Coalition had been taught not to repeat the errors of 1793; and the allied chiefs were in a very different mood from the Yorks and Brunswicks of a former day. Towards the close of December 1813 they set in motion their immense hosts; and Blücher and Schwartzenberg crossed the Rhine in two masses from Coblentz to Bäsle, while to the North Bernadotte invaded Belgium, and Wellington, to the South, advanced to the Adour. This sudden and overwhelming invasion completely disconcerted Napoleon's projects, and for several weeks met no resistance on the theatre where it was most formidable. Driving before them some feeble French detachments, and masking, as it is called, the fortresses on

Napoleon thinks only of a death-struggle.

His preparations.

The Allies invade France, Dec. 20—26.

their way, Blücher and Schwartzenberg soon passed the Vosges; and by the middle of January, 1814, their converging armies reached the end of the vast plain which, watered by numerous streams, extends through Champagne to the capital of France, from the western hills of Lorraine and Franche Comté.

The military situation of Napoleon seems hopeless.

The military situation of the French Emperor at this juncture appeared hopeless. He had raised only a small part of the levies he had intended to collect; and he had probably not 250,000 men, including the remains of his Spanish armies, to oppose to the hosts of the Coalition, which numbered fully 500,000, supported by enormous reserves. His troops, too, were in part worn-out and demoralized, and his lieutenants had lost their wonted confidence; while the allied commanders were flushed with success, and their armies burned with fierce national passions. France also seemed without hope and prostrate; and even the obsequious Bodies of State, and the new *noblesse* of the Revolution, had begun at last to show dangerous symptoms of open insubordination and anger.

Prostration of France.

Campaign of 1814.

Napoleon, however, did not despair, and prepared to encounter Blücher and Schwartzenberg, though these leaders had more than 200,000 men, within easy reach of each other in Champagne, and he had hardly more than 70,000 in hand. His first operations were unfortunate; in a daring attempt to separate the Allies, he fought an indecisive battle at Brienne, and was beaten with heavy loss at La Rothière; and had his antagonists followed up their success, or even acted with ordinary skill, they could have made the issue of the campaign certain. But Blücher and Schwartzenberg had advanced

Battles of Brienne and La Rothière, Jan. 29, Feb. 1, 1814.

1814.   *Fall of Napoleon.*   253

on divergent lines, and were alienated by mutual dislike and jealousy ; and, accordingly, at this critical moment they divided instead of uniting their forces, and began to march on Paris by distant roads, one along the Marne, the other along the Seine. The opportunity was not lost by the great warrior who stood in their path, and whose powers were never, perhaps, more evident than when in a position of this kind. Availing himself with consummate art of the obstacles formed by the double rivers, and leaving a detachment to hold Schwartzenberg in check, Napoleon, in the first days of February, marched against Blücher, who had spread his forces along the Marne with careless confidence; and the result was worthy of the General of 1796. Breaking in on the side of the Prussian army, Napoleon met its separate divisions, and multiplying his swift and terrible strokes, routed them one after the other in detail, at Champaubert, Montmirail, and Vauchamps; and in less than a week the discomfited chief was driven, completely beaten, on Chalons, with forces reduced to half their numbers. The Emperor now turned against his second enemy, descending from the Marne to the Seine; and in a short time the army of Schwartzenberg, which had also pressed forward with little caution, was pierced through and compelled to retreat, after a double defeat at Montereau and Nangis. The losses of the Allies had been so great, that Schwartzenberg actually sought an armistice; and at the close of February the invading host had fallen back to the positions in Champagne, from which it had moved a month before.

Napoleon interposes between the allies.

Battles of Champaubert, Montmirail, Vauchamps and Nangis, Feb. 10—18, 1814.

These operations rank justly among the finest specimens of Napoleon's skill, though

Astonishing success of Napoleon.

made possible only by the errors of his foes. Negotiations were now set on foot, and had he abandoned Belgium and Italy, he might have preserved part of the revolutionary conquests; but he refused, either from indomitable pride, or confidence in his late extraordinary success. The Coalition resolved to continue the war; and events on other parts of the theatre contributed largely to confirm their purpose. The arms of Wellington progressed in Gascony; Eugène Beauharnais was being driven from Italy; and Murat, with the disloyalty of a revolutionary age, was actually preparing to march from Naples, and make common cause with the allied armies. It was, therefore, evident that the British commander would occupy a large part of the Imperial forces—the Army of Soult at this juncture was in fact superior to that of his master—and that a fresh attack would be made from the east; and it was thought impossible but that the allied armies would at last crush their still dreaded antagonist. Hostilities were resumed in the beginning of March; and, in order to make success certain, Bernadotte was directed to advance to the Meuse, Schwartzenberg refusing otherwise to move; though united to Blücher, he was still immensely superior to the French Emperor in force. Napoleon proceeded to renew against Blücher his late manœuvres; and he had nearly caught his stubborn foe, who, though daring to a fault, was wanting in skill, when Blücher was saved by the surrender of Soissons, and having joined the vanguard of Bernadotte, was able to offer battle in preponderating strength. Napoleon was compelled to recross the Aisne, after a bloody and disastrous action at Laon; and having thus failed to defeat Blücher, he thought himself

Success of the Allies in other parts of the theatre.

Fresh forces raised against Napoleon.

Battle of Laon, March 9–16, 1814.

unequal to assail Schwartzenberg; and threatened with destruction by their uniting armies, he formed a resolution which, though fatal in the event, was worthy of his art as a military scheme ;" and, in other times, might have proved successful. Considerable forces were locked up in the fortresses on the Meuse and the Moselle—those on the Oder and Vistula had been lost—and the Emperor determined to fall back on Lorraine, to add these garrisons to his army in the field, and then, descending on the rear of his foes, with a force stronger than he had yet possessed, to oblige them to fight in a position in which a single defeat might prove as ruinous as that of Melas had been at Marengo. He broke up from the Aube towards the end of March, after a short conflict with the enemy on his way; and, concealing the movement by a screen of horse, his columns sought the roads to the Moselle. *Napoleon falls back on Lorraine, to rally his garrisons, and strike the rear of the Allies.*

This march of Napoleon would have certainly made the Allies pause, on ordinary occasions, and might have exposed them to his strokes; but though Blücher and Schwartzenberg had suffered heavily, the Coalition held firmly together, and national passions inspired its armies. At a council of war held on March 24th, it was resolved to disregard the Emperor's movement, and to make a *The Allies march on Paris, March 25, 1814.* great effort to bring the war to a close, by marching directly on the capital. The condition of France, and of Paris itself, concurred to favor this bold design. The Nation, utterly exhausted by war, had become wearied of the Imperial rule ; the distress of most of the great towns had caused the royalist and republican parties, long silent, to raise again their heads ; and in the capital, the centre of thought and opinion, Napoleon's tottering throne was mined by intrigue. A sentiment had spread that could peace be obtained, and the interests of the Revolution be saved, the Emperor ought to be made a sacrifice; and it had made way among the aristocracy of wealth, which had worshipped Napoleon in the day of success, among the Bodies of State, which, in this manner, avenged themselves for the slights of power, and among the masses of a thoughtless populace demoralized by the events of the last twenty years. Thus everything led the Allies to believe that the fate of Paris would prove decisive; and their great armies were set in motion, converging upon the defenceless capital, which for so long a time had been the ardent focus of trouble, disturbance, glory, and empire. Driving before them a few weak bodies of troops which attempted in vain to retard their advance, they had soon reached the hills overlooking Paris; and after a brief but sharp struggle the city surrendered on March 30. The hopes of the Allies were soon verified: on an assurance that the rights which had grown up since the Revolution would be guaranteed, the once humble and flattering Senate declared the Crown of Napoleon forfeited; the example was followed by the different Bodies which represented the Nation or the State; and, as in the presence of the hosts of Europe, no other choice could have been accepted, the Bourbon Monarchy was re-established in the person of the Count of Provençe, the second brother of Louis XVI. Some interested demonstrations of joy were made; but though the Nation, on the whole, acquiesced, and changed the Empire with the same suddenness with which it had changed the extinct Republic, it felt intensely the humiliation of defeat, and received the Bourbons without sympathy;

1814.   *Fall of Napoleon.*   257

nor did thousands forget the name of Napoleon, even when, under the stress of crushing disaster, it was widely denounced as the symbol of ruin.

While these memorable events were occurring, the Emperor had pursued his march eastwards; but on the news of the allied movement, he retraced hastily his steps through Champaigne. He arrived at Fontainebleau, with about 70,000 men, as the capitulation was being signed; and for a moment he formed the desperate design of falling on the Allies, who had divided their forces negligently upon the Seine, in the confidence of assured success. His lieutenants, however, protested against an attempt which might have destroyed Paris, even though, as he insisted to the last, it was promising from a military point of view; and one of them, Marmont, having, without their knowledge, placed his divisions in the power of the Allies, the conqueror's sword fell broken from his hand, and he was left defenceless in the midst of his enemies. In a few days he abdicated the throne; and the fallen Lord of five-sixths of Europe, deserted by those whom he had raised to greatness, though his soldiery clung with devotion to their chief, was left to muse, unheeded and alone, on the instability of human things, and the punishment of unbridled pride and ambition. The small island of Elba had been given him in exchange for the Empire he had lost; and, after a touching farewell to the veterans of his Guard—the Tenth Legion of the modern Cæsar—he set off for his insignificant realm, the populace of the maritime towns having more than once beset him, on his way, with execrations which made him feel the misery caused by the Continental system. Thus fell from the loftiest height of grandeur attained by man in the modern world, that mighty pro-

Napoleon hastily retraces his steps.

He abdicates, April 4, 1814.

S

duct of the French Revolution—the Lucifer, as he has been called with some truth, of the gigantic strife of the first part of the century. Those who regard Napoleon as a mere tyrant, destructive, cruel, inhuman, selfish, see only a very small part of his character, and pervert it by this imperfect estimate. Many as were his faults and, we may say, his crimes, this wonderful being conferred benefits on France which she has not forgotten; and if his despotism was an evil from the first, and contained the germs of future disaster, and if his ambition was always perilous, his government was able and moderate for a time, and even his blood-stained career of conquest was not without good results in Europe. His fall is the old tale of the terrible effects on the conduct of men of unbounded power; and the potentate who, after the Treaty of Tilsit, set himself to oppose the laws of nature, invaded Spain with perfidious insolence, plunged into the frozen deserts of Russia with Europe conspiring on his homeward path, and preferred to challenge the world to arms to the surrender of a worthless ascendency, seems a different person from the Bonaparte of Luneville and the author of the Concordat and the Code. For the rest, if Napoleon had few scruples, and was pitiless in carrying out his aims, this may be accounted for, in some measure, by the moral confusion of the France of his time; and if he made self the centre of his hopes, he associated self with national greatness. As a General he created modern war; and though his passionate and daring imagination made him over-confident as a military chief, and his strategy of invasion was not always safe, he stands pre-eminent as a leader of armies, was a master of his art in all its departments, and was wholly unrivalled in those great combinations which form the highest problems of military science.

His greatest fault as a politician was the contempt of national feelings and instincts, which led him into innumerable mistakes; nor did he, perhaps, give proof of the gifts which distinguish statesmen of the first order; but he had good reason to despise and distrust the popular movements of the France of his youth; and he possessed in the very highest degree the faculty of administration, and even of government. Let it be added, too, that perhaps his despotism was inevitable in the existing condition of France, that for years it was the glory of Frenchmen, and that, to this day, it has been, in part, justified by the noble institutions and great measures, with which History will always connect it. The offspring of the Revolution and yet its controller, Napoleon stands on the tracts of the Past, the most prominent figure of a wonderful age; and the shadow of the great name along the path of Time seems to blight the pretensions of rulers alien to his own race in the land he swayed.

In the readiness of France to throw off Napoleon we see a fresh proof of the national character; and the manner in which French officials of State and dignitaries of every kind abandoned the master to whom they owed everything, stands in marked contrast to the steadfast loyalty of Austrian and Prussian nobles to their Kings after such calamities as Jena and Austerlitz, and to the constancy of the Allies in 1813-14. Before, however, we censure Frenchmen generally, all the circumstances must be taken into account, and condemnation must be largely qualified. After making efforts such as never, perhaps, have been made by a European State, France was utterly broken down when the invasion came; and in this condition of affairs we can hardly feel surprise that she deserted a Sovereign who, at the moment, appeared

Reflections on his fall.

the existing cause of her sufferings and whose chief title to her obedience was success. As for the conduct of the marshals and ministers who forsook Napoleon in the hour of misfortune, it was such as has more than once been seen in the case of a mere *noblesse* of functionaries, the new-made instruments of new-made power, and without the traditions, and the sense of honor, that distinguish an aristocracy worthy of the name. Apart, however, from the national temperament, the inevitable result of the Revolution was to weaken in France every tie that binds the State and even society together; and, accordingly, when it was put to the proof, the authority of Napoleon suddenly collapsed, and could not bear the strain of disaster, the truest test of institutions and men. Still we must not imagine that all classes were indifferent to the fall of the Empire; the remains of the Army mourned their chief, and his name retained its spell in parts of the country. Nor can we ascribe to the Revolution alone the precarious nature of his unstable rule, for the Monarchy of the Bourbons was overthrown with greater facility than the Empire, and left, perhaps, fewer adherents behind. In fact, the corruption of the old order of things had blighted loyalty and faith in France before the events of 1789; and we must not ascribe the whole difficulty of establishing power in that country to the period of disorder that followed, though this has certainly been a principal cause. We must add, too, that it was not only those of new origin, and recent dignity, who betrayed Napoleon or fell away from him; his imperial consort shook him off as lightly as she would have shaken off a disagreeable dream; his discarded plebeian wife died of a broken heart "at the ruin of her Cid."

CHAPTER XV.

THE HUNDRED DAYS AND WATERLOO.

FRANCE, after the capitulation of Paris, was at the mercy of the victorious Coalition. Owing, however, to the interposition of England, the conditions of peace were less onerous than the vanquished Nation might have expected; though stripped of all her revolutionary conquests, she was left with her ancient boundaries intact, and if her influence was relatively lessened by the tendency of large to absorb small States, which had been one effect of the late disorder of Europe, she remained the France of Louis XVI. The Peace of Paris, as it was called, was followed by a Congress, to resettle the Continent, held at Vienna in the autumn of 1814; and at this great Council the Northern Powers exhibited an ambitious lust for dominion not unworthy of Napoleon himself. Russia threatened to swallow the whole of Poland; and Prussia, not contented with the enormous spoil she had acquired by taking part alternately with France and the allied Power, aspired to annex a large part of Germany ; and their pretensions became so intolerable that a fresh general war seemed for a while imminent. Meantime Louis XVIII., the new King of France, had endeavored to consolidate his power; but the difficulties in his way were, perhaps, invincible. The Bourbon Monarchy was soon felt to represent national disaster and disgrace ; if France had eagerly grasped at peace, she

Peace of Paris, May 30, 1814.

Congress of Vienna, Sept., 1814, March, 1815.

Unpopularity of the Government of Louis XVIII.

quickly learned to dislike her position as a conquered Power not of the first class, and she charged on her rulers the bitter consequences of humiliation, subjugation, and defeat. The government of the King, too, made several mistakes, and the associations which gathered round it contributed to excite alarm and suspicion. The old Imperial army was broken up, and deprived of the far-famed Tricolor; many of the new revolutionary interests were menaced, if not openly attacked; invidious distinctions were drawn which disturbed the civil equality won in 1789; and plans were formed for changes which seemed to shake the innumerable titles founded on the immense confiscations of bygone years. The general feeling of ill-will was increased by the attitude and conduct of the surviving *émigrés* who had returned with Louis from exile; these representatives of a detested past, who, it was bitterly said, "could neither forget nor learn," talked loudly of restoring the feudal abuses, and of taking their own in due time; and, high placed and caressed at court, they delighted to display towards the upstart *noblesse* of the "Corsican monster," as he was called, the refined insolence of an exclusive caste. The fine ladies of this worthy order of men were singularly skilful, as may be supposed, in this exhibition of the breeding of Versailles.

Conduct of the émigrés.

The general result of this state of things was that, within a few months after his elevation to the throne, France became hostile to her new monarch, and, filled with sullen jealousy and discontent, began to hope wistfully for some unknown change. The sentiment of irritation soon proved intense in the army still true to its mighty chief; and it was shared by the whole class of younger officers, though the ennobled marshals of the fallen Emperor felt or feigned respect for the restored dynasty. All this was not lost on the extraordinary man who, from his island speck in the Mediterranean, kept his eyes fixed on the state of Europe ; and by degrees Napoleon conceived the design of escaping from the kind of royal captivity in which he had been lately placed. His preparations were not long in being made, and on February 26, 1815, he set off on the most daring enterprise which even his sanguine mind had· formed—that of recovering his lost Empire in the face, as it seemed, of all Europe against him. A few hundred men of the Imperial Guard, left about him incautiously by the Allies, accompanied the adventurer in a flotilla; and it is but just to say that if his attempt was a breach of faith as regards Europe, it was hardly so as regards Louis XVIII., who had been intriguing against a still feared rival. On the 1st of March the little expedition set foot on the shores of Provence, not far from the spot where years before the youthful Bonaparte had returned from Egypt; and the strange apparition was soon welcomed with sentiments of exultation and joy, for the neighboring peasantry had not forgotten how Marengo had freed them from foreign invasion. In a few hours the exile was threading his way through the defiles of Dauphiny, issuing on his path proclamations appealing to French patriotism ; and his march before long began to resemble the rapid spread of some mighty influence which, for the moment, nothing can resist. Regiment after regiment, sent to check his progress, threw down their arms at the well-known sight of their loved and unforgotten commander; and in a short time his insignificant band had gathered into a con-

Napoleon leaves Elba. Feb. 26, May, 1815.

He lands in France, March 1, 1815.

His triumphant march to Paris.

siderable force, which multiplied at every stage of his advance. He was at Grenoble on March 9, and by the 10th had taken possession of Lyons; and, as he moved onwards, hostile authority seemed to disappear and perish before him. The whole army was now in revolt; and Ney, one of his most brilliant lieutenants, having been swept away in the general torrent, the Bourbon cause soon became desperate, and Louis XVIII., fled across the frontier. On March 20 the restored exile was once more in his place at the Tuileries; and, before a fortnight had passed, a faint show of royalist opposition had been quietly put down. Yet though in Napoleon's expressive phrase, "his eagle had flown from steeple to steeple with the Tricolor to the towers of Notre Dame," the Revolution which had reseated him on the throne was in the main the work of the army; and if France, fascinated, as it were, at the sight, seemed to welcome her returning master again, she rather rejoiced that the Bourbons were gone than believed or even hoped that the Empire could live.

Pacific overtures of Napoleon. Napoleon, upon regaining the throne, assured the Great Powers of his desire for peace, and soon afterwards proceeded to offer a more liberal Constitution to France than she had possessed at any previous time, with a double Assembly, and guarantees for freedom. It is useless to inquire whether the Emperor was sincere; but it is not surprising that he was not believed, and he was quickly undeceived even if he imagined that he could play the part of a "Napoleon of Peace." *The Allied Powers declare war, March 25, 1815.* At the intelligence of his return from Elba, the discords of the Coalition ceased; and after proclaiming Napoleon an outlaw, the Great Powers set their armies in motion to crush the usurper and invade France again.

1815.   *The Hundred Days.*   265

Left thus to contend against Europe in arms, Napoleon tried to confront the approaching tempest; and notwithstanding all that detractors have said, his efforts were great and worthy of him. He did not indeed, appeal to the Nation, true to the last to his despotic instincts, or revive the memories of 1793, and France was still much too worn-out to display the enthusiasm of that time; but he effected all that ability could effect; and if he ultimately failed, it was because the nature of the present contest had nothing in common with that in which the Convention triumphed. One fortunate circumstance was in his favor; many thousands of prisoners had returned home, and by making use of these old soldiers and turning to the best account the resources of France, he raised the French army from a state of impotence to a force of not less than 600,000 men, of whom 200,000 were ready for the field. Two strategetic combinations were now before him: he might either await the attack of the Allies around Paris, which he had hastily fortified, or he might suddenly assume the offensive, and, falling upon one of their separate masses, endeavor to divide and beat them in detail. Adhering to his usual system of war, he resolved to adopt the second plan; and if possibly it was the less prudent, it was in some particulars extremely tempting. On the extreme end of the front of invasion on which the hosts of the Coalition would move, the two armies of Blücher and Wellington lay encamped in Belgium from the Scheldt to the Meuse; and they were exposed to a fierce and sudden attack, as they were extended along the French frontier, and their supports were

Great efforts of Napoleon to restore the French army.

Campaign of 1815.

Two plans of operations open to Napoleon.

He resolves to attack Blücher and Wellington in Belgium.

still on the Elbe and the Oder. It might be possible, thus, to assail and divide this detached wing of the hostile arrays, and to destroy successively its isolated parts; and if a decisive victory were won, who could tell what the results would be? And if the Emperor should be inferior in force, many a field of fame could attest that his genius had been able to turn the scales of fortune when placed in a position of this kind.

Concentration of the French army on the frontier. In the second week of June the movement began on which the Emperor had staked his destiny. The French divisions, their movements concealed by false demonstrations with exquisite skill, drew together rapidly from Lille to Metz, while the Imperial Guard pressed forward from Paris, the Emperor's object being to combine his forces secretly and swoop on Belgium. Napoleon left the capital on June 12; and by the evening of the 14th his whole army, concentrated with extraordinary art, was collected on the edge of the French frontier, immediately around the banks of the Sambre. It numbered about 130,000 men; but though a sudden rising in La Vendée had deprived its chief of 20,000 more, and the united armies of Blücher and Wellington were fully 220,000 strong, Napoleon drew, from what he had already achieved, a hopeful augury of brilliant success. On the morning of the 15th the march began, but though skilfully delayed by a Prussian detachment, the French columns advanced rapidly; and having passed the Sambre and seized Charleroi, made straight for the centre of the allied line, the great road from Namur to Brussels, which, as Napoleon calculated, was but weakly defended. The French army, before night had closed, lay between Gosselies, Frasne, and Fleurus; and if it had not got

It advances on June 15, 1815.

quite so far as its leader had wished, it was even now in a most formidable position, within easy reach of the advanced posts of its foes, not as yet concentrated in adequate strength. On the 16th the French advanced again; and Blücher, who, with his wonted daring, was eager to fight as soon as possible, offered battle to Napoleon near Ligny, though his forces were not nearly collected, and Wellington had urged him not to run the risk. The engagement was one of the fiercest on record, each side contending with a national hatred; but the skill of Napoleon at last triumphed; and the Prussian army, pierced through the centre, was driven with heavy loss from the field. Meanwhile Ney had attacked Wellington at Quatre Bras, a few miles to the left: but though the British chief could send no aid to Blücher, he held Ney in check, and preserved the Prussians from an attack on the flank designed by the Emperor, which would have made Ligny a second Jena. An accident, however, alone prevented this consummation from being otherwise attained. Ney had left a part of his forces in his rear; and Napoleon having perceived from Ligny that his lieutenant was making but little progress, he ordered this division to advance and accomplish the task of Ney, and complete the defeat of Blücher. Ney, however, severely pressed by Wellington, called this detachment to him at the critical moment; and this misadventure probably had a decisive influence on the result of the campaign.

Battle of Ligny, June 16, 1815.

Battle of Quatre Bras, June 16, 1815.

These operations had given the French a brilliant triumph over the Prussians, had brought them upon the allied centre, and had prevented Blücher and Wellington

Result of the operations of June 16.

joining on what was their proper line of junction, the before-named road from Namur to Brussels. Still the Prussian army had not been routed as the Emperor had had good reason to hope; and the allied chiefs might yet find the means of uniting by activity and zeal, an event which might lead to Napoleon's ruin. The Emperor, however, after Ligny, appears to have thought that, for some days at least, he had got rid of the defeated Prussians, and that he would have ample time to turn against Wellington; and this conclusion would probably have been entirely correct in his earlier campaigns. Events, however, were soon to show what the energy of the allied chiefs and the passions which sustained the Prussians could effect. The Prussian army, though beaten at Ligny, had not been in the least cowed; Blücher had rallied it with heroic vigor; and he had soon concentrated his whole forces, and made them ready for a new effort, in position only a few miles from Wellington. The British commander prepared to approach his colleague by a corresponding movement; and thus, though forced from the first line, the allied generals were not really divided, and were beginning to approach each other on a second. The French, meanwhile, had been allowed to halt, worn-out by continued marches and fighting, nor had the movement of the retiring Prussians been watched and followed with sufficient care; and, accordingly, when about mid-day on the 17th, Napoleon broke up to assail Wellington, he had no conception that the Prussian army was not far off, and was drawing towards the British. He left Quatre Bras with about 72,000 men, having detached Grouchy with 34,000 to "observe the Prussians and com-

Blucher rallies the Prussians, and moves to join Wellington.

On a second line.

Movements of Napo-

plete their defeat;" but Wellington was already falling back; and by the evening he had taken a position beyond the little village of Waterloo, resolved to accept battle on a pledge from Blücher—who, at this time, had his whole army at Wavre, twelve miles away—that he would come up and assist the British. Meanwhile Grouchy, who had completely lost sight of the Prussians, and even of the line of their march, and who, besides, like the Emperor, thought they could not yet venture to join Wellington, had advanced only a short way from Ligny; and, ignorant what dispositions to make, had halted in the neighborhood of Gembloux, at a considerable distance in the rear of Napoleon, and separated from Blücher by no small interval.

<small>Position of Wellington on June 17, 1815. Miscalculations of Napoleon.</small>

By these arrangements it had been made all but certain that the allied armies would unite at Waterloo in sufficient time to overpower the French; and the chances were faint that Grouchy at Gembloux would be able to arrest the march of Blücher. The Emperor, however, either still convinced that the Prussians were far away from the field, or that Grouchy possessed the means to stop them, thought only of bringing Wellington to bay; and as Wellington had only 69,000 men, composed in part of second-rate troops; and was very inferior in horse and guns, his adversary felt assured of victory. Napoleon wished to attack at daybreak on the 18th; but the night and morning had been dense with rain, and he delayed the attack for several hours, in order to allow the ground to harden, and to give his manœuvres more effect—a sure proof that he had no conception that Blücher was already gathering on his flank. The battle began by an assault on Hougoumont, an advanced post on

<small>Results of the operations of June 17.</small>

Great battle of Waterloo, June 18, 1815. the British right; but this was intended to be a feint; and it was succeeded by a tremendous onslaught on Wellington's left and left centre, which met a brilliant and decisive repulse. Meanwhile Napoleon had been informed that about 30,000 men of Blücher's forces had advanced from Wavre, and were close at hand; and, accordingly, at about mid-day he sent part of his reserve against this unexpected foe, though he still hoped it was a stray column which he would be able to hold in check. The plan of Napoleon's battle was thus much disturbed; but he turned fiercely against the British centre; and, after a series of furious attacks, the French became masters of La Haye Sainte, a farm-house in front of Wellington's line. The violence of their efforts now became intense; the French calvary streamed up the slopes of Mont St. Jean, and fell desperately on the British position; but nothing could break the infantry of the defence, which in solid squares "seemed rooted to the earth;" and after a succession of fruitless charges, the horsemen, who were unsupported by foot, were obliged, cruelly mutilated, to retreat. During all this time the Prussian detachment had been striking hardly at Napoleon's right; and this had given Wellington relief not sufficiently acknowledged by English writers; but about seven this attack seemed spent; and Napoleon seized the opportunity to make a last attempt against the British centre. The greater part of the Imperial Guard, the veterans of a hundred fields, marched resolutely to this fresh encounter; but Wellington had skilfully strengthened his line; and, after a short but terrible struggle, the Guard was repulsed and swayed slowly backward. It was now the turn of the British to advance; and just at this moment the remaining masses of Blücher appeared upon the field, and rending asunder the French right, converted defeat into a frightful rout. Except the Guard, which fought to the last, Napoleon's army became a mere chaos of despairing fugitives pursued by the Prussians; and only a fragment of the ruined host was ever seen in arms again. Grouchy, who had broken up from Gembloux late, and had refused, when urged, to approach Waterloo, only reached Wavre to find Blücher gone, and merely detained 15,000 Prussians from the scene where the Empire had succumbed. *Defeat and rout of the French army.*

Volumes have been written on this memorable struggle, yet the general facts are sufficiently plain. The first operations of the French Emperor were a masterpiece of military skill; and the result was that, in spite of a very great preponderance of force, Blücher and Wellington were in peril on June 16, and probably, but for a mere accident, Ligny would have been an overwhelming defeat. The Emperor's movements after the 16th have been condemned by the worshippers of success; but all that can be fairly said is that he sanctioned certain errors of detail, for which a commander-in-chief can be scarcely blamed, and that he made a single false calculation, fatal in the event, but extremely natural. The delays of the French on the 17th should be ascribed to the fatigues of the troops; if the Prussians were not sufficiently watched, surely the fault lies mainly with the French staff; and as for the supposition that Blücher could not join Wellington for some days, Napoleon's views were warranted by his earlier campaigns, and had proved correct on similar occasions. It was in fact most unlikely that the defeated Prussians would be able to make a critical march and fight at Waterloo on June *Reflections on the campaign.*

18; and that such a movement became possible was largely caused by a moral element—the passions that stirred the army of Blücher. Nor did Napoleon neglect the Prussians; he detached Grouchy to hold them in check; and the conduct of his lieutenant was wretched, even if we may doubt that with 34,000 men he could have stopped Blücher with 90,000. Napoleon was not a "mere shadow of his former self" in 1815; and if he met ruin on the field of Waterloo, it was not because his powers had declined, but that—apart from the overconfidence which we see in this as in other campaigns—his antagonists supported each other better than any allied chiefs had ever done before, and especially that the Prussian army, sustained by a principle he undervalued, baffled reasoning, founded on experience, indeed, but fatally untrue in the actual contest. If this view be right, the defeat of Napoleon was largely due to his characteristic contempt of some of the strongest feelings that animate man; and the frequent errors of the politician confounded the schemes of the military chief. As for the conduct of the allied commanders, it exposed them to danger at the outset; and as Blücher ought not to have fought at Ligny, it revealed at first the divided councils so often disastrous to allies. But all this was nobly repaired; and the constancy of Wellington on the field of Waterloo, and the heroism of Blücher in overcoming defeat, are fine specimens of great qualities. Yet though Waterloo was a splendid triumph, the fame of Wellington does not rest on the campaign of 1815 as a whole; his real title to renown depends on the admirable sagacity with which he perceived the weak point in Napoleon's strategy, and illustrated a discovery, big with great results, by his memorable defence of Torres Vedras.

1815. *The Hundred Days.* 273

Napoleon abdicated after the rout of Waterloo, the French Chambers, already hostile, rising against him in the hour of disaster; and before long he was on his way to the last scene of his eventful history, the solitary island of St. Helena. France, trodden under foot by the allied hosts, accepted the Bourbons in 1815, as she had accepted them the year before; but though Louis XVIII. was a sagacious ruler, such a dynasty could not become permanent. A sudden heave of the revolutionary forces which, though long quiescent, retained life, deprived Charles X. of his crown; and a Constitutional Monarchy was set up in his stead, in favor of the son of the Duke of Orleans, the Royal Jacobin of 1793. This government, of which the chief feature was a corrupt and weak parliamentary system, met the fate of its immediate forerunner, and it was followed by a short-lived Republic, which, after agitating Europe in 1848, perished unlamented in 1851. Long before this time the great name of Napoleon had regained its magical power in France, and the nephew of the departed conqueror, a grandson of the divorced Josephine, was raised to the throne as Emperor of the French, assuming the title of Napoleon III. The Second Empire was a feeble image of the first, without the military genius of its chief; and it disappeared in the great war of 1870, in which Prussia, heading a united Germany, more than avenged the disaster of Jena, and has torn from France Alsace and Lorraine, spared in 1814 and 1815. A provisional Republic has been since in power, its history marked by a national defence as gallant as that of 1793, but less noticed because a failure, and by a terrific outbreak of Jacobin frenzy which awed Europe in 1871; but this settlement is felt to be only for a time; and France remains torn by revolutionary troubles kept under only

Conclusion.

T

by the power of the sword in the hands of a soldier brave indeed, but not a chief of the first order. The general results of these events, which all run up to 1789–1815, are that Government in France is never secure, and that the nation appears to have lost some essential elements of general welfare; and though the great convulsion of the last century is not the only, it certainly is a principal cause of this evil disorder. If the material progress of France, too, since the fall of Feudalism has been immense, there has been no corresponding moral improvement; and if, within the memory of living man, she swayed Europe from the Tagus to the Baltic, her military reverses have since that time been awful, and the Tricolor has been plucked down from Metz and Strasburg, which once floated on Madrid and Moscow. The consequences of the Revolution outside France, have been, on the whole, more fruitful of good; they have tended to civilization and national progress, but they have been accompanied all over Europe by frightful wars and general disturbance; and we see the evils in the prodigious armaments and fierce animosities of the Continent, and in the disregard of the rights of the weak, and the ignoble flattery of force and success, too characteristic of modern politics. ' We end as we began; it is at least doubtful whether the mischief done by the French Revolution does not preponderate over its benefits. The greatest of English historians remarked, a few years before 1789, that the era of wars seemed about to close, and that Europe would be for all time secure from the barbarism of the savage hordes which had overturned Imperial Rome. What would Gibbon have said had he lived to witness Borodino, Leipsic, Waterloo, Sedan, and the atrocities of the Reign of Terror, and of the Commune of Paris in 1871!

APPENDIX.

AN ABRIDGED BIBLIOGRAPHY

OF THE

FRENCH REVOLUTION.

BY ANDREW D. WHITE.

AMONG the things which most astonished Arthur Young, as he looked upon the first stir of the French Revolution, he notes, especially, the flood of Revolutionary literature issuing from the press.

From that day to this that stream has continued—growing less in breadth, but greater in depth, until its volume is enormous.

In all this great current four phases may be clearly distinguished.

The first of these includes the works of the Philosophers of the Eighteenth Century, and the whole mass of writings by those interested in the Revolution, down to the overthrow of the Triumvirate in 1794. The main characteristic of this literature, of whatever tendency, is clearness of conviction and earnestness of purpose. From Voltaire defending Calas, to Marat clamorous for

Lafayette's head, it is a militant literature—looking backward to some principles and forward to some policy.

In all this period there is little attempt at writing treatises strictly historical. The first series of the history by *Deux Amis de la Liberté*, and that by Rabaut are the only histories of importance, and these are thoroughly tinged by the earnest spirit of the time.

The second phase extends from the downfall of the Triumvirate to the death of Louis XVIII. in 1824. This is the first reaction,—the period of hopes crushed, of illusions lost, of grudges to be fed, of disgust taking refuge in luxury and ceremony and cynicism; and by this the literature of the times is thoroughly tainted. There is no historian of the Revolution during this period who reaches the first rank, and few who reach the second. Lacretelle and Montgaillard are the best the time affords.

The third phase extends from the accession of Charles X. in 1824,—through the Revolution of 1830,—to the Revolution of 1848. This is the time of reaction against reaction; dislike of the monarchy has revived, justice begins to be done to many Revolutionists, and, often, more than justice. Disappointed old statesmen and ambitious young politicians see that here is a current which may carry them to power,—that deification of the military genius of Hoche, or Moreau, or Bonaparte, is the best means of bringing contempt on the memory of Louis XVIII., who could not mount on horseback,—that deification of the patriotic devotion of Lafayette, and Bailly, and Condorcet, is the best means of bringing contempt on Charles X., who is the incarnation of dynastic views as opposed to patriotic,—that deification of the patriotic enthusiasm of Mirabeau, and Vergniaud, and Danton, is the best means of bringing contempt on Louis Philippe, who is cold and shrewd,—and, finally,

Appendix. 277

that by glorifying the strength, and stir, and triumphs, and disasters of the Revolution, they can best bring contempt upon the common-place hum-drum Bourbon and Orleans Restoration.

Therefore, this is by far the richest period in brilliant histories, and among their authors are such as Mignet, Thiers, Guizot, Louis Blanc, Michelet, Henri Martin Barante, and Quinet. In almost all these there is a tendency to pamphleteering; party spirit runs high, and the roots of parties strike down into the Revolution, still every one of these men has too much regard for the position of a historian to sink into the mere party attorney. Whatever partizanship there may be is generally compensated by a clearness in drawing and vigor in color, which enables us to get at the truth all the better.

The next phase extends from the Revolution of 1848 to the present day. It is not the time of great histories. There has been a surfeit of glowing pictures and dramatic effects; new men have taken pens; the old party struggles have comparatively little personal bearing; it is the period of close study of particular events and individuals, of revision of judgments made in anger or enthusiasm, of search for exactness and fairness; and of the writers who best represent the historical research of this period are such as De Tocqueville, Mortimer Ternaux, Janet, Lanfrey and Von Sybel.

Of course, these phases are not absolutely defined divisions. There are many cross-currents of thought, and many counter-currents; there appeared some cool, intriguing writings in the hottest period of the Revolution, and some filled with a true enthusiasm during the Restoration; treatises aiming at judicial fairness appeared before 1848, and treatises brilliant in party advocacy have appeared since; but the whole body of historical literature of the Revolution is unquestionably divided, as has been stated.

The following bibliographical sketch has been prepared to give useful hints to those who seek profit or pleasure in studying a period which a very thoughtful writer has pronounced "the best worth studying since the Crusades." This sketch may be thought, by some, to omit too much; to such I would say that my aim is to give a practical aid, not an exhaustive treatise. Some may think that this sketch includes too much; to such, when I say that my own collection alone, of works relating to the Revolution, numbers more than six thousand titles, it will, perhaps, appear that less than the present number was hardly to be expected.

The period treated has been narrowed to its smallest limits, beginning at the events immediately leading to the calling of the States-General, and ending with the Consulate.

The historical works named are mainly those of recognized value.

As to Memoirs, but few have been named. A student who reads any of the standard histories will find in them the best clews to this part of the Revolution Literature.

As to newspapers, I have given a small selection of the most influential. The names of others can be found in Hatin or Gallois.

As to rare or curious works, only those have been named which throw especial light into leading events and tendencies.

CORNELL UNIVERSITY, *Feb., 1875.*

Appendix. 279

I. GENERAL HISTORICAL WORKS.

ALISON, Sir Archibald. History of Europe. (First Series, 1789 to 1815. Second Series, 1815 to 1852.)
The American edition, though wretchedly inferior to the English in paper and print, is worth more to the American reader on account of the valuable notes upon Alison's treatment of American questions.

This work presents everything from the High Tory point of view; but is as judicially fair as it can be under such circumstances. It is full in matter, honest in treatment, and in the main, clear in style.

A student who has not access to Arthur Young's travels, and the leading memoirs, will find the summary in the first volume well worth reading. The later parts have also a considerable value, at times, from the direct acquaintance of the author with so many men and events of the period studied.

BLANC, Louis. Hist. de la Révolution Française. Paris. 12 vols., 8vo. The introduction and a portion of the first part have been translated and republished in the United States.

The introduction covers much ground, and is very brilliant at times in its treatment of events which even very remotely helped to bring on the Revolution.

The study of details in the history itself is very careful, but their presentation as a whole is none the less readable. The studies of character, especially in the days of the Triumvirate, are admirable. No other writer has, for example, given so striking a portrait of Robespierre. Despite its socialistic bias it is the most fascinating history of the Revolution, save Carlyle's. The account of the downfall of Robespierre and his associates, is, doubtless, what its author claims it to be—the most complete in existence.

BREWER, Rev. Dr., of Trinity Hall, Cambridge. Political, Social, and Literary History of France brought down to the middle of the Year 1871. Lond. 12mo.

A sort of lift for the lazy; and, as such, perhaps, not without its uses. Its main design, as hinted in the preface, is to aid candidates for the military, civil service, and Oxford local examinations. It would be of use to any student in reviewing extended courses of reading in French history. But it is too much of the potted meat and desiccated vegetable sort for good mental digestion under ordinary circumstances.

BUCHEZ AND ROUX. Histoire Parlémentaire de la Révolution Française, ou Journal des Assemblées Nationales depuis 1789, jusqu'en, 1815. 40 vols., 8vo.

This is not only a good narration of events, but is the most important by far among the collections of historical materials for the Revolutionary history. It gives the proceedings of the Assemblies, Societies and Clubs, with copious extracts from their discussions, the doings, regular and irregular, of the Commune and the Tribunal, and keeps the student in the current of the times by large citations from newspapers, pamphlets, reports, etc.

Carlyle, while jeering at its generalizations, gives it very high praise as a mass of skillfully arranged material.

CARLYLE, Thomas. History of the French Revolution. (Various forms and editions.)

A prose poem, full of its author's merits and defects,—probably his most brilliant work,—not just, not complete,—yet some of his judgments seem inspired, and many of his pictures are marvellous. As, for example, the death of Louis XV., and the flight of Louis XVI. to Varennes. The characteristic vice of Carlyle is seen in his ill-treatment of such men as Bailly and Lafayette, and in the glory given Mirabeau and Danton.

CONNY, Vicomte Felix de. Hist. de la Révolution de France. Paris, 1834. 14 vols., 12mo.

A mass of reactionary matter, without the earnestness of De Maistre and Gaume, or the piquancy of Veuillot.

DES ODOARDS, Fantin. Abrégé Chronologique de la Révolution de France, à l'usage des Écoles publiques. Paris, 1802. 3 vols., 12mo.

The best thing about this book is the motto on the title page, from Tacitus: "Mihi Galba, Otho, Vitellius nec beneficio, nec injuria cogniti." The author appears a goodish man, but the book is poor. As a sample of his largeness of view, we may take the expression of his belief that Robespierre and the rest

mingled gunpowder in wine to work up their satellites to the pitch of fury required for the massacres of September.
Montgaillard's history, on the same general plan, is infinitely better.

DEUX AMIS DE LA LIBERTÉ. Histoire de la Révolution de France. Paris, 1792. 20 vols., 18mo. (Including index.)

Carlyle says: "It is, perhaps, worth all the others, and offers (at least till 1792, after which it becomes convulsive, semifatuous, in the remaining dozen volumes), the best, correctest, most picturesque narration yet published." Carlyle's distinction between the first and last series is abundantly accounted for by their difference in authorship. Kerverseau and Clavelin only wrote the first part. It has all the merits and surprisingly few of the defects of a history of such a time written by men deeply interested in the events. Alison cites largely from it. Many others quote without acknowledgment.

DURUY. Histoire de France. Paris, 1858. 2 vols., 12mo.

Of all the short summaries of French history, this is probably the best. Duruy was a faithful professor, and one of the best ministers of public instruction that France ever had. His tragic struggle with the Church for the improvement of education in France, is too little known. The book is rendered especially valuable by beautiful historical maps of France at various important periods, and by engravings illustrating the progress of French art, and especially of architecture. The history is given not only by periods, but by topics. The view taken is wisely liberal.

GAUME, Mgr. La Révolution Française. 4 vols., 8vo. Being part of "*La Révolution, Récherches Historiques sur l'origine et la Propagation du Mal en Europe, dépuis la Rénaissance jusqu' à nos Jours.*" Paris, 1856. 12 vols.

Mgr. Gaume is one of the leaders in the French Hierarchy, and this book is mainly a tirade against the Rénaissance. The author is crazed, almost, against classical learning and education, believing it the great cause of the evils of modern society, and especially of the Reformation and French Revolution.

He lays especial stress on the fact that the Triumvirate were classically educated, and that Madame Roland read Plutarch at the age of nine years, and Tacitus afterwards; that Camille

Desmoulins knew nothing but antiquity, and that the paper money bore portraits of Brutus, Cato and Publicola; and of course he finds plentiful confirmation of his view in the universal adoption of antique modes and phrases during the Revolution.'

It cannot be denied that the book possesses much ability; but with an American, it will pass simply for a curiosity of literature.

GONCOURT. E. and J. Histoire de la Sociéié Française pendant la Révolution. Paris, 1864. 1 vol. 3d Ed.

A rapid journalistic sort of account of daily life, during the Revolution. It dwells rather too much on the vile side.

GRANIER " de Cassagnac " A. Histoire des causes de la Révolution Française. Bruxelles, 1851. 2 vols. 12mo.

One of several reactionary treatises by an author whose tongue, pen and duelling pistols, have been for forty years at the service of slavery in the colonies, and despotism in France.

The depth of his thinking can be gauged in his statement: that "in the first years of Louis XVI., there was in public affairs no cause of trouble, and in men's minds no germs of sedition," and that "the excessive and inopportune reforms of that prince, gave public opinion its first impulse." No one can seriously consider him an authority on a subject which tasked the ripest years of De Tocqueville.

JANET, Paul—Philosophie de la Révolution Française. Paris, 1874. 8vo.

A discussion, in an excellent spirit, of the various leading views of the Revolution,—with the conclusion so necessary of enforcement in France, that although the main aims of the Revolutionists were founded in right reason, the despotic methods of reaching them have proved and must always prove, a curse to the nation. After so much screaming of parties at each other, this book affords grounds for hope that some large and quiet thinking will some time be done.

JOMINI, Le Lieutenant Général. Histoire Critique et Militaire des Guerres de la Révolution. Bruxelles, 1841. 4 vols. 8vo.

The work universally acknowledged the best on the military operations of the Revolutionary Epoch.

LACOMBE, Paul. Petite Histoire du Peuple Françõis. Paris, 1872. 1 vol. 18mo.

A very thoughtful little book, giving the development of the evils which the Revolution swept away. It has one advantage for an American reader, over most French treatises, in that it explains many of those things of which a knowledge is generally pre-supposed by writers for the French public.

LACRETELLE. Histoire de France, pendant le 18ième. Siecle. Paris, 1812. 6 vols. 8vo.

This history was once regarded as a classic, but is now little read. The same may be said of other historical works by the same author.

LANFREY. Histoire de Napoléon. [Translated.] Paris, 1870. 4 vols. 12mo.

One of the greatest historical works of this century. Very severe in its treatment of Napoleon; but its severity is that of a just judge charging against a prisoner whose guilt is clearly proven.

Among the most interesting parts of the book, is the brief account of the early life of Bonaparte, in Corsica; and among the most valuable, is the exhibition of his almost supernatural duplicity previous to the treaties of Campo Formio and Tolentino. Nothing could be more convincing than the comparison made by Lanfrey between the letters to the Directory on the one hand, and to the Venetian Senate, and the Papal court on the other. The sketches of his false bargain with Prussia, and his dalliance with Russia, are well done; but perhaps best of all is the unravelling of his monster intrigue in Spain, and the exhibition of the uprising of the Spanish peasantry.

LAVALLÉE, Théophile. Histoire des Français. Paris, 1865. 4 vols. 12mo.

Volume 4 is devoted to the Revolution, and is a fair summary.

LEO, Dr. Heinrich. Geschichte der Französichen Revolution. Halle, 1842. 1 vol., 8vo.

This is a slice from Leo's "Weltgeschichte," and, like that, is characterized by fullness of knowledge and vigor in presentation; but all is subordinated to North German pietistic conservatism.

——— Histoire de France à l'usage de la Jeunesse. A. M. D. G. * * *. 6iéme. édition, Lyons, 1820. 2 vols., 18mo.

This is the famous history of France written by Father Loriquet of the Society of Jesus, and prepared, as the A. M. D. G. * * * indicates, for the glory of God and the inculcation of what was considered, at the Restoration, as " sound knowledge." Its purpose was to put safe views into the youthful mind of France regarding French history in general, but especially regarding the Revolutionary and Napoleonic period. In the final table of contents, the name of Napoleon is carefully left out of the list of French sovereigns, and Louis XVII. follows closely upon Louis XVI. Five small pages contain the history of the Empire down to the Spanish catastrophe; and at the close of the history of the Empire, the downfall of Napoleon is compared with that of Nero.

For a very characteristic touch, see Vol. II., page 242, *note*, on the fate of the relics of Saint Géneviéve in the hands of the sans-culottes. It was this work which Prince Napoleon quoted with such bitterness against the Ultramontane party in the French Senate, when they claimed to be supporters of the Second Empire. But it is only fair to say that the book has been made to appear much worse than it is. Father Loriquet has successfully defended himself against the charge of having represented Napoleon as simply " Le Marquis Bonaparte Général des armées du Roi,"—a calumny which at one time it was republican orthodoxy in France to believe and spread.

MARTIN, Henri. Histoire de France. Paris, 1867. 16 vols., 8vo.

There is an American translation in four octavo volumes, covering the period from Louis XIII. to the Revolution. The last two of these volumes are most directly important for the student of the French Revolution. Public sentiment seems to have settled down upon Martin's History as the most useful of the extended works on French History in the large.

MICHELET, J. Histoire de la Révolution Française. Paris, 1847. 7 vols., 8vo., (translated).

Pictures of the Revolution from a democratic point of view,—sometimes with miraculous exactness in lines and coloring,—sometimes wildly fantastic, yet always on a groundwork of solid knowledge of men and events. The praise won by Michelet from John Stuart Mill, would of itself raise a very strong presumption against those who choose to call him a declaimer.

MIGNET, F. A. Histoire de la Révolution Française. Paris, 1836. 2 vols. English translation in one small volume, published in Bohn's series.

Thorough enough for the general student, thoughtful, just, clear in style, compact in matter; the best, by far, of all the short histories. Carlyle confesses this, while he scolds that Mignet "jingles and jumbles a quantity of mere abstractions and dead logical formulas and calls it thinking,"—by which is meant simply that Mignet believes in the desirability of Constitutional Liberty, and gives honor to Statesmanship rather than brute force, and presents the result of calm and wise thinking rather than philosophical pyrotechny.

MONTGAILLARD. Histoire de France, ou Revue Chronologique depuis la prémière convocation des Notables jusqu' au départ des troupes étrangères, 1787–1818. Paris, 1823. 8vo.

A very valuable chronological summary, giving the events day by day as above, with tables of statistics short and to the point, when needed. Its prejudices, which are strong, do little harm in a book of its kind, which is used mainly to get the bearings of facts upon each other by their relations in time,—very little more harm than geographical relations presented in an atlas made by a strong partisan.

QUINET, Edgar. La Révolution. Paris, 1860. 2 vols., 8vo. [6th Edition.]

Takes up suggestive thoughts and discourses upon them; and is especially good in going to the bottom of various charges that have been made against the Revolution. It is evidently the result of a reaction against the melodramatic method, and is an earnest attempt to get at truth somewhat in the style of De Tocqueville.

Very interesting are the copious original contributions from the unedited memoirs of Baudot, of which perhaps the most interesting is his account, in the chapter on the Festival of the Supreme Being, of the jealousy of Robespierre which Baudot heard and saw among Robespierre's immediate followers in the procession on that occasion. Only one account of Robespierre's downfall is more suggestive of thought, and that is the simple, unvarnished record in the MONITEUR.

RABAUT, J. P. Précis Historique de la Révolution Française. Assemblée Constituante. Suivi de Réflexions politiques sur les circonstances. Septième édition. Paris, 1819. 18mo.

The historical part is interesting as the view of a man who enjoyed a very great reputation during the first years of the Revolution, who sought to humor the popular will, but to restrain it from atrocities, and whose life was sacrificed to it at last.

But by far the most interesting part is the "*Réflexions politiques.*" These reflections are in sixty-three statements, often pungent, and always valuable as showing the faith in an approaching political millenium, among strong men of affairs at that period. Some are almost pathetic to us, who look back upon all the intervening disappointments and miseries. Of these No. LX. is a type, in which Rabaut joyfully declares, that now that kings have ceased to excite nations against each other, and "nations are sedentary," their hatred will cease. And this was just before the convention, twenty years of bloodshed, and the addition of two new dynasties to the plagues of France.

SYBEL, H. Von. History of the French Revolution. (Trans.) London, 1861. 4 vols., 8vo.

Thorough and careful. Von S. had access to masses of material, in the Continental Archives, untouched by the earlier historians; and these throw new light upon the dealings of the other powers with France, during the Revolution. Various important questions are handled well, even when but little space is given them, as for example, financial expedients upon which most French historians simply declaim.

THIERS, A. Histoire de la Revolution Française. Paris, 1827. 10 vols., 8vo. (And a multitude of Editions in various modern languages since.)

The most successful history of the Revolution ever written. In spite of the character of its first volumes which have much of the political pamphlet about them, and a frequent looseness of statement, they hardly deserve all the bitter censures passed by Croker.

The first part derived a fictitious value, without doubt, from the fact that its pictures of the opening glories of the Revolution were not only drawn by a skilful hand, but came at exactly the right time in the tide of reaction against the Bourbons.

The latter part, relating to the period of the Thermidorians, Directory, &c., is really far more valuable, for in this Thiers' wonderful skill in intrigue, enables him to find and follow clews which would be lost by most historians.

This latter part is written, mainly, in accordance with his noted essay on the writing of history, in his "*avertissement*" at the beginning of the twelfth volume of his History of the Consulate and Empire, but nothing can be further from it than the first part.

II. SPECIAL AND COLLATERAL TREATISES.

ADOLPHUS, John. History of England from the Accession to the Decease of King George the Third. London, 1840. 7 vols., 8vo.
The view of affairs in France is worth little, but the view of affairs in England, as influenced by the Revolution in France, is, in spite of prejudices, of much practical value.

BARANTE, A. G. P. Histoire de la Convention Nationale. Paris, 1851. 6 vols., 8vo. Histoire du Directoire. Paris, 1855. 3 vols., 8vo.
Ponderous works by a statesman and scholar; valuable for reference, worthy of all respect for accuracy and judicial fairness.

BATBIE, M. Turgot,—Philosophe, Économiste et Administrateur. Paris, 1866. 8vo.
A life of the great statesman who proposed the only means which could arrest the Revolution; by a living statesman fitted by study and experience to understand his subject. Among other things from which American statesmen can learn much, this volume presents with care Turgot's views on paper money, —views, which had they been adopted would have been nearly as valuable to the Revolution as would have been the views on general reforms, to the old monarchy, had not they also been rejected.

BERRIAT SAINT PRIX. La Justice Révolutionnaire. 2iéme edition. Paris, 1870.
An exceedingly valuable contribution, embittered though the author is at times. Aided by some of the foremost lawyers of the provinces, he has ransacked the archives at Paris, and in the departments, for materials bearing upon the administration of justice during the Revolutionary period. Its spirit is best revealed in his citation from Louis Blanc, " It is false that the Reign of Terror saved France. On the contrary we can affirm that it broke down the Revolution."
A good example of his thoroughness in hunting down a lie may be found in vol. 1, pp. 80–91, where he proves that, horrible as the *noyades* were, the story repeated by such a multitude of historians, regarding " *les mariages républicains*," is pure fiction.

BLANQUI, J. A. Histoire de l'Économie Politique. Paris, 1845. 2 vols., 12mo. (Third edition.)
Chapter 37 of the second volume is devoted to the economical doctrines of the French Revolution. As a rapid summary it has a certain value; but the student who is thorough enough to consult the book at all, will probably be disappointed by its want of fullness.

BRUNET, Charles. Marat. Notice sur sa vie et ses ouvrages. Paris, 1862. 12mo.
Mainly bibliographical; but the last chapter on "False Marats," as well as sundry other parts of the book, bring out the fact of Marat's popularity in a very suggestive way.

BUCKLE, Henry Thomas. History of Civilization in England. N. Y., 1858. 2 vols.
The part directly bearing upon the French Revolution is comprised in chapters 8–14, vol. 1, and whatever may be said of other parts, it can hardly be denied that these chapters form an epoch in the writing of history. If but one thing be read on the events introducing the Revolution, this should be that one thing.

The part of Chapter XII. showing the influence of English thought on French, is one of the marvels of thoughtful research. It probably marks the limits of the application of the positive method to History in this age.

BURKE, Edmund. Reflections on the Revolution of France. London, 1790.
A work abounding in shrewd judgments, brilliant pictures, bitter denunciations and striking prophecies; the work of a great statesman and thinker, yet always so one-sided, and at times, so outrageously unjust, that Buckle has thought it only to be explained on the hypothesis that Burke had lost his reason.

Burke's remarks on the formation of the States-General seem almost to justify Buckle's view.

CARNÉ, Comte Louis de. Études sur l'Histoire du Government Représentatif en France, de 1789 à 1848. Paris, 1855. 2 vols., 8vo.
A work somewhat heavy, and of what Carlyle would call the "rumbling" sort, but giving the ripe thoughts of a statesman. The author follows *doctrinaire* principles, but not blindly, and many important points are treated judicially. If, for example, a student wishes a well-weighed estimate of the Girondists, after Lamartine's deification and Louis Blanc's depreciation of them, he will find it in this book.

CONDORCET, J. A., Marquis de. Vie de Turgot. London, 1786. 8vo. Also in his collected works. Paris, 1847. vol. 5.

The shortest of the more important biographies of Turgot, and in some respects the best. Condorcet, by purity of character, thoroughness of knowledge, vigor in reasoning, and close personal acquaintance with Turgot, was one of the few statesmen France has produced fitted to sketch such a career. The work is of peculiar value also, as throwing light on the ideas of Condorcet himself, whose life was one of the noblest, and whose death was one of the saddest in Revolutionary annals.

DESMAZES, Charles. Le Parlement de Paris. * * * Avec une Notice sur les autres Parlements de France. Paris, 1859. 1 vol., 8vo.

The Parliament of Paris plays such a large part in the beginning of the Revolution that the student may wish to examine it closely. For this purpose there are many more ponderous works than this, but probably none more to the point.

DESPOIS, Eugene. Le Vandalisme Révolutionnaire. Fondations Littéraires, Scientifiques et artistiques de la Convention. Paris, 1868. 12mo.

A pithy statement of the vigor in creating institutions shown by the National Convention. Its sketches of the various plans of education, and of such creations as the Polytechnic School, the Normal School, the Conservatory of Arts and Trades and others which experience has proved admirably fitted to the wants of the nation, are very valuable. This little book is an excellent antidote to the more unjust parts of Alison and Burke.

DONIOL, H. La Révolution et la Féodalité. Paris, 1874. 8vo.

A very thorough discussion of the social condition of France at the outbreak of the Revolution, of the good reforms which were attempted, and of some evil expedients which were adopted.

DROZ. Histoire du règne de Louis XVI. pendant les années on l'on pouvait prévoir et diriger la Révolution Française. 3 vols. 8vo, 1839.

Faithfully done, with a love of liberty, but with no attempt at mere dramatic effect. It gives a very careful summary of the various administrations which tried to hold the Revolution in check.

U

DULAURE, J. A. Histoire de Paris : Physique, Civile et Morale. Paris, 1859. 6 vols. 8vo.
Contains a multitude of curious details, many of them of much use to a student not familiar with Parisian customs and localities.

DUVERGIER de HAURANNE. Histoire du Gouvernement Parlémentaire en France. Paris, 1859. 3 vols. 8vo.
A heavy work, not likely to repay an American reader.

FLEURY, E. Babœuf et le Socialisme en 1796. Paris, 1859. 1 vol.
Of value to any one who wishes to study the Paris mob from the days of Henry III. to the recent doings of the Commune.

FLEURY, Edouard. Élections aux États Généraux en 1789. Laon et Paris, 1869. 1 vol. 8vo.
Very interesting to the careful student as exhibiting samples of the *Cahiers de Doléances*, and practical political expedients of various sorts.

GALLOIS, Léonard. Histoire des Journaux et des Journalistes de la Révolution Française, Paris, 1849. 2 vols. 8vo.
Some of the lives—as those of Peltier and Marat—give extracts of much value in exhibiting the bitterness of parties.

HATIN, E. Histoire Politique et Littéraire de la presse en France. Paris, 1859. 8 vols., 8vo.
The part devoted to the Revolution is very minute. It is in all respects the best work on the subject.

KINGSLEY, Charles. Three Lectures delivered at the Royal Institute on the Ancient Regime as it existed on the Continent before the French Revolution. Lond. 1867. 1 vol. 12mo.
An off-hand sort of treatise made up from a few leading authorities, and given with the author's well-known earnestness of purpose and ease of style.

LAMARTINE, Alphonse de, Les Girondins. Various editions and translations.
A prose poem deifying the brilliant orators of the Gironde. A book which proves the profound truth of Goldwin Smith's exhortation, " Let us never glorify revolution."

Probably no work, save possibly Thiers' History, has done so much to make revolution chronic in France. If reason was given us for any useful purpose, this book is of no particular use to any American student.

LAVERGNE, Léonce de. Les Assemblées Provençales, sous Louis XVI. Paris, 1863.
A thorough and useful study.

LEWES, G. H. Life of Maximilian Robespierre. Lond. 1849. 1 vol. 12mo.
Although not to be compared with the same author's life of Göthe, it is spirited and well worth reading, as one of the first attempts to picture Robespierre *as he was*—neither making him out to be a demon or *un grand homme incompris*.

LOMÉNIE, Louis de. Beaumarchais and his Times. (English translation.) Lond. 1856. 4 vols. 12mo.
His connection with the Court of Louis XV., his suit against Goezman, which did so much to upset the old French judicial system, his aid to our own Republic, in supplying arms to the armies of our war of the Revolution, his authorship of the "Mariage de Figaro," which did so much to undermine the French Monarchy and Aristocracy, and his career during the most stirring period of the Revolution, in relations both with the Democrats and Monarchists, make his life one of the most interesting in French history, and this book gives it reasonably well.

MACKINTOSH, Sir James. *Vindiciæ Gallicæ*. Defence of the French Revolution, and its English admirers against the accusations of the Right Hon. Edmund Burke; including some strictures on the late production of M. De Calonne. Lond. 1791. 1 vol. 8vo.
If any person finds time to read Burke, he ought to find time to read Mackintosh. A deep strong current of liberal thought sweeps through the book, which gave it great power in its day, and makes it still worth reading.

MARON, EUGENE. Histoire Littéraire de la Révolution. 1 vol. 12mo. Paris, 1856.
Has some few points of value, but is generally declamatory with the usual stock antitheses between Mirabeau and Siéyès,— Danton and Robespierre, etc.

MORLEY, John. Rousseau, 1 vol. 8vo. London, 1873. Voltaire. 1 vol. 8vo. London. 1871. 1 vol. 8vo.

In these works the relations of the two leading thinkers of the 18th century to the Revolution are brought out with great ability. There is none of the conventional suppression of truth in this book, which spoils so many English treatises touching upon the French deists of the last century.

STAËL, Mad. de. Considérations sur les principaux, événements de la Révolution Française. Paris, 1820. 2 vols. 8vo. 3d Ed. (Various translations.)

Interesting from the personal characteristics and experiences that enter into it, but warped by her admiration for her father, and by various prejudices.

SOULAVIE, J. L. Memoires Hist. et Polit. de France pendant le Règne de Louis XVI. 6 vols. 8vo. [Translated].

The usual taint of prejudice and inaccuracy, which hangs about most French memoirs attaches to this, but it is full of valuable materials out of which the truth can be obtained. Its first volume evidently supplied much of the rough material which Carlyle worked into his master-piece, the picture of the last days of Louis XV.

STUDENTS' HISTORY OF FRANCE.

The part given to the French Revolution is dry and one-sided.

TERNAUX, Mortimer. Histoire de la Terreur, 1792-4. d'après des documents authentiques et inédits. Paris, 1862. 7 vols., 8vo.

The most complete and conscientious of all histories of the Reign of Terror. Highly praised by Von Sybel.

TISSOT, J. Turgot; sa vie, son administration, ses ouvrages. Paris, 1862. 8vo.

An excellent study of the greatest French statesman of modern times, and none the less great because both the ancient régime and the Revolution utterly rejected his best ideas.

TOCQUEVILLE, A. de. L'Ancien Régime et la Révolution. (Translated.) 1 vol., 8vo.

A work in which the labor and thought of many years are brought to bear on some fundamental points in Revolutionary history. There is much that is profound, but, in the midst of it, not a little that is fanciful, and over all a cloud of doubt and disappointment. Yet with all this it is one of the most valuable books on the Revolution ever produced

Appendix. 293

VIEL-CASTEL, Horace de. Marie Antoinette et la Révolution Française. Paris, 1859. 12mo.
Contains materials of interest obtained from Austrian sources. Also,

———— Les Travailleurs de Septembre, 1792. Paris, 1862. 8vo.
A careful research into the doings and motives of the leaders in the September massacres.

YOUNG, Arthur. Travels in France during the years 1787-88-89. London, 1794. 1 vol., 4to. 2d Edition.
One of the two or three most valuable books regarding the Revolutionary period. Young was a very intelligent country gentleman, who traveled, mainly, in the interest of agriculture; but his observations extended over a much wider range. At Versailles, for example, he dines in company with a number of the leaders of the States-General, and gives the conversation. He stops in coffee-houses in remote parts of France, hears the discussions, and notes the want of real ability in political matters arising from the lack of popular education; he talks with poor peasants on the roads, and enables us in a short conversation to see more of the real misery of France than many historians can give in an elaborate volume. The causes which led to the Revolution become wonderfully clear as we go on with Young's most attractive narrative; and no one can fail to go with him in his occasional outbursts of indignation. These are all the more striking when his natural conservatism is considered. The book in English is at present difficult to obtain. It ought to be reprinted.

———— A Comparative Display of the Different Opinions of the most Distinguished British Writers on the Subject of the French Revolution. London, 1793. 2 vols., 8vo.
The principal writers cited are Burke and Mackintosh.

III. HISTORICAL ESSAYS AND LECTURES.

ADAMS, Prof. Charles K. "Democracy and Monarchy in France." N. Y., 1874. 1 vol.
Ten lectures and essays upon the most important periods, questions and men of French history, from the first stir of Re-

volutionary thought in the eighteenth century, down to the catastrophe of 1871. Apart from what seems a want of full appreciation of the work of the Constituent Assembly, and thorough discrimination between the Constitutions of 1791 and '93, it is masterly.

Especially thoughtful are the chapters on "The Philosophers of the Revolution," "The Restoration," and the "Revolution of 1848."

The chapters on the first and second Napoleonic periods give the very facts which are most difficult of access, and which a thinking man most wants to know. The Chapter on "The Ministry of Guizot," is one of the very few adequate judgments upon the work of that unfortunate statesman.

BONALD, M. de. Mélanges Littéraires, Politiques et Philosophiques," etc. Paris, 1838. 2 vols., 8vo.

Various short pieces, and especially the essay in Vol. 2, entitled, "Observations sur l'ouvrage de Madame de Staël," are held in the highest esteem by the reactionary and clerical party in France, and are therefore, perhaps, worth the short time it takes to read them.

Their spirit can be understood by the following passage: "Ce n'est pas de la haine que les hommes éclairés ressentent pour la Révolution, c'est un profond mépris."

BROUGHAM, Lord. Historical Sketches of Statesmen who flourished in the Time of George the Third. London, 1843. 3 vols., 8vo.

The third series contains, "Remarks on the French Revolution," which are valuable as the comments of a statesman who was associated intimately with men of that time, and who was not carried away by reaction.

There are also essays on Robespierre, Danton, Desmoulins, St. Just, Siéyès, Fouché and others.—all having excellent points, as, for example that on Siéyès gives an account of Brougham's interview with him, and a very striking statement of views regarding him expressed to the author by Carnot and Talleyrand—so respectful as to prove a perfect antidote to the sneers of Carlyle.

CARLYLE, Thomas. Essays.

Especially noteworthy are those on Voltaire, Mirabeau, The Necklace Affair, the criticism on the Histoire Parlémentaire, and, for an admirable bit of historical satire—his exposure of Barère's account of the sinking of the *Vengeur*.

Appendix. 295

To all except the last the same remarks apply as to his History.

CHATEAUBRIAND, F. A. de. Essai Historique sur les Révolutions Anciennes et Modernes.
Utterly worthless from every point of view. The whole work is made up by forcing facts, ancient and modern, into historical parallels. His memoirs are valuable.

CROKER, J. W. Essays on the Early Period of the French Revolution. London, 1857. 8vo.
Contains the most searching of all criticisms on Thiers. Several interesting studies of important points in Revolutionary history are given, all of course from an ultra Conservative point of view. The study on the Guillotine is a strange piece of research—illustrated with curious wood-cuts, showing conclusively that the Revolutionary mode of decapitation was by no means a new thing.

MACAULAY, T. B. Essays (Various editions and dates.)
The essay on Lord Mahon's "War of the Spanish Succession" gives some interesting details collateral to the history of France. That on Frederick the Great, in alluding to the defeat of the French at Rosbach, gives some statements and remarks as to the military decline of France just before the Revolution. In the essay on Dumont's Recollections of Mirabeau, he makes incidentally a sharp attack on some of Burke's positions which have been considered strongest; and the essay on Barère is a searching review of the career of probably the vilest public man that the Revolution produced.

MACCALL, William. Foreign Biographies. London, 1873. 2 vols., 8vo.
Contains readable biographical essays upon Joseph de Maistre, Paul Louis Courier, Saint-Martin, Cadoudal, Carnot, and others.

MAISTRE, Joseph de. Considérations sur la France. Paris, 1786.
The most important, probably, of all the French reactionary works; vigorous and bold, while it is hopelessly in the wrong, as events since have shown.

REEVE, Henry. Royal and Republican France. London, 1872. 2 vols. 8vo.
Several essays of excellent workmanship. Reeve and Croker probably know more of the nice points of the French Revo-

lutionary history than do any other Englishmen. The essay on Mirabeau is, perhaps, best because it aims to give a just view, which, after the deification by Carlyle and the melo-dramatics of Thiers and Lamartine, is worth much.

The essays on St. Simon and Marie Antoinette are valuable. The latter is presented from what Carlyle stigmatizes as the "Custos Rotulorum point of view," which is probably much nearer the enlightened view of posterity than is Carlyle's own.

SAINTE-BEUVE. Causeries de Lundi. Paris, 1857. Various series, several volumes.

Scattered through this are sketches, always elaborate, and often pungent, of the various characters and events of the Revolutionary period.

SMYTH, William, Professor of Modern History at Cambridge. Lectures on the History of the French Revolution. Bohn, Lond., 1855. 2 vols., 12mo.

An excellent series of studies of the main events in their order. There are also valuable chapters showing the cotemporary current of English thought.

STEPHEN, Sir James. Lectures on the History of France. London, 1857. 2 vols., 8vo.

The last half dozen lectures are very valuable as a general introduction to the study of the Revolution, but do not give sufficient details for an exact judgment.

THACKERAY. Paris Sketch Book. London. Various Editions.

The essay giving recollections of Versailles is in Thackeray's best style; and the sketch by his own hand of Louis XIV. goes into the vitals of the old regime.

IV. MEMOIRS AND CORRESPONDENCE.

BERTRAND DE MOLLEVILLE. Memoirs. Paris, various dates and editions.

Worthy of special mention as containing probably the most absurd exhibition of the fatuity of the Court-party in the whole history of the Revolution. This was the "claque scheme," a plan to revive loyalty and put down republicanism by means of a hired corps of applauders. Full details of the scheme and its results are given.

BERVILLE ET BARRIÈRE. Collection des Mémoires relatives à la Révolution Française. Paris, 1821. 68 vols., 8vo.
This collection contains nearly all the more valuable memoirs, such as those by Besenval, Campan, Weber, Georgel, Thibaudeau and others.

BONAPARTE, Joseph. Mémoires et Correspondence Politiques et Militaires du Roi Joseph. Paris, 1855. 10 vols.
Interesting, especially as regards the Spanish difficulties, and the restiveness of Napoleon under his first real check.

CRÉQUI, Souvenirs de la Marquise de. Paris, 1834. 7 vols., 8vo.
Unfortunately, the witty Marquise left no memoirs, and this book, which at first seems so valuable, is a forgery throughout. It is a sample of a class of memoirs made up by speculators and attributed to noted personages, against which the student of French history needs to be especially upon his guard.

DANGEAU. Memoires. Paris, 1839. 4 vols., 8vo. Translated and condensed into 1 vol., 8vo.
The easiest of reading, and while giving a relief to more severe studies, useful in letting the student into the daily life of the old monarchy.

DUMONT. Souvenirs sur Mirabeau et sur les deux Prémières Assemblées Législatives. Paris, 1832. 8vo.
This work, though it throws much light upon the boldest man at the beginning of the Revolution, and upon the men and things about him, no longer retains the relative importance it held when Macaulay wrote his essay.

GUIZOT. Memoirs to Illustrate the History of my Time. London, 1858. 4 vols., 8vo.
Worth reading, of course, but will probably disappoint every reader. Under the circumstances, it could hardly fail to degenerate into a piece of special pleading, and it produces the effect of a series of orations or sermons in which the personality of the orator is much more important than the events discussed.

MALLET DU PAN. Memoirs and Correspondence. English translation. London, 1852.
Mallet was a Swiss intriguer who put himself at the service of the Reaction. In carrying out those secret intrigues, he found out some things of use, and his revelations have a certain value.

MEMOIRS.
The collection of Berville and Barrière is very large, but by no means complete. Besides these, those of Barère, Segur, Fauche-Borel, Malouet, Lafayette and others, are important; but the leading histories will best introduce the reader to them. The first part of those usually named in connection with the Napoleonic period, often throws much light on the later period of the Revolution. Thus, Beugnot's Memoirs begin with the Necklace affair, and Dumas' with the War of American Independence. The space allotted to this appendix, forbids an extended catalogue.

NAPOLÉON. Correspondence Publiée par Ordre de L'Empereur Napoléon III. Paris, 1858. — vols., 8vo.
The first part throws great light on the period of the Directory. Their value will be appreciated by any one who sees the use made of them by Lanfrey.

ROBESPIERRE, ST. JUST, PAYAN, et al., Papiers Inédits trouvés chez Robespierre. Paris, 1828. 3 vols. 8vo.
The introductory report by Courtois, is simply a ferocious oration. The remainder is exceedingly important and interesting as showing the wheels within wheels during the government, by the Committee of Public Safety. Under the head "Guérin" will be found secret reports of Robespierre's spies, upon his intimate associates; and some of them throw a flood of light over the spirit of the Reign of Terror. Thus, Vol. 1st, Page 366, it is reported, " People noticed that Légendre showed *Ennui*," * * * and "spoke mysteriously" to a friend; and of Bourdon it is reported that, in the Convention, " He gaped while good news was announced."

ST. SIMON. Memoirs. Translated and abridged, by Bayle St. John. London, 1857. 4 vols. post 8vo.
No other writer has given so living a picture of the social condition which had its centre in the Courts of Louis XIV. and Louis XV.; but the original generally frightens away readers by its length. This abridgement is well done, and brings the whole within the leisure of a short vacation.

VÉRON, R. Mémoires d'un Bourgeois de Paris. 5 vols. 8vo. 1853.
Veron was a *bon-vivant*, and man about town, and from the Restoration to the culmination of the second Empire, mingled with all ranks and parties, and had all persons worth knowing at his table.

Appendix. 299

V. NEWSPAPERS.

CONDORCET, Rabaud St. Étienne and others. Chronique de Paris. Paris, 1789-93. 9 vols. 4to.
A moderate republican Journal advocating a federal system.

DESMOULINS, Camille. Le Vieux Cordelier.
For extracts from this very influential Dantonist newspaper—a paper conducted in what is in these days known as the "sensational style"—see memoirs of Desmoulins in Berville and Barrieres' collection.
The Révolutions de France et de Brabant are also of importance.

HÉBERT, Le Père Duchesne. Paris, 1791—93. 11 vols. 8vo.
Unutterably vile. The organ of a class never thoroughly understood until the "Commune" of 1871.

LAVAUX, Rousseau, Th., and others. Journal de la Montagne. Paris, 1793—5. 7 vols. 4to.
A newspaper thoroughly in the Jacobin interest.

MALLET DU PAN, and others. Le Mercure, 1772-'92.
Often cited, but of little value, as it expressed no convictions, but represented mainly personal interests and grudges; hence the reader in these days can never know what allowances or corrections to make.

MARAT. L'.Ami du Peuple. Paris, 1789—1793. 18 vols. small 4to.
The organ of Marat's blood-thirsty policy. The most vivid descriptions of historians are poor compared with almost any number of this Journal, taken at random.

MONITEUR. 1789—1868.
Although the publication of the Moniteur was not begun until after some of the most important of the early events of the Revolution, it must always remain the great repository of facts regarding the modern history of France. Any person who has access to it will find that even a few short studies upon it are of great value. Nothing can give more vividness to one's knowledge of the French Revolution than a rapid run over the issues on the two or three days succeeding the downfall of Robespierre. There are brought together first the timid mention of Robespierre's arrest; then the vigorous denunciations by Billaud, Varennes, Tallien and Barère,—the account of the execution of

the Triumvirs, the long lists of those sent to the guillotine, including a large batch of aged widows, and, immediately following one of these, the list of plays at the various theatres for the same evening, followed by the burning of the paper money, &c., &c., &c.

MONITEUR, ANALYSE DU. Paris, 1801. 5 vols., 4to.
This is the key to the Moniteur, being the index by persons and subjects.

PELLETIER, Rivarol and others. Les Actes des Apôtrés. Paris, 1789-91. 10 vols., 8vo.
A Royalist newspaper, full of wit. As an example of its comments the following will suffice: "Six months ago Louis was master of twenty-four millions of subjects, to-day he is the sole subject of twenty-four millions of kings."

PRUDHOMME. Les Révolutions de Paris 1789-94. 17 vols. 8vo.
A vigorous democratic newspaper; its editor well acquainted with events as they were developed.

ROBESPIERRE. La Défenseur de la Constitution.
Lasted but a short time during 1792. Valuable, but with far less clearness and shrill force than his speeches.

VI. ILLUSTRATIVE MATERIAL.

BEAUMARCHAIS. La Folle Journée; ou le Mariage de Figaro. Paris, 1785. 1 vol., 8vo.
This play is well worth rapid reading, in view of the ideas it stimulated, and the stir it made at the beginning of the Revolution.

BULLETIN DU TRIBUNAL CRIMINEL. Paris, 1793. 6 vols., 4to.
One of the most important though one of the rarest documents throwing light upon the proceedings of the terrible Tribunal. The mere reading of two or three of these trials, which are generally very short, will greatly deepen the reality of the student's knowledge of the period.

C * * *, Théophilanthropes, Manuel des. Paris, 1798. 1 vol., 12mo.
This was the prayer-book of the sect of Deists which attempted to give a new religion to France, toward the close of the Revolution, but which encountered the truth enunciated by

Thiers, that "the only altars that are not ridiculous are old altars."

The book has, as its frontispiece, the picture of a priest in suitable robes, and contains prayers, hymns with music, catechism and all that was apparently necessary for establishing a new form of worship.

CHALLAMEL, Augustin. "Histoire Musée de la République Française." 2 vols., 8vo. Paris, 1858.

A very useful and amusing collection of Engravings of Revolutionary scenes, portraits, medals, caricatures, autographs, documents in *fac-simile*, paper money of various issues, &c., &c. The later editions are much more complete than the earlier; no work easily accessible gives a more living idea of the daily play of passions among the French people during the period which it treats. Every day philosophy, poetry, fun and blackguardism are faithfully reflected from it.

CHALLAMEL, A. Les Français sous La Révolution. 1 vol., 8vo. Paris, N. D.

A review of well-drawn sketches of typical persons in the Revolution, useful in clearing up our knowledge of the period.

CHAMPFLEURY. Histoire des Faïences Patriotiques sous la Révolution. Deuxième edition. Paris, 1867. 12mo.

Text of little value, but interspersed with a large number of engravings of the pottery of the period, which by its inscriptions and designs throw much light upon popular conceptions of men and events.

CHÉRUEL, A. Dictionnaire Historique des Institutions Mœurs et Coutumes de la France. Paris, 1855. 2 vols., 12mo.

An exceedingly helpful little work to a student, in any period of French history, and especially in the Revolutionary period. Such articles. as "Féodalité," "Gabelle," "Parlement," "Taille," etc., though not exhaustive, carry one through the difficult points very satisfactorily.

COLLIER, Admiral, Sir George. "France on the Eve of the Great Revolution." 1 vol. London, 1865.

Collier passed a little time in France in 1773, and has left some details, amusing, but of trifling value compared with those of Arthur Young; and of little interest compared with the sketches in Mercier's "Nouveau Paris."

CONSTITUTIONS DE FRANCE, 1791–1830. Paris, 1830. 12mo.

One of many collections of the sort. For others more or less complete, see Challamel, Tableaux de la Révolution, and other similar works. Despite Burke and all who have since given us dilutions of him, the Constitution of 1791 is well worth study, and the ultra radicalism of that of 1793, the ultra conservatism of that of 1795, and the singular expedients resorted to in those made afterward, render them worthy of attention.

DICKENS, Charles. A Tale of Two Cities. London. Various editions.

With many variations from exactness, it sketches in a striking way, some phases of society during the Revolution, as well as before it.

ERCKMANN-CHATRIAN.

Various historical novels, by these two writers; several of them translated. These delightful works well deserve their great success. They cover a period beginning with the confusion before the States-General in 1789, and continuing to the Plébiscite under Napoleon III. Not only is the *couleur locale* admirably preserved, but the very spirit of those who took part in the events is reproduced. Very striking examples of this are seen in the pictures of the preparation of the Deputies for the States-General, in the expression of feeling by soldiers in the army of the Republic, as compared with those in the armies of Napoleon, and by the peasants who voted at the will of the leaders of the Second Empire. No more delightful and profitable relief from severe studies on the entire Revolutionary and Imperial periods can be imagined.

GILLRAY. Caricatures. London. 1 vol., large folio.

There is also a second edition, in which the plates are good enough for the purposes of the historical student. The most valuable, perhaps, of all things of the kind for exhibiting the feelings of the English nation toward the French during the Revolution. All the plates are interesting and valuable, but those bearing upon the early part of the Napoleonic period are perhaps most so. Probably most important of all, as showing the culmination of English injustice toward the French Revolution, is the one which glorifies the atrocious murder of the French envoys by the Austrian hussars at Rastadt.

There is a volume sold separately, for obvious reasons, which has no great historical value.

LAHURE. Histoire Populaire de France. 4 vols., 4to. Paris, 1865.

Text worth little, but the wood-cuts are of that spirited sort which none but the French can make, and which throw much light over the history.

LIVRE ROUGE or RED BOOK. Being a list of Secret Pensions paid out of the Public Treasury of France. London, 1790. 1 vol., 8vo.

This is a translation of one edition of the famous Livre Rouge which, when brought into light, provoked such a bitter feeling against the old monarchy. This English edition contains notes such as are not to be found in the original French edition presented to the Assembly by Camus. These notes profess to show the reasons why the pensions were granted to various persons about the Court, and are full of the most biting satire.

LOUIS XVI. Réflexions sur mes Entretiens avec M. Le Duc De Vauguyon. Paris, 1851. 1 vol., 8vo.

For a long time this was supposed to be a pious fraud like Dr. Gauden's Eikon Basilike; but the argument now weighs altogether in favor of its authenticity. It shows Louis as a docile young man with a fair stock of very serviceable knowledge and thought.

MERCIER. Le Nouveau Paris. Brunswick. 1800. 3 vols. 12mo.

Often cited for the light it throws on every-day life in Paris, during the Revolution; but it requires much knowledge of events to make the proper allowance for prejudices and exaggerations.

NECKER. Compte Rendu au Roi. Paris, 1781. 1 vol. 4to.

This was the first statement of French finances ever made clear to the nation. The Memoirs dwell at great length on the stir produced by it. It is a book easily found, and worth examining.

SOREL, A. "Le Couvent des Carmes, et le séminaire de St. Sulpice pendant la Terreur." Paris, 1864. 12mo.

Of some value as showing the feeling of the Parisian mob, toward the clergy.

TABLEAUX HISTORIQUES DE LA RÉVOLUTION FRANÇAISE. Paris, 1802. 3 vols., folio.

A large and precious collection of views, scenes, portraits and documents, beginning with the oath of the Tennis Court, and ending with the Concordat and kindred documents.

There are sixty large and beautifully engraved portraits, of leaders of the Revolution, with accompanying sketches of more or less value, also the full text of each of the five constitutions of France, beginning with that of 1791.

VII.—MAPS.

ALISON'S HISTORY OF EUROPE.—The English edition has a valuable atlas with battle plans, &c.

CROKER'S ESSAYS.—Contains, as a frontispiece, a carefully studied plan of Revolutionary Paris, not encumbered with minor details.

DURUY'S HISTOIRE DE FRANCE.—Contains small, but very distinctly engraved maps showing variations in interior divisions and in frontiers, at various periods during the Revolution.

SPRUNER'S HISTORISCH-GEOGRAPHISCHER ATLAS.—Contains maps showing old ecclesiastical divisions, and changes made under the "Civil Constitution of the Clergy"—also many other maps carefully drawn; but its plans of Paris are almost too much confused with details of minor importance.

THIERS' HISTOIRE DE LA RÉVOLUTION. The best Editions have an atlas admirable in all respects.

VIII.—SKETCHES OF COURSES OF READING.

A.

1. BUCKLE.
History of Civilization in England, Vol. I., Chapter VIII., to XIV.; being the part on French history before the Revolution.

2. MIGNET.
History of the French Revolution, giving a rapid but thoughtful survey of the whole period.

3. ADAMS, C. K.
Democracy and Monarchy in France, which will give a rapid

Appendix.

review of the history treated in the two books previously read, with an exhibition of its effects on French affairs since.

And it would suggest much thought and give much vividness to the narration to read:—

Between 1 and 2, *Arthur Young's Travels in France in 1787 and 1789*, or, as the book is difficult to obtain, Alison's introductory chapters, which give copious citations from Young.

Between 2 and 3, *Dickens' Tale of Two Cities, Macaulay's Essay on Mirabeau and Barère, Carlyle's History of the French Revolution*. This brief course will give a general history written by master hands, from the time of Louis XIV. to the war between France and Prussia in 1871.

B.

[*A More Extended Course.*]

1. BUCKLE.
History of Civilization in England; Chapters 8—14 on the History of France before the Revolution.

2. ARTHUR YOUNG.
Travels in France from 1787 to 1789, or introductory chapters of Alison's History of Europe.

3. DE TOCQUEVILLE.
Ancient Régime and Revolution.

4. MIGNET.
History of the French Revolution.

5. SYBEL and THIERS.
Selections bearing upon points where the reader desires a fuller discussion than that given by Mignet.

6. ADAMS, C. K.
Democracy and Monarchy in France.

7. LANFREY.
History of Napoleon.

8. THIERS' CONSULATE AND EMPIRE.
Selections covering points upon which the reader wishes to see a judgment more favorable than that given by Lanfrey.

V

For collateral reading the following may be named:

Between 1 and 2, *St. Simon's Memoirs*, translated and abridged by Bayle St. John; or, *Dangeau's Memoirs*.

Between 3 and 4, Memoirs of *Madame Campan* and of *Besenval*.

Between 5 and 6, *Carlyle's History of the French Revolution*.

Between 6 and 7, *Macaulay's Essay on Barère*.

Between 7 and 8, Memoirs of the Duchess of Abrantès; and, perhaps, selections from Bourrienne, de Beausset, Fain, and others.

And to add life to the whole period, the Erckmann-Chatrian novels *ad libitum*.

For summary histories of the various European States which were brought into relations with the Revolution, the reader will find them generally well given in Alison's History of Europe.

FINIS.

www.ingramcontent.com/pod-product-compliance
Lightning Source LLC
Chambersburg PA
CBHW031856220426
43663CB00006B/652